KV-384-794

JO

WITHDRAWN FROM

OF

KA 0432646 6

Host Cities and the Olympics

Rather than interpreting the Olympics as primarily a sporting event of international or national significance, this book understands the Games as a civic project for the host city that serves as a catalyst for a variety of urban interests over a period of many years from the bidding phase through to the event itself. Traditional Olympic studies have tended to examine the Games from an outsider's perspective or as something experienced through the print media or television. In contrast, the focus presented here is on the dynamics within the host city understood as a community of interacting individuals who encounter the Games in a variety of ways through support, opposition, or even indifference but who have a profound influence on the outcome of the Games as actors and players in the Olympics as a drama.

Adopting a symbolic interactionist approach, the book offers a new interpretive model through which to understand the Olympic Games by exploring the relationship between the Games and residents of the host city. Key analytical concepts such as framing, dramaturgy, the public realm, and the symbolic field are introduced and illustrated through empirical research from the Vancouver 2010 Winter Games, and it is shown how the social media and shifts in public opinion reflected interaction effects within the city. By filling a clear lacuna in the Olympic Studies canon, this book is important reading for anybody with an interest in the sociology of sport, urban studies, event studies, or urban sociology.

Harry H. Hiller is Director of the Cities and the Olympics Project and Professor of Urban Sociology at the University of Calgary. He has been lecturing and publishing on the Olympics from an urban perspective for more than twenty years.

Routledge Research in Sport, Culture and Society

Host Cities and the Olympics

An interactionist approach

Harry H. Hiller

UNIVERSITY OF WINCHESTER LIBRARY

Routledge
Taylor & Francis Group

LONDON AND NEW YORK

First published 2012
by Routledge
2 Park Square, Milton Park, Abingdon, Oxon OX14 4RN

Simultaneously published in the USA and Canada
by Routledge
711 Third Avenue, New York, NY 10017

Routledge is an imprint of the Taylor & Francis Group, an informa business

© 2012 Harry H. Hiller

The right of Harry H. Hiller to be identified as author of this work has
been asserted by him in accordance with sections 77 and 78 of the
Copyright, Designs and Patents Act 1988.

All rights reserved. No part of this book may be reprinted or reproduced
or utilized in any form or by any electronic, mechanical, or other means,
now known or hereafter invented, including photocopying and recording,
or in any information storage or retrieval system, without permission in
writing from the publishers.

Trademark notice: Product or corporate names may be trademarks or
registered trademarks, and are used only for identification and explanation
without intent to infringe.

British Library Cataloguing in Publication Data
A catalogue record for this book is available from the British Library

Library of Congress Cataloging in Publication Data
Hiller, Harry H., 1942–
Host cities and the Olympics : an interactionist approach /
by Harry H. Hiller.
    p. cm.
    1. City planning–History. 2. Municipal government–History.
3. Municipal services–History. 4. Olympics–History. 5. Olympics–
Planning. 6. Olympics–Management–History. I. Title.
HT166.H526 2012
    307.1'21609–dc23   2011051739

ISBN: 978-0-415-52241-0 (hbk)
ISBN: 978-0-203-12133-7 (ebk)

Typeset in Goudy
by Wearset Ltd, Boldon, Tyne and Wear

UNIVERSITY OF WINCHESTER

Contents

Figures

Acknowledgments

The analysis presented in this book has benefited from visits to and interactions with people in a number of bid cities such as Östersund, Sweden, and Cape Town, South Africa; Olympic cities such as Athens, Salt Lake City, Turin, Beijing, London, and Rio de Janeiro; several meetings in the Olympic capital city of Lausanne; and discussions with many city representatives at meetings of the World Union of Olympic Cities. The relationship between host cities and the Olympics has always been an "on the ground, first person" focus for me rather than merely an analytical view from afar. Therefore, I am very grateful for the opportunities I have had to walk and talk with people from many cities where the Olympics have been on the agenda.

The Cities and the Olympics Project of which I am Director became particularly active as the result of the Vancouver 2010 Winter Olympics, when a number of unique research initiatives were begun, which are discussed in this book. The willingness of Angus Reid Public Opinion and its representative Mario Conseco to share their data with me has been invaluable. I especially want to thank my colleague Richard A. Wanner for his statistical expertise and collaboration on the analysis of the public opinion data, which is reflected in Chapter 7. Dick's colleagueship on this aspect of the project has been superb. My gratitude is also expressed to Kevin McQuillan, Dean of the Faculty of Social Science at the University of Calgary, who provided assistance for this project. My thanks are also extended to cartographer Robin Poitras, who created the map of the public realm.

The interactionist perspective developed in the book also benefited from discussions with students in my course "Cities and the Olympics." These students played an important supporting role in helping to formulate the interpretations which were developed out of what was observed in our fieldwork in Vancouver. They included Adam Zendel, Sara LaMarre, Ravneet Chima, Heather Gagnon, Andrew Gilbert, Balreen Gosal, Tegan Sly, Liz Hendrick, Chris Ly, Nav Mann, and Nigel Istvanffy. Adam Zendel was a particularly able research assistant, who taught me much about the social media and assisted with Chapter 6. I am grateful to colleagues at many academic institutions who responded to my many requests for information about their research or perspectives about the Olympics. Arizona State University and Richard Fabes, David Altheide, and John

Johnson provided a welcome workplace and colleagueship where much of this manuscript was prepared while I was on leave from the University of Calgary. The efficient and expeditious work of Simon Whitmore, Joshua Wells, and Peter Harrison in the publication process at Routledge also made preparation of this book an enjoyable experience.

As always, I am grateful to my wife, Edna, who shares my life with grace and beauty.

Harry H. Hiller
University of Calgary

Introduction

The rationale for a new approach

It is one thing to read about the Olympics and learn about their principles of operation, their philosophy, their controversies, and their impact. It is quite another thing to live in the city in which the Olympics are hosted. My first direct experience with the Olympics was the 1988 Calgary Winter Games. Somewhat unexpectedly, I observed how the Olympics monopolized the urban agenda before the Games even began, and then how the city was transformed by the Games themselves. During the Games, it was not so much what was happening at competition sites but what was happening on the streets and in homes and in other public and private spaces that caught my attention. And city residents themselves seemed surprised by what they were experiencing. Even more difficult to identify, there was energy in the city or a mood transformation during the Games that was unusual and that spilled out into public spaces. From a host city resident's point of view, it was clear that hosting the Games meant more than sporting events, the Olympic industry (athletes, sport organizations, and sponsors), the presence of global media, and the dreams of the city's elites. Outsiders might have viewed the Olympics as a vehicle for corporate marketing or as a symbol of transnational power, but local residents had a different perspective. They were aware of how the Olympics were an international trophy for their city, yet at the same time that preparation for the Games meant repeated waves of controversy and political wrangling. Once the Games began, there was something about the Olympics as an event that captured their imagination and set in motion a response not characteristic of routine city life. In some ways, who was winning medals almost seemed irrelevant. Since that time, and after reviewing the burgeoning literature on the Olympics, it occurred to me that what I experienced, and what has been reported in other host cities, has been missing in the analyses of the Olympics. And I wondered whether it was not time for a fresh perspective in the analysis of the Olympics. The focus on the host city, and particularly host city residents and how they experience the Games, has been a recurrent theme in my own thinking, speaking, and writing since that time, and was re-energized by my direct experience with the Vancouver 2010 Winter Games. This book, then, represents more than twenty years of my thinking on the topic, although it uses the most recent Olympic Winter Games in Vancouver to illustrate the perspective that I have developed.

The traditional way of viewing Olympic host cities is that they are the sites for sporting events and that the role of host cities is to provide the support systems required by the Games. The Olympics are about athletes, medal counts, and the ability of the city to stage the Games in an efficient way. Energy and resources must be mobilized to ensure that all is ready for the competitors, the many segments of the Olympic family, the media, and spectators. From this perspective, the host city is the container in which the Games operate. The city provides the backdrop for the Games, and when competitions are transmitted to the global audience, the skyline of the city or unique points of architectural or cultural interest serve as contextual sidelights. What is really important is close finishes, heroic performances, or the personal stories of medal winners. In this scenario, host cities are a minor aspect of the Olympic story.

Over the past twenty years, analysis has shifted to demonstrating how cities that host the Olympics operate in a field of international forces in which globalization serves as the dominant theme. Political-economic factors are seen to be at play in the geopolitical debates about which cities should host the Games, transnational forces are understood to shape how the Games are marketed, host cities strategize how to use the Games to transmit messages to a global audience, and elites are understood to manipulate the Games for their own interests. Host cities are viewed as launching pads for international marketing objectives, and the International Olympic Committee (IOC) is understood as a powerful emergent global institution. From this perspective, a host city is perceived as a franchise holder obligated to acquiesce to IOC requirements, in which the city struggles with the paradoxical role and interstitial nature of the IOC being nonprofit yet profit-making, and non-government while yet being dependent on governments (Rustin 2009:4–5). These have been the dominant themes that have captivated analysts of the Olympics in recent years.

The analysis presented in this book takes a different perspective. First of all, host cities are understood as dynamic places in themselves and not merely as backdrops for the Games or playgrounds for international forces. Second, host cities are composed of people as residents who encounter the Games not uniformly but from a variety of perspectives and in a variety of ways. The Olympics cannot be understood only in terms of official rhetoric or its local or international institutional face because the host city consists of a plurality of individuals who are part of social groups that interpret the Games in different ways. Third, the Olympics must be understood as a public policy choice by governing elites, a choice that generates a range of responses and consequences because the Games intrude into the normal functioning of a city. The study of the Olympic host city from this perspective, then, aims to understand how the city itself is the central focus and not merely a sidelight to the sporting competitions, and it does so by making local residents and their constituent groups a key part of the analysis. Rather than viewing the city as "a site of economic production or an object of governance" (Liggett 2003:ix), the approach pursued here understands cities as places of social production in which local residents themselves are active participants and not just a passive audience of spectators. In contrast to the view that the Olympics are something that happen to a city, the view developed here is that the Olympics are something that happens in a city and, in turn, reflect the dynamics of urban processes, conflicts, and issues in which local residents are participants. The question of how the Olympics impact a city needs to be supplemented with the question in which the direction is reversed, namely, how city residents encounter the Olympics as a civic project.

Because the Olympics are a mega-event of extraordinary proportions bridging the local with the global, they capture the attention of host city residents, though with differential impact, and draw them into its orbit in a way that few events do. The Olympics are both a spectacle and a project; a production with external components but also produced locally; an event and a happening; both experience and participation. City dwellers are not just a supporting cast but an integral part of the event itself, as co-participants in its production and outcome. As we will see, the Olympics are a drama that involves performances by people at a wide range of levels and many locations throughout the city, and over a longer period of time than just the seventeen days of the Olympics.

There has been a tendency to marginalize the role of host city residents to include only those involved in opposition activities or to focus primarily on the role of elites or decision-makers (Lenskyj 2008; Burbank *et al.* 2000). When other local residents are included, their participation is viewed as ephemeral. The Olympics are sometimes described as "a circus" in which locals are transmuted from the harsh realities of urban living by a short-term extravaganza that entertains them and then leaves them with debt and many problems (Whitson and Macintosh 1996; Eisinger 2000). When local residents are acknowledged as participants, their collective action is described as "a party" which then leaves them with "a hangover" (Hall and Hodges 1996; Cashman 2006). Activities that do have a party quality in that large numbers of people congregate in a joyful atmosphere are explained away and are not interpreted in their urban context. The descriptions and characterizations utilized in this way minimize a very complex phenomenon and ignore the multiple ways in which urban residents encounter the Games. Words like "circus" and "party" also appear to be built from an ideological bias about the Games rather than the result of a more comprehensive analysis. These terms are rooted in criticism and social activism that object to the fiscal priorities of the Games and seek to address the more urgent needs of the marginalized. For example, the Bread Not Circuses movement, which began in Toronto, has played an enormous role in shifting the focus of Olympic organizers to lasting legacies that address urban issues beyond the Games themselves (Kidd 1992).[1] The value of these actions, however, cannot displace the need for an analysis of the broader ways in which host city residents encounter the Olympics as an event and an experience. This book is meant to provide a first step towards that more comprehensive account of this interface by using an interactionist perspective.

In the discussion presented here, the Olympics are understood from an urban sociological point of view. The focus is on people in interaction within a city that has adopted the Olympics as a project to which there will be responses of varying position and intensity. The Olympics are understood as "a project" because they represent a highly focused task that interrupts the urban agenda and commands the mobilization and redirection of people and resources across all segments of the city. The event's fixed time frames catalyze and structure the energy that is required for collaboration to meet the Games requirements. And when the Games are over, the "project" is deemed completed and the city returns to normal functioning – almost as if the Olympics had never happened. People return to their usual roles and deal with other issues that are more pressing or that have been neglected. Infrastructural changes and memories are all that remain, and the city moves on, with many of the pre-Games issues submerged in the need to move forward. As a "project," the Olympics have a beginning and an end from the point of view of the host city, and it is the social dynamics of this urban project that this book seeks to address.

Applying an interactionist approach: Vancouver 2010 and its context

The purpose of this book is to lay out the basic principles of an interactionist approach to understanding the Olympics. While this interactionist approach has broader value than what is proposed here, the focus will be on the host city. In order to illustrate its utility as an interpretive scheme, the experience of Vancouver with the 2010 Winter Games will be discussed in some detail. However, what will be presented is not meant to be a history of the Games in Vancouver and certainly will not attempt to cover all aspects of the Games. The goal is to develop a theoretical interpretation of the Games with illustrations from Vancouver. But in doing so, it is selective in what it reports. There is so much more detail, so many elements of the historical record of the Games that are not mentioned here. During the Olympics, my own observations were supplemented by a student research team whose members were on the streets daily. Even since the Games ended, many anecdotes of personal experiences have been voiced, or observations made by residents shared, which could easily result in an interesting ethnography of the Games. While little from these accounts is mentioned in this book, they have provided me with further illustrations about how local residents interacted with the Games.

The selection of Vancouver as a case study is not just a matter of convenience. In fact, it is my contention, as will be shown in the pages that follow, that Vancouver is an especially interesting case in which to apply an interactionist perspective. The president of the IOC, Jacques Rogge, exclaimed at the conclusion of the Games that

> [t]here was this extraordinary embrace of the entire city of the Olympic Games, something that I have never seen on this scale before. This is really

something unique and it has given a great atmosphere for these Games. The whole world will understand how totally involved this city was in the Games.

(IOC Marketing Report, Vancouver 2010:12)

Rogge did not describe the Vancouver Games as "the best ever," as former president Samaranch was wont to say, but clearly observed that it was not so much the efficient operation of the Games that made these Olympics so distinctive; rather, it was the way the city responded to the Olympics that was so unusual (see also Kines 2010). The same IOC report claimed that the residents of the city embraced the Games "in a way that has rarely been witnessed before" and that "the undoubted story of the Games was the friendly atmosphere created by Vancouver's residents." Many long-time Olympic observers also commented that public response to the Olympics during the Games period in Vancouver was remarkable. However, the action in public spaces that served as the basis for much of these assessments masked a much more complex situation of multiple undercurrents that were present in the city. It is this mixture of conflicting forces and emotions that makes Vancouver a particularly interesting host city in which to apply an interactionist perspective.

Vancouver is a relatively young city on the west coast of Canada – a country largely settled from east to west by Europeans – but a city with strong British ties, as the name of its province, British Columbia, suggests. The city was incorporated in 1886 and really only obtained its lifeline to the rest of Canada when the Canadian Pacific Railroad arrived, in 1887. While Vancouver's intermodal capabilities from sea to rail enhanced its role as a transportation hub for the rest of Canada, the country as a whole was oriented more to Europe than to Asia, and the city's growth languished. By 1941, Vancouver's population was only 250,000. Perhaps more than any other single factor, the shift from rail to air as a dominant transport mode played a major role in shifting Vancouver's orientation from Europe to Asia as the city became the Canadian gateway to the Pacific Rim. The establishment of a new immigrant classification system for those bringing capital to invest in Canada and to provide employment particularly played a role in opening the door for immigrants from Hong Kong and Taiwan to settle in Vancouver in the latter half of the twentieth century. However, immigrants from other Asian countries (and especially Southeast Asia) also came to the Vancouver metropolitan area in large numbers. Vancouver was particularly impacted by immigrants who brought considerable capital with them, which led to escalating prices in the housing market (Ley and Tutchener 2001; Moos and Skaburskis 2010), with bittersweet consequences for Vancouver residents. For much of the first decade in the new century, Vancouver metro averaged 25,000 immigrants arriving per year. Because large numbers of them were of Chinese and Indian (Southeast Asia) origin, the social composition of the city changed dramatically. As will be shown in Chapter 5, the foreign-born population virtually reached parity with the native-born population in some of the metro municipalities by the time of the Olympics. While the city was generally welcoming to this population invasion, it did produce some tensions, the most notable of which was what it did to the housing market. It is no surprise, then, that the argument that the Olympics would put the city on the world map or encourage more foreign investment – the typical economic argument for hosting the Olympics – rang hollow to many city residents who had already experienced urban transformation through globalization forces. Furthermore, hosting the Expo/World's Fair in 1986 had already supposedly accomplished the objective of place marketing.

It is also useful to understand Vancouver's role within the national and international economy. In a province where the products of lumbering and fishing had been major export commodities, it is not surprising that Vancouver played a key role in the control and distribution of the staples economy. Consequently, Vancouver has no history as "a classic industrial city" (Barnes and Hutton 2009) because federal government tariffs ensured that the British Columbia market for manufactured goods was serviced by the central Canadian manufacturing juggernaut in Ontario and Quebec. The central role of shipping as an economic catalyst for the city ensured that supporting industries such as iron, steel, and concrete were all located along the waterfront, where rail and sea met. Sawmills and fish packing were also located there, although all were eventually phased out, leaving waterfront locations with derelict buildings, such as old warehouses and machine shops, and brownfield sites. The sale of the Expo waterfront lands to Concord Pacific developers, owned by Li Ka-Shing of Hong Kong, played a major role in the remediation of some of these sites but also contributed to the large-scale development of high-rise housing. A warehouse district known as Yaletown was transformed into residential and consumptive spaces for a new class of residents. By this time, staples had been left behind as the dominant industry in the city, and a new economy based on creative industries such as media and information services, software and computer systems, advertising, and architecture took hold. Gentrification became a huge issue by the turn of the century as older buildings housing people of modest income were replaced largely with upscale condominiums. In fact, high-rise condominiums became the norm in the downtown peninsula – even to the point that the city council expressed concern in 2004 that housing was replacing employment in new building construction. Coal Harbour and False Creek, for example, became highly desirable waterside residential locations, and it was anticipated that the last piece for waterfront development on False Creek, which became the place where the city built the Olympic Village, would be an equally desirable revenue-producing investment for the city. Needless to say, this housing boom only accentuated the social polarization that was occurring in the city, as housing became very expensive and those on low incomes were particularly disadvantaged (Hutton 2004). The Downtown Eastside became the poster district for Vancouver and for all of Canada of the poverty, breakdown, and marginalization that this kind of urban growth produced.[2]

By the time of the Olympics, the city of Vancouver itself had a population of around 600,000, but its metro population was over 2.1 million people. Density in the city was 5,039 people per square kilometer compared to 736 persons per square kilometer in the metro area. The city had a thriving tourist industry in which the Alaska cruise ship season served as its anchor in the summer and the ski industry anchored the winter season. As a coastal city, Vancouver became "the largest, warmest, wettest metro area ever to host the Games" (Judd 2009:41). The city possesses spectacular scenery bounded by the Pacific Ocean and the mountains, and the Vancouver Olympics sometimes were referred to as "the sea-to-sky Games." Its coastal location in a large country with vast distances, and especially far removed from the fulcrum of power in central Canada with its two dominant cities, Toronto and Montreal, created a political climate of its own making. Perhaps more than any other province, British Columbia, the province in which Vancouver is located, became known for its polarized electorate and voting patterns, shifting between strong right-wing and left-wing parties. The New Democratic Party, with a left-wing orientation, was in power from 1991 to 2001, including during the time when the bid was being mounted. However, the more right/center Liberal Party government elected in 2001 strongly endorsed the bid and made it a central part of its public policy. Prior to the Olympics in 2009, Gordon Campbell (leader and premier) and the Liberals won their third election in a row, suggesting considerable political stability approaching the Games. Shortly after the Games concluded, there was considerable turmoil on the political front because of two things: the surprise announcement of a new harmonized sales tax (HST) that was about to go into effect, and the issue of a large provincial deficit. Public opinion polls showed a dramatic drop in support for the Liberals, and especially for the premier. Much of the anger coalesced around the HST, and a referendum and recall petition related to this initiative began. By November 2010, Premier Campbell resigned. Eight months after the Olympics, the euphoria of the Games had not protected its most visible government supporter.

Civic politics in Vancouver is organized around locally based political parties that also span the ideological spectrum from the more left-wing Coalition of Progressive Electors (COPE) to the more centrist Vision Vancouver to the center/right Non-Partisan Association (NPA). Instead of candidates for civic elections running as independents on a territorial or ward system, which is the norm in most Canadian cities, the party system with its well-known ideological orientations tends to shape voter decisions. Even though the parties are not directly linked to provincial or federal parties in name or in practice, voters are aware of ideological links between them (Cutler and Matthews 2005). Given the fact that Canadian cities are all subject to provincial oversight and fiscal provisioning, civic voting is often related to provincial issues. This background is important because of the close relationship of the Olympic project to local and provincial politics.

The Vancouver Games were organized at a time of considerable cost inflation, only to be followed by the economic meltdown that began in the United States in 2008 but whose effects reverberated around the world. Cost inflation meant that Olympic construction was subject to significant cost overruns, which increased public anxiety and public pressure in relation to the Games. The economic meltdown was triggered by the subprime mortgage lending crisis and led to the collapse of financial institutions in the United States, which impacted lending to Olympic projects, especially the Athletes' Village. The tightening of credit and the rise of interest rates, the decline of corporate profits, stock market losses, and the effect on national economies through further recession-induced debt and controversial stimulus programs all contributed to what has been called a global financial crisis. This was a difficult time in which to mount an Olympic Games and contributed to considerable public uncertainty in the host city of Vancouver about the fiscal implications of hosting the Games.

These introductory comments about the context of the 2010 Winter Olympic Games in Vancouver, although brief, provide the background that is necessary in order to understand the analysis that follows. Much more could also be said about the city of Vancouver, its urban form and evolution, its ideological contrasts and contradictions, and its unique contribution to urban planning and design (Berelowitz 2005; Harcourt and Cameron with Rossiter 2007). It should also be pointed out that, for strategic reasons, the emphasis in the analysis developed in this book is on what occurred in the city of Vancouver, and especially in the downtown core, rather than its suburban municipalities. Suburbanites participated in the Vancouver city events but suburban municipalities also dealt with their own issues and had their own collective experiences of the Games. The city of Vancouver was the dominant player in the decision-making and hosting of the Games, but in other ways the Games were very much an event of the metropolitan region. Finally, it must be acknowledged that an intensive study such as this gives one a deeper appreciation for the Olympics as a complex and truly multifaceted event for a host city.

1 Building an interpretive model

From macro to micro

In the popular mind, the Olympics are all about competitions between the world's best athletes every two years, alternating between the summer and winter games in different host cities. Analysts, however, have been quick to point out that there is much more to the Olympics than that. There are the ideals of the Olympic Charter that establish sport as a philosophy of life promoting peace, human dignity, and universal ethical principles, principles that are constantly being tested by public scrutiny, thereby challenging the structure of the International Olympic Committee and its affiliated organizations. There is also the link between the Olympics and marketing programs that align the Games with globalization and corporatization. The Olympics can also be viewed as caught in the crucible of international politics, reflecting ambitions or antagonisms between nation-states, ideological shifts, or new phases of economic development. More recently, the Olympics have been shown to be at the forefront of emerging trends such as in surveillance and securitization. In all these instances, the Olympics are understood as more than sport and not just an event that lasts seventeen days. Instead, the Olympic Games are positioned in relation to wider global processes and issues that are more typical of macro analyses.

The macro approach to analyzing the Olympics has been very fruitful. It has led to a focus on institutions and structure as well as global shifts and evolving trends and how these matters are reflected in Olympic activities. It has become clear from such analyses that not only are the Olympics at the forefront of conflict and change in the Olympic Movement's own operations, but the Games as mega-events participate in other global processes of conflict and change. Key themes and concepts such as transnationalism, corporate capitalism, urban entrepreneurialism, neoliberal ideology, post-industrialization and urban regeneration all point to macro processes in which the Olympics operate, and help to explain how the Games have evolved and the purposes for which they are used. Notwithstanding all that can be learned from a more macro perspective, and especially the lens of political economy, is there room for a more micro approach to understanding the Olympics? Rather than institutions, structure, and global processes, the Olympics also involve people in interaction. And the host city is a critical location where this interaction can be observed.

The Olympics as a mediated event

How does the public encounter the Olympics? For most people, the Games are a mediated event because they are not physically present and they depend on reports presented by others, either electronically or in print. These reports are filed by the official media but are now increasingly being represented in the social media. There are four dominant ways in which the public encounters the Olympics through these forms of mediation. First, the media inform the public about the athletes and the events in the Olympic sport competitions as well as the results of the riveting contests of victory and defeat. Television ratings in particular show a broadening global audience for the Games. Most people do not have direct access to athletes or to the events in which they compete, so they depend on the media to tell them. The primary focus in these reports is on athletes representing the country in which a member of the receiving public lives, but there are also narratives that go beyond merely reporting the results to the personal stories of athletes that humanize the Games and create wider public interest. Again, the media play an enormous role in making the Olympics into a drama that heightens viewership or readership.

Second, the public also encounters the Olympics through controversies that keep the Olympics high on the public radar. Again the media play an enormous role in informing the public about the Olympics as an issue or a matter of crisis or debate. In contrast to the Games themselves, these issues, whether IOC, National Olympic Committee (NOC), or International Sport Federation disputes, scandals, various forms of cheating or corruption, or controversies related to bidding cities or the host city preparation process, are all constantly under public scrutiny in non-Olympic years as well as Olympic years. So, not only are the actual Games a mediated event for most people, but also the media (and increasingly the non-official media, as represented by the role of the internet) keep matters pertaining to the Games in public consciousness even outside the period of the Games itself. While some people tend to view the Olympics primarily in terms of their sporting aspects, it is clear that other members of the public view them more in terms of the controversies and issues in which the Games becomes embroiled.

Third, some members of the public primarily encounter the Olympics through their pageantry and ceremonies. The television audience for the opening and closing ceremonies is usually the highest for any of the Games activities and obtains an audience far beyond the sporting world. There is often much media discussion of the contents of the ceremony as representing not only Olympic traditions but especially the host nation's culture (de Moragas *et al.* 1995). Images of these ceremonies are quickly flashed throughout the world and easily attract persons not normally interested in sport. For example, the acceptance of the Olympic flag at the closing ceremonies of the Turin Games by Sam Sullivan, the wheelchair-bound quadriplegic mayor of Vancouver, the next host Winter Olympic city, had an impact that went far beyond sporting circles.[1] The parade of athletes from all participating countries is also part of the pageantry and engenders interest from among those in each nation looking to observe their own representatives in this international forum.

Fourth, the public also encounters the Olympics through advertising, particularly from those corporations that have become official sponsors (TOPS) and have exclusive access to advertising opportunities. The use of the Olympic rings in their advertising helps to make these rings one of the best-known brands in the world. Organizing committees also enlist as sponsors large numbers of national and local businesses that want to use this affiliation to accomplish their own marketing or public relations objectives. Since sponsors use the media to link their own brand with the Olympic brand through various forms of saturation and strategic marketing, the public encounters the Olympics in relation to the goals of corporate capitalism. Winners and losers, controversies, big show, and advertising – these are the predominant ways in which the Olympics as a mediated event are encountered by the general public.

If most people around the world experience the Olympics as a mediated event, then being a resident in a host city potentially changes that relationship to a more direct experience. People who are part of the Olympic family/industry – whether associated with the IOC or NOCs, athletes, coaches, sponsors, or various consultants, or a layperson with the financial means to travel to the Games and access to tickets – are members of a select group who always have the opportunity of experiencing the Games directly. But it is host city residents who experience the Olympics in a different way in that they discover that the Olympics as a project intrude into their own urban space and dominate their city's agenda. They are a project that shapes civic political debate, affects urban planning and urban finances, may reorganize part of the urban landscape, and may rearrange some people's activities. Moreover, local media always play a major role in making the Olympics a prime topic of discussion within that city. The preparation period, in particular, can generate considerable anxiety about how the Olympics as an event will change people's normal routines as announcements are made about disruptions that will occur. While some may see the Olympics as an intrusion into their normal routines and an unacceptable selection as a city project, others view the Olympics as a "once-in-a-lifetime" opportunity to host a unique, highly sought-after event. To be chosen to "host the world" is a perspective that warrants considerable exceptions to the normal urban agenda and legitimizes action and the mobilization of resources. In either case, host city residents discover that the Olympics are almost inescapable and that they will have some kind of direct experience with the Games as a civic project, and in some way be subjected to their impact. Clearly, not all aspects of the Olympics will be directly experienced and some mediation will still occur, but residents of an Olympic city have a unique vantage point that has often been overlooked.

Developing a micro perspective

The host city is an important place to start for this analysis because it can move us away from structure and help us focus on the people who inhabit the city.

Typically the Olympic host city has been interpreted more as a location or a context, or at best a political entity, rather than as a community of people. Beijing, Salt Lake City, Athens, or Sochi may be unique places understood in terms of the local or national culture but usually their residents are only understood as people to be mobilized for the Olympic event and the hosting of visitors. As Roche (2000:222) notes, staging the Games in itself requires such a wide range of participation that it is "an effective model of collective action." Rather than the Olympics being a project just of urban elites, the residents of the host city are an integral part of the event as individuals and within groups. They participate in the Games in multiple ways, both directly, as in the case of official volunteers or employees, and indirectly, as in the case of food service workers, security staff, residents living near competition sites, patrons of bars and restaurants, and consumers of the myriad forms of merchandising, among others. Baby-sitters of parents who volunteer for the Olympics are part of the Olympic interaction just as much as politicians who support the Games or those who choose to protest the Olympics either during the Games or in the months or years preceding the Games. Announcements about road closures or the creation of special Olympic lanes, the reconfiguring of working hours, or the rebuilding of parts of the city to the neglect of other parts clearly impact urban residents directly or indirectly. Olympic rhetoric fills the air, and most host city residents would truly agree that the Olympics have an inescapable presence. Without the many forms of participation and interaction that come from local residents, and without their presence, indeed it is difficult to imagine the Games being what they have become. People in host cities often report about the mood transformation that they experienced during the Olympics, and much of this came from the awareness that they were not spectators but active participants in what was happening. The host city is not just a location, nor is it just a context; instead, it is a community of diverse people who interact with the Olympics as a dominating urban project that impacts their world. While there is often tacit recognition of this element of the Olympics, there has been little room for it in our theorizing or our analysis.

There are, then, three conclusions that result from this approach. One is that the host city must be understood as a community of people with diverse interests who interact with the Games through all aspects of the Games cycle, from bidding, to planning and preparation, to the actual event itself. Their story begins not with the opening ceremony but many years before and continues well after the Games (Hiller 1998). Second, people do not respond to the Games as one voice but with a plurality of voices. They interact not just verbally but through a variety of symbolic forms that indicate their approval, disapproval, apathy, or indifference, and these responses often change over time. Third, from this perspective the Olympics are not just about officially sanctioned events but include the myriad "unofficial" ways in which people respond to the Games. These actions and reactions show how the Olympics provoke and evoke a variety of forms of responses and participation. Virtually none of these responses occur in isolation; rather, they are social in nature. The question is, how can this approach be included in our Olympic analyses?

The analysis proposed here builds from a micro perspective. Instead of a top-down perspective that focuses on structure and power, the approach taken here is a more bottom-up approach that emphasizes interaction and agency. The fundamental question in this approach is how do host city residents encounter the Olympics? It is answered by saying that they encounter the Olympics through interacting with other people about the idea of the Olympics and its appropriateness for their city as well as announced operational plans and ultimately the event itself. All of this occurs through interaction with significant others in homes, with peers at work, with neighbors across the fence, with friends in bars and restaurants, and even with the public in general through the mass media. Residents develop their own opinions, attempt to determine how and whether they will be affected, and need to decide in what way they might respond. Their assessments are based on their interpretations of what they see and hear, their interpretations of leaders and advocates of the Olympics as a local project, and their interpretations of the Olympics as represented by IOC leaders and national Olympic officials, as well as athletes. Rather than beginning with multinational organizations and global processes of change, we begin more fundamentally with individuals in interaction at the level of the host city.

The Olympics are typically understood from a political economy and organizational perspective. The International Olympic Committee or international sport federations are understood as powerful international bodies dealing bureaucratically with other powerful organizations such as national governments or multinational corporations following protocols, regulations, and established policies. Even host cities are understood in terms of the power relations that have emerged to support the Games, whether they be local or regional governments, local business and real estate elites, or the boards that are created to endorse or deliver the Games. People in power roles who head all these organizations do not make decisions in a vacuum but interact with others in order to accomplish objectives. Numerous accounts of the experiences of leaders of bid cities or leaders of organizing committees of the Olympic Games (OCOGs) are replete with stories of who talked to whom, and when and where, as part of their account of the Olympic project in their city. Books written by the CEOs of OCOGs or bid leaders demonstrate the importance of face-to-face interpersonal relationships (Ueberroth 1985; McGeoch with Korporaal 1995). Analyses of the IOC and how it works have also stressed the role of interpersonal relationships (Pound 2004). The failure of some cities that have bid for the Games, particularly in the Third World, has even been attributed to the lack of strong interpersonal relationships with power brokers (Swart and Bob 2004). The Olympic movement is best understood as people encountering one another as human beings in relation to this common focus. Even the IOC as an organization is primarily interpreted through its leaders (e.g., Juan Antonio Samaranch or Jacques Rogge), whose personalities, backgrounds, style, and use of words in interaction with others communicate much more than the official policies and procedures.

At each level of the Olympics as a multidimensional entity, there are numerous interpersonal encounters that shape outcomes, involving individuals ranging from athletes to officials to representatives of media and host governments. The story of virtually every Olympics is that there are always local people who initiate, organize, mobilize, and energize others through interaction with them. This interaction brings about support, opposition, or uncertainty, responses that help us to understand the outcomes. The purpose of this study is to use this approach to understand how host city residents encounter the Games. While it is tempting to view the hosting of the Olympics as merely a top-down decision, it is in reality much more than that. Host city residents respond to the Games through interpreting and negotiating meanings about the Games with others.

The analysis of cities and the Olympics needs a fresh start. The focus for too long has been on the questions of why cities want to host the Olympics, who promotes that agenda, and whose interests are served by hosting the Games. The answers invariably are all the same, namely that cities want to host the Games to obtain global recognition that will result in economic benefits, that this agenda is promoted by elites, and especially by those who will benefit the most, while the needs of the general populace are ignored (Whitson 2004). Terms like signaling, reimaging, globalization, and inter-urban competition are the rationales for hosting the Olympics, while residents are promised economic benefits from inward investment or tourism that seldom materialize to the levels proclaimed. City inhabitants are viewed as captives to an agenda in which they have little voice but who might be enthralled by the spectacle and excitement of the circus of the Games themselves. Such a view represents observations from a distance, imputes motivations, and, above all, does not understand how cities consist of people with a plurality of perspectives and points of view about the Olympics. Urban residents interact with the idea of the Games as well as the actual operation of the Games. Much of the color and energy of the Games from the host city's point of view comes from inhabitants evaluating and responding to what they see and hear, whether their reaction is one of apathy, enthusiasm, or opposition. Through interaction with others, citizens encounter the Games as active residents of the community. Claiming to understand the role and meaning of the Olympics for a city without including an analysis of the responses of urban residents is to impute actions and motives that render people passive and powerless.

Symbolic interactionist theory and the Olympics

The interpretive model of the Olympics developed here borrows heavily from the symbolic interaction perspective, which has many different advocates and interpreters. The common denominator among them is a focus on interaction that takes place in interpersonal encounters. It is the context of local interaction that is considered "the micro foundation of civil society" (Fine and Harrington 2004). Randall Collins (2004:260) has argued that the basic unit of analysis is the situation or the encounter rather than the structure, and "micro encounters are the ground zero of all social action." When two or more people are bodily co-present (physically assembled in the same place), when participants have a sense of who is included and who is not taking part, when they have a common focus on an object or activity, and when they share a common mood or emotional experience, Collins calls this an interaction ritual (IR). "Everyday life is the experience of moving through a chain of interaction rituals, charging up some symbols with emotional significance and leaving others to fade.... [W]e are constantly being socialized by our interactional experiences throughout our lives" (2004:44). Interaction rituals accumulate over time into chains depending on the person's stock of social resources that mesh with previous encounters. Macrostructures, then, must be seen as linking a series of interaction rituals that connect people and networks through the presence of common symbols. Macro patterns are aggregates of face-to-face interactions that are chained over time (Summers-Effler 2006). It is through a plurality of interaction rituals that society is produced, so it is with interaction rituals that any analysis must begin.

The most basic question of symbolic interaction is how do people create meaning in their lives? As Geertz (1983:34) has said, the goal is to understand how behavior is linked to its sense rather than to its determinants. Meaning emerges when people interact with one another through communication, communication that can occur discursively (verbal) and non-discursively (gestures, dress). Human life requires that we use symbols that have a shared meaning in order to communicate with each other. Language is the most important symbol system that we use, but the meanings of symbols emerge from and can be transformed through social interaction. Not only do words have symbolic meaning, but how the words are delivered (with laughter, with tears, on a platform, in a costume) also convey meanings. Wordmarks and logos found on signs or lapel pins, or types of clothing that distinguish a police officer from a football player or a nurse, are also symbols which communicate meaning. How these symbols are interpreted may vary with the persons interpreting them. Meanings may have widespread consensus but meanings may also be disputed. The key is that the meaning of symbols is created through interaction.

The symbolic interactionist tradition understands humans as actors who continually adjust their behavior to the actions of others. Rather than being passive objects of socialization, human beings creatively participate in constructing their social worlds through the process of interpretation (giving interpretations to their own actions as well as the actions of others), which utilizes symbols. Building on the work of George Herbert Mead and others, Blumer (1969) coined the term "symbolic interaction" and argued that people act towards things or other people on the basis of the meaning that they give to them. Meaning emerges through the interpretive process that occurs in interaction between people where negotiation takes place about the meaning of things in order to obtain a consensual understanding. For example, in interaction with others we develop a name for a four-legged creature called a dog that everyone understands. But through further interaction, we are able to develop more refined language to distinguish a pit bull from a Chihuahua. And as we describe our experiences with a pit bull, we may associate terms like "fear" with that dog, and such terms are also commonly understood – even by those who have never personally encountered a pit bull but who have learned that meaning from people who have had an encounter with a dog of that breed. But there may be others who own a pit bull and love this breed of dog, and even though fear might be a common meaning attributed to pit bulls, pit bull lovers and owners have their own meaning system attached to this dog. In a similar way, while there may be some things that have a common meaning and symbol system within our society, there are other things for which meaning is variable and dependent on negotiated interaction between individuals and groups of people. Interpretations and meanings, then, are not fixed, and humans may modify their interpretations and meanings as the result of emerging norms or the influence of others in interaction.

The crucible of meaning construction for symbolic interactionists occurs in face-to-face interaction rather than in macrostructural institutions. When the individual attempts to understand something, a process of reflection occurs in which the meanings that have been handed to the person by society or by their social group are examined. W. I. Thomas referred to this as the "definition of the situation," which then can serve as the basis for interaction with others. The quotation for which Thomas is well known and which demonstrates the action orientation of this assessment states: "If men define situations as real, they are real in their consequences."[2] How a person thinks and what a person chooses to do are dependent on their definition of the situation, which then affects that person's behavior. This definition, though, is subject to input from interaction with others and therefore is not fixed. It is also variable because of the tension between a handed definition and a more spontaneous definition that emerges from the individual. The family and friendship network serve as the most important reality-defining agencies, and while community-wide defining agencies exist, they are sometimes challenged. So, definitions of the situation may vary from person to person, vary with different circumstances and the way social cues are interpreted, and are variable with the different resources and worldviews that people bring to the situation. Individuals have to learn how to balance their own definitions of the situation with the customs, traditions, and norms of society and their social group. Our actions are based on the meanings something has for us, but the sources of these meanings are derived from and modified by the interpretive process that occurs in interaction with others. It is also important to acknowledge that power also plays a role in relationships, because some persons' definition of the situation dominates that of others.

Symbolic interactionists find meaning in people's behavior through how they express themselves in interaction with expressive others. Communication does not occur just through language as one expressive symbol system but through a variety of non-verbal forms of communication such as gestures, facial expressions, bodily postures, eye movement, dress, and behavioral choices (Goffman 1959).

We do not communicate in interaction just through our words, but also through our actions and our behavior. Goffman is particularly helpful in this analysis because he uses the metaphor of the theater to explain how interaction is based on the roles we play. We act differently in different settings dependent on our understanding of our selves and the image we want to project. In this dramaturgical perspective, our actions are a type of performance in which we play roles and engage in impression management. Goffman notes that the front stage is the more visible part of our performance that is available to others, in which we work hard to project the image we prefer that suits our character role. The back stage is the private side where we can step out of character because there is no audience. For example, an executive may act very differently in the office or at a shareholders' meeting, where a certain decorum and role expectation with appropriate dress are observed, in comparison to the way he or she acts at home, where the mask comes off, relaxation can occur, and casual dress is the norm. All this suggests that human interaction varies with time, place, and audience and cannot be understood just in terms of macro forces and structures.

The theoretical work of Randall Collins builds from this foundation, but he goes further to include emotions more explicitly to show how some interaction rituals (IRs) are more successful and more energized (using terms like "rhythmic entrainment" and "emotional energy" (EE)), while other interactions fail and drain energy.[3] Some IRs are mediocre, bland and unnoticed, and other IRs fail, creating passivity or alienation. When IRs are successful, they generate outcomes that are transitational, create feelings of solidarity, and engender respect for the symbols of group belonging. They also develop feelings of morality or a sense of rightness in adhering to the group and its symbols (2004:49). The key is that the strongest interaction rituals between people are those that build strong collective emotion, and Collins utilizes Durkheim's term "collective effervescence" for the outcome of this phenomenon. The IR, then, may generate a range of emotions from fear and anger to laughter, joy, or solemnity, which makes ritual experiences with different people unique. Interaction rituals help us to understand affective ties and solidarity as well as competition and conflict (Rossel and Collins 2006). When ritual experiences with others have a common emotional outcome, a sense of solidarity results not only among those participating in that ritual experience but also in the series of other interactions that build from that experience, interactions that have a similar outcome, resulting in growing intensity. Collins refers to these groups within society as "pockets of solidarity" (2004:15) that give the individual an identity and sense of belonging but also create social conflict.

The symbolic interactionist tradition allows us a new starting point in analyzing the Olympics because it begins with the intersubjectivity that occurs as people interact with one another rather than with institutions and structures and organizations.[4] While there is considerable variation within the tradition, this does not mean that structure is ignored (Fine 1991). It is not that the interaction order is just a chain of occurrences but rather that it establishes a reciprocal feedback between agency and structure (Srinivasan 1990). As Edgley puts it,

[d]ramaturgy certainly includes, and perhaps even requires a conception of structure to show how the actor forms his or her conduct against certain institutional and organizational backdrops. But it turns the structural argument on its head, noting that it is in the doings of people that the social structural features of social life emerge.

(2003:153)

Edgley goes on to say that instead of dealing only with how structure constrains behavior, the symbolic interactionist tradition explains how people act within the contexts that are available to them and thereby helps us to understand behavior and behavioral outcomes beyond what structure alone makes possible. Symbolic interactionists are voluntarists because they believe in self-reflexivity. Yet they can also be considered "soft-determinists" because they understand how interaction can be influenced by structural forces, although not be determined by them (Sandstrom *et al.* 2001). Interactionism stresses the role of agency and self-reflexive behavior, but in the context of the constraints of social structure.

In what way are these perspectives from symbolic interaction relevant to an interpretation of the Olympics within an urban field? At the outset, it is important to understand the Olympics as a symbol whose meaning is open to a variety of interpretations. It is often assumed that there is a high degree of consensus about what that meaning is, but closer examination reveals that different groups of people interpret the Olympics differently. For some, the Olympics are about sport, but for others the Olympics may be about "elitist" sport (a different twist than just sport), pageantry, commercialism, politics, or global corporatization. For host city residents, the Olympics may be a symbol of pride but it can also be interpreted as a financial sinkhole or an intrusion. The Olympics, then, are a symbol with contested meanings. Thus, what is important to understand is how people develop their own interpretations of the Games and how these interpretations may evolve over time.

Furthermore, the Olympics need to be understood as a symbol system that dominates host cities for a significant period. Collins (2004:42) acknowledges that there are certain moments in history or particular occasions that have a high degree of mutual focus of attention which promotes more intersubjectivity than others.

Intense moments of interaction ritual are high points not only for groups but also for individual lives. These are the events that we remember, that give meaning to our personal biographies, and sometimes obsessive attempts to repeat them: whether participating in some great collective event such as a big political demonstration; or as a spectator at some storied moment of popular entertainment or sports … these moments have a high degree of focused awareness and a peak of shared emotion.

(ibid.:43)

There are many points in time within cities where there is a high degree of mutual focus of attention. Civic elections, festivals, and special holidays all normally generate considerable enthusiasm and public interest, drawing people into interaction around that focus. All of these events, however, occur with regularity and are part of the normal routine of city life.

The Olympics, on the other hand, are a one-time mega-event that is obtained through a global competition and a lengthy process of adjudication that generates considerable attention from the international media. Winning the bid to host the Games is usually interpreted as an achievement in itself and is viewed as a form of validation of urban strength and capacity-building.[5] Winning the bid also puts the host city into the global spotlight, with media exposure far beyond that generated by normal, recurring events. As Short (2008:337) observes, hosting the Games is often viewed as "winning the gold medal of inter-city competition." The result is that most urban residents are well aware that the Olympics are a special or unique project which the city has undertaken, one that is outside the rhythm of normal city life. Frequently it is unclear what this all means, but by the time that the Games commence, the city has been well immersed in Olympic rhetoric. This kind of focused awareness means that emotions naturally intensify over time in enthusiasm, opposition, or, at the least, interest based on curiosity. The Olympics are arguably an event that is unique in the contemporary world in having that kind of urban impact.

The decision to host the Olympics means that there is an official interpretation of the meaning of the Olympics and its value to the city. Host city residents, on the other hand, have to process this interpretation through their own meaning systems. This reflexivity is the natural outcome of the significance of this event for residents' personal and collective lives, and occurs in social interaction. How will the Olympics affect me? Is this really a good idea? Where will the money come from to pay for this? Do the benefits surpass the costs? Should I get involved? These kinds of discussions are not only natural but inevitable.

If we begin with local interaction contexts rather than with macrostructures, urban residents encounter each other in small groups as distinct individuals. The local provides a stage for action and creates a lens for interpretation (Fine 2010). It is through small-group interaction that participants come to define a situation (framing) and decide in what way and whether to act (mobilization) (Fine and Harrington 2004). It is in interpersonal interaction that macro issues are defined in more local (personal) terms and interpretations are shared. Gamson (1992) uses the term "micromobilization" to refer to the fact that it is through interpersonal encounters that people develop their own views and develop responses and action choices, which they share with others. As MacAloon (2006:17) also notes, most people's Olympic encounters occur "in small-scale, even intimate social settings and according to behavioral logics that are anything but spectacular." As we will see later, the notion of the Olympics as spectacle ignores this important dimension.

Micro-interaction Olympic scenarios

In order to show how micro-interactions can be related to the Olympics, scenarios are presented in this section which illustrate how host city residents engaged in reflexivity with each other and discursively encountered the Olympics within their own meaning systems. These scenarios are based on observations and reports of interaction in Vancouver obtained by our research team. They are not verbatim quotations but are reconstructed. As excerpts from longer conversations, they illustrate how local interaction contexts provide occasions whereby people with diverse perspectives encounter the meanings that other people hold and influence each other. The thirty-four scenarios presented are divided into three time frames: the pre-Olympic period, the actual Olympics, and the post-Olympic period.

Anticipating the Olympics

Scenario 1
"I hear that the Olympics are coming. Sounds exciting" (eyes lit up with enthusiasm).
"Ya. Big deal. Doesn't do anything for me" (screwing up his face).
"Why are you so negative? Just think. The best athletes in the world are coming here" (joyful, happy tone).
"You know what? It will come and go and leave us and me with nothing" (strident anger, pounding table with fist).
"I never thought of it that way."

Scenario 2
"Why did you buy that shirt [official Vancouver Organizing Committee shirt]? It actually looks good."
"Because I am so proud that our city was chosen to host the Olympics."
"Ya. I guess you are right. We must be the best in the whole world. I think that the mascot they've got is so cute. I think I will buy it for my little Anna."

Scenario 3
"I hate the Olympics. Every time I hear that Gordon Campbell (premier) speak about it, it makes me mad."
"Ya, me too. I never liked his politics and I certainly did not vote for him."
"He has all these corporations behind him and now they are pushing the Olympics too."
"Ya. The Olympics is just an orgy for money-making."

In all three cases, urban citizens were responding to the Games. Their responses were each different and the conversation provided an opportunity to share opinions and perhaps influence the other person. In Scenario 1, two contrasting points of view and two contrasting emotional states encountered one another. Meaning was conveyed through facial features and gestures as the light-hearted booster came face to face with the angry person who saw no benefits. The end result was that both communicated something for the other person to think about – whether it immediately or eventually changed their point of view or not. The communication had both verbal and non-verbal aspects.

In Scenario 2, the positive view about the Olympics was communicated through the symbolism of the T-shirt. It was reciprocated by the other person, who either liked the shirt or valued its message, and who then decided to purchase a different symbol of association with the Olympics. For these two persons, owning Olympic paraphernalia reflected pride in their city and its association with the Olympics, and was reinforced by the interaction.

In Scenario 3, interpreting the Olympics could not take place without also evaluating the politician who was the Olympic advocate. The association of the Olympics with the politician who was not liked made it difficult to separate the Olympics from their political base. Criticizing the politician because of his perceived backers supported other views about how the Olympics were associated with big capital. Disliked politicians and "big money" were symbols that summarized their positions.

In Scenario 1, the interaction produced opposing points of view that were instructive to both parties about what the issues were. In Scenarios 2 and 3, the point of view expressed by the initial speaker seemed to have brought out supporting thoughts from the other person. Whether they both had totally similar views about the Olympics is not clear, but in that conversation they took the same position and supported each other. In all three cases, meanings were transmitted through both verbal and non-verbal symbols.

These are the kinds of interactions that took place all over the city. People developed their own viewpoints and shared their viewpoints with others, who then shared their thoughts in return. In some ways, these viewpoints were shaped by the structural context: the political context of Vancouver and British Columbia, the euphoria of winning or hosting the Games as promoted by elites, or the marketing of consumer items by profit-seeking organizations. But as reflexive beings, people also developed their own individual responses, and they did so through interaction in which their viewpoint was validated and supported, or criticized, or through which they learned from the opinion of others.

Scenario 4

"Bob [my husband] reads the paper and I don't. I think the Olympics are a good idea but he has me thinking now because he tells me about all of the issues and now I don't know anymore whether it is good or bad."

Scenario 5

"All of my co-workers are really against the Olympics. It seems like there has developed a kind of groupthink about it. Some people are quite vocal about it and the only things that are talked about are the critical things. One guy always tells us the latest that he gets from a website. But you know what? In reality, I know that some have different ideas – they just don't talk about it when we are all together. Yesterday I even learned that one co-worker has applied to volunteer. But all this negative talk has affected me, I think."

Scenario 6

"I actually don't know what to think about the Olympics. When I am with some of my friends, they are very pro the Olympics and I get drawn in. But some of my other friends are very anti-Olympics and when I am with them, I fit in with them. So I have learned to adjust to the people I am with. I can see both sides. Sometimes I think that I just don't care. Whatever happens, happens, and I'll enjoy it when it comes."

Scenarios 4–6 demonstrate how interaction with others through debate and discussion about the Olympics impacts people's own opinions. People learned from each other and were influenced by social contexts in which they interacted about the Olympics. There was an acknowledgment that there was no simple answer about whether the idea of hosting the Olympics was good or bad. These interactions could also lead to higher-order networking among those with similar opinions, as in the following examples.

Scenario 7

"One of my friends applied to be a volunteer and then it became the cool thing to do among all our friends to apply as well. Volunteering is not everyone's thing but the fact that a number of us became volunteers led to a sense that we were all a part of this big thing and it was exciting."

Scenario 8

"Once I discovered that there was a way in which I could register my concern about whether the Olympics would benefit our city in the long term rather than just be "a poof" for 17 days, I sort of became involved with the Community Coalition (to monitor the impact of the Olympics). I didn't join or anything but that organization resonated with my thinking and I wanted to support it.

Scenario 9

"I was given the job at work of helping us prepare for the Olympics. I went to a bunch of meetings and had to draft a plan. We were not directly involved in the Olympics in any way but we needed to determine how the Olympics might affect us, from staff time to how our workplace should become involved. This made me realize what a big thing this really was. When VANOC [the Vancouver Organizing Committee] made all kinds of announcements about Olympic lanes and traffic corridors and other things, we knew that we had to develop our own plan."

Scenarios 7–9 point out that responses to the Olympics did not just remain at the most basic micro level. Rather, the Olympics led to more organizational involvement where interaction was a key part of how people encountered the Games. This is not to imply that all people had this kind of experience, but many tended to gravitate towards those with similar views to themselves. Consider the following scenario, based on apathy.

Scenario 10

"I honestly don't care about the Olympics. They can do whatever they want. It doesn't affect me in any way. Most of my friends feel the same way. We hardly ever talk about it. It is in the background but it is just not part of our lives."

Notice that this person identifies with those for whom the Olympics are a marginal fact in their lives. It is a perspective that appears to be shared with others and not just a lone opinion. Interaction, then, can support indifference, just as it can inspire support or opposition.

The Olympic period

The illustrations above come from the pre-Olympic period. But what was the experience of urban residents during the event itself?

> Scenario 11
> "My son told me that he went downtown on the first day of the Games and he said that the atmosphere there was something else. So I said to my husband that we better go there and see what it is all about."
>
> Scenario 12
> "When I saw the pictures on TV about how many people were on the streets, I said that I wanted to be a part of that as well. I just had to be there. So, all my friends and I got on the SkyTrain and we went together to take it in. And we went back several other times as well."
>
> Scenario 13
> "I really didn't care about the Olympics at all but when everyone was talking about it, I figured that I would see what it was all about. Eventually I decided that I wanted my children to feel a part of this special experience that will never come to Vancouver again."
>
> Scenario 14
> "I was opposed to the Olympics and still am. My friends and I agreed that we would not support it in any way. We did not buy any of the stuff they sold and we did not go to any event that required tickets. But I have to admit that we did go to a sports bar to watch the hockey games with everybody else. That was fun but I still do not support the Olympics."

In every one of these scenarios, there was a clear interactional element to how people encountered the Olympics. They did not go downtown by themselves. They went with significant others in their lives. They did not encounter the Olympics as a mass experience but related to the phenomenon of a bigger group through more personal relationships (e.g., family or friends). The Olympics may have been reported as a mass experience but people participated in it via smaller groups.

Physical presence with other people, a common focus, and a shared mood became the dominant (though not the only) public expression of the Olympic experience in Vancouver during the Games itself. The downtown core of the city was transformed through street closures that allowed thousands of people to pack the streets. Long lineups at pavilions and celebration sites were the order of the day. The mood of the city was transformed by these expressions of jovial and good-natured interaction. Symbolic communication took place in a number of different ways. One was obviously through dress.

Scenario 15
"We needed something to express our participation. It did not seem that you were part of it in the same way if you just wore your regular clothes. So we did what others were doing too. My friend said she would wear a Canada shirt so I went out and bought one too, and we went down together. I guess I got in the spirit, you might say."

Scenario 16
"I thought the mittens were more of a souvenir but then all the girls in our group got them and we went downtown and we stood on a corner and sort of formed a wave effect by lifting our hands in a wave pattern. That was a hoot."

Scenario 17
"I decided that our whole family should dress in red and white [Canada's colors], so I wore my red sweater, my husband had a jacket that had red and white on it, and I bought Canada shirts for my children. I am not much for dressing alike but I guess doing something like this as a family made it special."

Scenario 18
"We can't afford to buy all the stuff they were selling and I don't agree with that anyway but I have to admit that the mascots – Quatchi, Sumi, and Miga – were great. We just bought the small ones and our kids loved them. Their favorite was Quatchi. It was sort of our way of being part of the Olympics even though we did not have tickets."

Scenario 19
"I got the idea of dressing up from seeing some people from the Netherlands wearing orange outfits. I did not even know that orange meant the Netherlands but it seemed like a fun thing to do, so we decided to dress up in Canada colors. One of my friends did not have anything red and white so he just wore his Vancouver Canucks [Vancouver's National Hockey League team] jersey and we said, 'What the heck, that will do, Canadians are Canucks anyway.'" [Canucks is a slang term for Canadian.]

The symbolism of sharing some sort of common apparel was the result of what smaller groups of interacting individuals thought was appropriate given what the larger group was doing. In every case, there was personal emotion attached to such participation, and apparel symbolized some form of participation. It is also noteworthy that deliberately not buying Olympic commodities also became a signal of oppositional group identity.

Scenario 20
"There was no way that I was going to buy any of this stuff they were selling. I did not agree with all this Olympic hype anyway. I love Canada but I was not going to support all those merchandisers and the companies that were looking to make a quick buck. In my son's school, they encouraged students to wear red and white and I said, 'No way.' I told my kids that we had to make a statement."

Scenario 21
"Whenever we got together to protest, we made sure that we did not carry any of those Olympic symbols on us. Two guys did have Olympic shirts on but they used ink markers to cross out words and put in their own words."

Scenario 22
"When we protested, we always carried signs that we had made because we knew that the media would pick that up and we would get our message across better. I carried a sign that said, 'Homes Not Games' and a guy with me had a sign that said, 'Resist the 2010 Corporate Circus.' One man who I passed said he agreed with the sign but he wore an Olympic shirt so I am not sure what he meant."

Clothing and signs were a form of communication and were symbols relating personal and collective identities. There were other sorts of appearance-related identities that were utilized. For example, face-painting was almost never done by single individuals. It was usually done by two or three (or more) friends who decided to express their relationship to what was happening around them together. People considered their appearance as a form of communication about their personal identity and their relation to the larger group.

Another symbolic form of participation was more verbal but had a collective tone to it. This usually occurred through the use of patriotic symbols. Almost always it was a few people who were together who started to cheer "Go Canada Go!" or "CA-NA-DA" and often it would then be picked up by others. The same thing could be said for the singing of the national anthem, "O Canada." Again a small group of friends would spontaneously start singing "O Canada" and then it might spontaneously spread throughout the crowd through other groups. This happened on street corners, in the streets, in bars, in lineups for the SkyTrain or any other lineup, and even in buildings or in SkyTrain cars. Whether it was sung on-key or off-key, sung too high or too low, did not matter. It was acting in the spirit of the occasion that drew people together.

Scenario 23
"I just showed up downtown. I wasn't into wearing all this Canada stuff. I don't even own any of it. I don't even sing. But there we were downtown with another couple and people started singing 'O Canada.' I saw that my girlfriend started singing and so was the other couple so I said, 'What the heck' and I started singing too. I guess that is how you become part of it without even knowing it."

Scenario 24
"I was on Granville Street last night and a small group were chanting 'U-S-A, U-S-A.' It almost seemed like they were daring us to respond – and boy did we ever. 'CA-NA-DA, CA-NA-DA.' It did not take long and we drowned them out completely."

Patriotic symbols became an important way in which people expressed their participation in the unofficial side of the Olympics in public spaces. More will be said about that later, but for the purposes of this chapter it is important to see that interaction at the grass roots involved people interacting in smaller groups, which, combined with other people in their groups, had a much larger impact, one that even captured global attention.

Perhaps one of the most important aspects of the Olympics from the host city's point of view was the elevation of emotions to a degree not typical of normal urban life in Vancouver.

Scenario 25
"Walking around downtown was an experience like I have never had before. It seemed like there were people everywhere and that in itself made you feel like something very unusual was happening. Crowds don't normally appeal to me but somehow this was different. I think it was because people were happy. The only thing that bothered me was that we had to wait so long to get on the train to go home. But that was even sort of fun as we stood in the long lines because people were in a good mood and everyone talked to each other in line."

Scenario 26

"I was on Robson Street near the beginning of the Olympics and all of a sudden I saw some people doing these dance moves in the middle of the closed street. It turned out to be a flash mob. I had never seen a flash mob before but it seemed like there were hundreds of people doing this dance all with similar moves at the same time. Whoa! I figured they must have practiced this before but I thought it was cool that a bunch of people would do this. I can't go on that street anymore without thinking about how much energy that activity put on that street. I'll never forget it."

Scenario 27

"I cannot get out like I used to but when I saw on TV all the fun people were having on the streets, I couldn't believe it. So I called my friend and she said that she could not believe how in not even being there, it lifted her spirits. So we talked about it every day after we listened to the reports. I don't think you had to be out of the house to be affected by it all."

Scenario 28

"The thing that I will never forget about the Olympics in this city is that people talked to other people who were complete strangers. I never do that otherwise. One guy told me about a pavilion that was really good and then told me that this other one was a waste of time. We talked for about five minutes and then I find out that he was from Toronto and I told him about a great restaurant he should not miss. Then he gave me his business card and said that if I am ever in Toronto and need help that I should call him."

All of these illustrations demonstrate that there was an interaction effect in which mood elevation contributed to different forms of interaction, sometimes even with strangers. The mood transformation in the city was especially difficult for those who were opposed to the Olympics. Solidarity with others who were opposed was somewhat difficult to maintain during the Games themselves, given the public mood.

Scenario 29

"We are totally against the Olympics but I have to admit that it was a big party for the whole city. And it was fun. The tough part for me was knowing how to deal with both of these things together – like when I was talking to people, if I told them I am against the Olympics, they would say, 'What are you? Some kind of party-pooper?' So I just shut up when I was talking to people and in a sort of way went along with things. It was too hard to be 'anti' all the time. I guess the dynamics of what was happening overpowered me."

Scenario 30
"I went to the protest on the first day and that was pretty invigorating. There we were all chanting our opposition and milling around while police horses lined up in front of the big domed stadium. I got a lot of energy from that. But I went to another protest at the Vancouver Art Gallery later in the week and there was hardly anyone there. Some organizer tried to hand out signs for us to hold and I took one, but I did not know anyone who was there, and eventually I just left."

Scenario 31
"My opinion about the Olympics has not changed. I still don't agree with it and I think it was a mistake. All my buddies who agree with me were disappointed that the opposition to the Games got drowned out, so we just decided to lay low. But once the Games are over, we will see the mess that is left and people will see we were right."

The Olympics were not a mass phenomenon or something impersonal to host city residents; rather, the Olympics were something that each person encountered through his or her own experiences and networks. There was no uniform response to what was occurring; each individual's interaction patterns shaped how that person confronted the event.

The post-Olympic period

After the Olympics were over, the opportunities for heightened emotions were considerably reduced. Collective gatherings were absent and the Olympic machine was essentially dismantled. Financial reports were forthcoming at a later time and the only issue of significant public interest focused on the slow sales of residential units at the Olympic Village, which mattered because the City of Vancouver had underwritten the project and it could leave a huge public debt. The bigger stories in the city focused on the disarray among provincial political parties, where leadership resignations created an unfocused political agenda on other issues. Consequently, the Olympics became primarily a memory in which interaction after the Games played only a minor part.

UNIVERSITY OF WINCHESTER LIBRARY

Scenario 32
"We have moved on. We have stuff around the house from the Olympics that remind us of the Games but what we cherish the most is the good times we had with our friends. When we get together, we often talk about the things we did with them during that time."

Scenario 33
"My best memory about the Olympics is that we did things as a family that we normally do not do outside of vacation time. We did not go in to work with regular hours and we were able to go downtown with the children, which we almost never do, and even watch some of the Olympics on TV together. I had not thought of the Olympics as more family time but it was. We talk about that part of it a lot."

Scenario 34
"I am just glad it is over. I hated the hype. I hated the way VANOC pushed us around. We talk about it a lot and all say that we still think that we are all going to pay for this for years to come. There is just no point in launching a crusade about it at this point. We can't get people together to fight something that is now over."

Clearly, the nature of the interaction occurring in the post-Olympic period was much more subdued and increasingly absent. Those opposed to the Olympics could not even hold their politicians responsible for any post-Games problems, because leadership had changed. The need for assembling for any purpose had gone and interaction rituals between people regarding the Olympics had subsided. What interaction did occur was through preserved symbols of the Games such as pictures from personal photography or purchased consumer items that stored interaction memories. The importance of these symbols was not in that they were material objects or that they represented the Olympics as an historic event but that they brought back warm feelings of people interacting with each other. It is the memory of these interactions related to the Olympics that generated the emotion that remained.[6]

Conclusion

The evidence is very strong that at the grass roots, face-to-face interaction was an important way in which host city residents experienced the Olympics and/or developed attitudes about the Olympics. This is similar to Fine and Harrington's (2004) argument that small-group interaction plays a significant role in framing and motivating thinking and action, and thereby contributes greatly to an individual's participation in public discourse within the wider society. It should also not be surprising that through interaction ritual chains, groups of people would develop who all had the same perspective or emotional reaction to the Olympics. A sense of solidarity would develop among these people based on their mutual response to the idea of the Olympics or its specific plans, while for others their interaction rituals produced apathy, indifference, or confusion and little social cohesion. Some interaction produced changes in attitudes over time while other interaction ebbed and drained emotion. It is in these interactions within small groups, and where people have cross-cutting affiliations and inter-actions between groups, that networks are created that serve as the basis for a civil society.

Among those for whom interaction rituals generated more emotional intens-ity, particularly in support of the Olympics or in opposition to the Olympics, collective symbols (the linguistic arguments defending their position, word-marks, terms or phrases, pamphlets, etc.) developed that motivated collective action and promoted group solidarity in the battle of public opinion. Collins (2004:75) uses the term "situational solidarity" to refer to moments of unity when symbols are shared among a group of people. These symbols will be dis-cussed further in later chapters.

Rothenbuhler's (1988, 1989a) research on television viewing during the 1984 Los Angeles Olympics provides an interesting illustration of how micro-interaction works even in mediated contexts. He found that half of the Amer-ican public planned their viewing of the Games by watching with friends, either in their homes or in a public place. These groups were larger than when they watched normal television and almost always also involved eating and drinking, i.e., intense socializing. While my argument goes beyond just watching the Olympics on television, this research provides additional evidence of how small groups serve as the base community for host city residents as they experience the Games through the Olympic cycle.

This chapter has provided evidence that the Olympics cannot just be under-stood in terms of the organizations that plan the Games or the official activities that constitute the Games. In every one of the scenarios described in this chapter, host city residents encountered the Olympics through a variety of sym-bolic forms and did so through interaction chains that involved small groups and often moved into response to and participation in larger groups. In spite of the structural forms that permeated the city (e.g., requirements of the IOC, VANOC's policies, corporate marketing objectives and civic regulations), indi-viduals formed their own patterns of response based on reflexivity and personal encounters with others, group expectations, and the norms and values that they embraced and shared. A theoretical base and its application have now been established, which enables us to analyze the Olympic host city in more detail.

2   The Olympics as dramaturgy

The imagery that is sometimes used to describe the Olympics is that of a spectacle (e.g., Tomlinson and Whannel 1984). A spectacle implies a phenomenon that is consumed, that uses powerful imagery to communicate and control and manipulate, and that exists in an othered position in relation to its consumers. The ceremonial and ritual aspects of the Games, as particularly represented in the opening and closing ceremonies or the medal ceremonies, as well as the packaging of Olympic events for mass consumption such as through television, makes audiences passive consumers of Olympic ideology. The spectacle is show business (Simson and Jennings 1992) and aims to send subliminal messages through impressive and compelling appeals to the emotions. From this perspective, host residents have little role except to serve as compliant participants in something in which they have little agency.

This chapter proposes that, instead of spectacle, the Olympics be understood as a drama in which there are many actors, scenes, episodes, and indeed many stages. Dramaturgy assumes that meaning is constructed by actors in social interaction and that their interaction constitutes a performance. The concept of drama is both a metaphor and a description of how life is lived (Hare and Blumberg 1988). The stage that is of specific interest here is the local stage and local players. Indeed, host cities are often referred to as "staging" the Olympics (Cashman and Hughes 1999). However, in this analysis the stage does not just involve athletes but also focuses on residents as local actors. The host city, then, serves as a performance platform in which there is an emerging plot with many characters and subplots. The imagery of drama is chosen because it emphasizes how players (host city residents) interact with one another in relation to the Games – some with lead parts and others with supporting or minor roles. The point is that the drama is not scripted (although there are attempts to script it), which means that there is a sense of agency among the actors that makes the moving of the plot and the outcome uncertain.

The city as stage

The host city takes on a unique identity by virtue of being the site for the Olympics. In an important sense, it becomes a distinct place, bridging both local and translocal forces. The host city has its own local particularities, form, and structure, and the Olympics have their own unique international composition and character. What gives the Olympics their power to local citizens is that they take local time and space and link it to transnational or global time and space. Being selected to serve as host city means that local urban spaces then become a stage for the drama of the interplay of local characters and culture with international players who work together for the Olympic performance. Roche (2000:137) has pointed out that "the Olympic games event is a 'show' which is permanently 'on the road', taking its 'caravan' from nation to nation and city to city every four years." But from the host city's point of view, it is now *the* stage for a performance involving local actors with a global audience. While there might be some traveling performers (e.g., athletes, officials, administrators) who have been on the stage at other places, every host city has its own unique cast of characters with its own special props and settings for the performance, so that the drama has its own character. This localization of global history has the effect of transforming everyday life in a host city through citizen awareness of being on the world stage. City residents are all part of the cast at the same time that they are also audience to the Olympics as a cultural performance. The paradox of being a local audience on a local stage while also being part of the performance observed by others on the world stage gives the Olympics a special position as a unique event.

As part of the drama, urban places are coded or recoded in terms of their relationship to the Olympics as the stage is set. For example, some streets are totally closed and used for security processing, other streets are closed to traffic but used by pedestrians, while still other streets have dedicated lanes for Olympic traffic only. Light standards are decked out with banners to give the city a festive look. Former parking lots have been emptied and are now used as exhibition sites or as vending locations. In Vancouver, even a park (David Lam Park) was remade into a LiveSite for pavilions and concerts. In another location, a new space (Jack Poole Plaza) was created for the Olympic cauldron, where people could make their pilgrimage for photos for only the seventeen days of the Games. People are also coded by what they wear in terms of their relationship to the Games. Security personnel wear one type of uniform and police officers wear another type and are present in much greater numbers than normal. Official volunteers are coded by their uniforms, known in Vancouver as the "blue jackets." People with special roles are coded with identification tags around their neck to facilitate ease of access. Getting the city ready to host the Olympics is like preparing the stage for the drama and clarifying roles with the appropriate costuming. But the drama actually begins much earlier.

The emergent storyline and the casting of the drama

In order for the drama to commence, the plot requires a beginning. The plot lines begin when someone proposes that the city mount a bid in a competitive environment to host the Games. Even though the bid may not always begin with government, eventually governments must become involved because of the need to mobilize massive resources. The idea of hosting the Olympics remains only an idea proposed by advocates until it achieves government backing. This escalates the drama, for the decision to host the Olympics is a form of government policy, which then opens it to more public debate. Governments can decide to adopt whatever projects they deem suitable for their constituency. These can be building a dam, a grand theater, or exhibition hall and convention center. They can also be medical programs, policies to stimulate business, aid for the poor, immigration programs – or hosting the Olympics. While these policies may be done in the name of the people, they are often open to debate. The point is that governments make policy decisions because they have been elected (at least in democratic countries) to do so, but once they initiate such actions they set in motion a plethora of reactions from civil society in which alternative policy options may be expressed. How can a symbolic interactionist approach help us to understand this process?

The Olympics have evolved into a powerful symbol in contemporary society. MacAloon (1981) has argued that it is an amalgamation of four performance genres (games, ritual, festival, and spectacle) that accounts for the popularity of the Games in this historical period. It is the combination of the competition of the games, the rituals which provide a sense of tradition and continuity; the festival motif, which draws out participation and celebration; and the sense of awe connected to aspects of the Olympics as a spectacle that has elevated the Games as "a crucible of symbolic force" and a stage on which the world plays out its dynamics (ibid.:4). The Olympics, then, are not just sport but an event that catalyzes symbolic energies. The Olympics do not just have one meaning, but meanings and interpretations are related to the interests of those who adopt the Games as a symbol. Because of its symbolic value (see also Chapter 5), the Olympics become a stage on which interests and values seek a performance outlet.

Hosting the Olympics requires the support of all levels of government within a country. Technically, the Host City Contract signed with the International Olympic Committee stipulates that the city has full responsibility for organizing and staging the Games (including the provision of services required, e.g., fire, police, athlete housing). The candidature file for bidding cities requires that a variety of covenants and guarantees be made by the host city in the event that the city is selected to host the Games.[1] The Host City Contract for Vancouver 2010 was signed in 2003 by the mayor of Vancouver, the IOC, and the Canadian Olympic Committee after Vancouver was selected to host the Games. The government of Canada (the host country) also signed a document indicating that it would respect the Olympic Charter and the Host City Contract, but it was clear that the prime responsibility for the Games would lie with the city. In order to convince the IOC of the city's viability even as a candidate, levels of government beyond the city also make commitments. While there is some variation from country to country, it is clear that city governments alone do not have the resources to finance all aspects of the Games. A higher level of government is required to stand behind the bid, which in the case of Canada meant the provincial government as well as the federal government. This is particularly an issue in Canada because cities have low taxation revenue and depend on higher levels of government for financial support. In Vancouver's case, the government of the province of British Columbia played the most important role in standing behind the bid. It is to the political leaders in the city of Vancouver and, especially, the province of British Columbia that we must look to understand the Vancouver Olympic drama context.

Most bids begin with a coalition of business leaders and sport enthusiasts, often with a highly motivated and/or charismatic leader.[2] A temporary bid organization is formed with links to government but not necessarily with direct ties to government. In less democratic countries, the links to government often are strong right from the beginning, but in western countries the idea of the Olympics is one usually initially cradled by local boosters. Sometimes it is the energy and entrepreneurial spirit of one person (e.g., Bob Scott in Manchester, Billy Payne in Atlanta, Peter Ueberroth in Los Angeles) that serves as the catalyst for networking and discussion about the Olympic idea (Cochrane *et al.* 1996). Often the concept of a bid is formulated in an independent organization funded by entrepreneurs, perhaps with some government contribution. In any case, a coalition of business leaders in conjunction with political leaders and government agency officials such as in tourism and sport is put together to promote the idea of the Olympics. This coalition is often described as an "urban growth machine" because it is assumed that the Olympics as a mega-event contributes to economic development and image transformation, and that this objective is a compelling reason for hosting the Games (Toohey and Veal 2007:67; Burbank *et al.* 2001). One perspective of this form of boosterism is that it is rooted in self-interest such as the commercial interests of merchants, tourism operators, or land developers, for whom economic growth is an important objective. Motivations of elites are often much more complex than this assumption, and local boosterism has many aspects, such as pride of place or the desire for the international recognition of their city which then can reflect favorably on them. It should also be acknowledged that many Olympic boosters are "big project people" who like ambitious new challenges, and creating a powerful working group for a special project can be particularly stimulating. The opportunity for some form of redevelopment of blighted areas or the construction of signature structures for the city also motivates persons who would not personally benefit economically from hosting the Games. So, while motivations may include personal economic interests, they cannot be simplified in that way.[3]

What we do know is that people in power roles sit together and discuss ideas, often with one or two friends or peers or a small group, who then take leadership and mobilize others who have positions of influence and with whom they are connected.[4] Frank King (1991), for example, the leader of the 1988 Calgary bid, discusses how the idea of hosting the Olympics was born in a small group called the Calgary Booster Club.[5] He refers to the numerous breakfast meetings and lunches with friends and acquaintances and their contacts, which awakened their "competitive spirits" (ibid.:11) and which led him to see the Games as a community project run by volunteers rather than government (ibid.:87). John Furlong's (2011) biography of his leadership of the Vancouver 2010 Games also describes how key business leaders, including Arthur Griffiths, former owner of the professional sport teams the Vancouver Canucks (National Hockey League hockey) and the Vancouver Grizzlies (National Basketball Association basketball), and especially big-project people in the development industry such as Jack Poole, pushed the idea of the Games. The key leaders then attempted to recruit elites from other segments of society to form a coalition from which they could obtain at least provisional support from appropriate levels of government. For example, Jack Poole, who was part aboriginal, reportedly had a series of coffee shop meetings with leaders of local aboriginal groups to create the Four Host First Nations concept as a way of recognizing that the Olympics would be held on their traditional lands (Cernetig 2010).[6] This model of operation is similar to what Boltanski and Chiapello (2005) refer to as a "projective city" in which short-term projects are carried out by informal networks and connections rather than hierarchy or bureaucracy.

Early interests in hosting the Olympics in Vancouver began with promoters of the Garibaldi/Whistler area as a destination ski resort in the 1960s and 1970s, when its development was in its infancy. The Vancouver/Whistler 2010 Bid Society was established in 1998 in a more serious yet developmental mode to explore the idea of hosting the Games. This society cradled the idea of the Games in a provisional way through various means with the community and various stakeholders and a $50,000 grant from the provincial government. The Canadian Olympic Association required Vancouver as bid city to endorse the bid even at this early stage, for which the city council sought and received indemnification from the province of British Columbia, which agreed to stand behind the bid financially. The understanding that the bid was regional (i.e., Vancouver–Whistler) rather than just the city of Vancouver provided further justification for the support of the provincial government. This essentially made the Vancouver Olympics project a policy decision of the provincial government. A much more serious and broadly based organization was created in 1999, known as the Vancouver–Whistler 2010 Bid Corporation, which became the structure that developed the bid plan and carried the bid forward. The pattern demonstrated here is that the idea for the bid was developed outside the formal channels of government among a few key members of the elite, but usually with connections to government leaders, who indirectly sanctioned the exploratory initiatives of the elite backers. In Vancouver, Jack Poole, a major real estate developer and highly decorated business leader who received honors such as the Order of Canada and was a good friend of the former Vancouver mayor and premier of British Columbia Gordon Campbell, played the leading role in the bid phase and also became president of VANOC. It is impossible to know all the details of the relationships between these people and other key leaders except to say that the *Olympics as a project* developed among people who interacted with each other informally at whatever venues were available to them. Obtaining the Olympics, from their perspective, was a symbol of global competitiveness and the ability to mobilize resources for a big project. One can only imagine the face-to-face interaction and the networking that occurred whereby people encountered one another in the evolution of this idea from board meetings, private clubs, arguments and disagreements to enthusiastic communication. The Olympics as a project and policy, then, began with micro relationships.

It is interesting to observe how a similar process occurred among those in opposition to the bid. Christopher Shaw (2008) discusses how a conversation that began among four people in a vehicle on the return trip from anti-globalization protest activities at the G8 Summit at Kananaskis, Alberta, in 2002 led to an awakening of ideas to counter the Olympic bid. Small-group discussions among anti-poverty activists and advocates for the homeless among others also helped to generate ideas that later were represented by organizations such as No Games 2010 and the Olympic Resistance Network. Opposition, then, was crystallized after considerable face-to-face interaction and the networks that were created through these kinds of discussions.

An unfolding drama

The main characters in the drama were now more or less in place but with an unscripted outcome. The interaction of people in dyads, small groups, and then increasingly larger groups formed the basic elements of the Olympic drama. The prologue to the play which we have seen so far was necessary for an intriguing script. The drama could not begin until the stage was set, with its intriguing storyline and a plot. In this case, the central question was whether bidding for the Olympics was a good idea, who would become its boosters and its opponents, and which side would win the day. And if the bid was won, what roadblocks, controversies, and struggles would intervene that might lessen the likelihood of a successful Games? These are the two high points in the drama, with the second fully dependent on the first. All good drama involves conflicts and subplots. And so it is with the Olympics in a host city. The decision to bid begins an unfolding drama in which people play various roles and in which there is little certainty over the outcome. Will they fail or succeed? Who will intervene? Will there be conflict between the protagonists and the antagonists, and in what way will that conflict be resolved (Benford and Hunt 1992)? There are tensions and conflicts in every act, and, while everyone knows that the storyline anticipates a successful Games, there is an air of suspense over whether that will indeed be the end result and what issues will serve as blocks or emotion-straining elements along the way.

While city residents are the audience and are caught up in watching the drama, they are also part of the drama as co-participants. Those on the margins may think of themselves primarily as observers of the drama, although, as has been shown, they do participate and become drawn in, especially for the final act or the climax (the Games themselves) of the drama. A few city residents play the role of major characters through their positions of responsibility, others are minor characters who appear in a small number of scenes, but most are extras who are part of the background. By virtue of endorsing the bid, government leaders become main characters in the drama. So also do leaders and advocates of the bid. Because the media respond well to the Olympics as drama, they help create the drama and sustain it. But they also help move the drama along in new acts of the play by moving from issue to issue, which helps to keep the audience's attention. By the actual Olympic Games, there are usually so many unresolved issues (e.g., what are the true costs? Who will pay? Was this a good idea?) swirling in the air that the audience (host city residents) may be polarized or confused. However, as may happen, the emotion of the final act or climax of the play can become so strong and convincing that most members of the audience can be sent home with euphoric feelings, leaving all the issues raised in the plot in a state of unsettled suspension. But as in any good drama, these issues become less important if there is a sense of a happy ending that is based on emotions rather than the rationality of the debated issues.

Viewing the Olympics through a dramaturgical lens helps us to understand more clearly the response of host city residents. Dramas stir emotions, and the Olympics as a drama stir emotions. From a local point of view, there are aspects of the Games' drama that are captivating, that create anger, that generate joy, and that produce heroes and villains. There are uncertainties, slow-moving parts, and distractions but the Games themselves as the final act in the drama heighten emotions to a level not at all typical of urban life, as city residents become both actors and audience. The key to this drama, however, is that there is no uniform response from the audience/participants. What sweeps one person off her or his feet may leave another person less affected. While the emotion of the final act may be more compelling to some people, the reactions to previous acts create a wider array of responses, including hostility and uncertainty about the facts that are part of the storyline. In other words, the audience/participants (host city residents) do not react as one piece but in a plurality of ways.[7] It is almost as if in the intermissions to the various acts, people talk with their friends and neighbors about what they think is happening and how they evaluate it. People state their opinions and learn from each other, and through this interaction they bring an interpretive lens to the next act. It is this process that makes it so difficult to come to simplistic conclusions about what urban residents think about the Olympics, because each act in the drama raises new issues that evoke a response.

The Vancouver Games are particularly amenable to a dramaturgical interpretation because bid boosters were quickly challenged by an opposition, setting the stage for all the necessary ingredients of a drama with protagonists, antagonists, heroes, and villains. The protagonists obviously worked from a power position, so their goals, leaders, and rhetoric were dominant. Regardless of their size and power, the antagonists who opposed the bid and ultimately opposed the Olympics, either for Vancouver in particular or in opposition to the Olympics in general, were visible enough to create the conflict that made the drama more compelling. As was noted earlier, the media played an enormous role in creating and transmitting the drama to the general audience.

The plebiscite as act 1: broadening and energizing public interest

Understanding the dramaturgical nature of the Olympics in the bid period in Vancouver is best illustrated by the most dominant event in that phase, the city-wide plebiscite. Prior to the plebiscite, there were a variety of scenes related to the pro-bid and anti-bid contingents such as at staged press conferences, debates on radio talk shows, and community meetings. But the announcement of the plebiscite best reflects the growing intensity of the drama.

On December 10, 2002, Vancouver City Council voted to hold a plebiscite (in the city of Vancouver only, rather than including its contiguous suburbs or the entire province) that was to measure support for the Olympics. This decision was primarily the result of a promise made by the new mayor, Larry Campbell, in the civic election campaign but it was also meant to be a response to those who saw the idea of the Olympics as an initiative by elites in which the people had no say. Making the Olympics amenable to democratic processes may have been acceptable theoretically but the bid committee saw it as a huge risk – especially since it was being held so close to the time of the visit of the IOC Evaluation Team. There was considerable anxiety that the bid could be derailed at this critical point even though the results of a plebiscite are non-binding.[8] The timeline for the plebiscite was relatively short, and about ten weeks after the decision was made by the city council, voting took place, on February 22, 2003. The question was as follows:

> "Do you support or do you oppose the City of Vancouver's participation in hosting the 2010 Olympic Winter Games and Paralympic Winter Games?
>
> ___ YES, I support the City of Vancouver's participation.
> ___ NO, I oppose the City of Vancouver's participation."

A brochure was distributed to every household on the first week of February with instructions on how to vote. The brochure itself acknowledged that there was a wide range of opinions about what it called "The Olympic Question" but said that "It's your city … have your say." The turnout for the vote was 46 percent (much higher than for typical civic elections), with a final result of 64 percent "Yes" and 36 percent "No."[9]

This plebiscite was a very important event for the Olympic project in Vancouver, especially given our symbolic interactionist interpretive framework. First of all, the plebiscite legitimated the Olympics as controversial from a city resident's point of view. If it was necessary to take a vote, the implication was that there must be something that was not obviously acceptable about hosting the Olympics. In that sense, No Games 2010 and its spokespersons, as well as opposing politicians, had been successful in capturing public attention. City documents that acknowledged the existence of a "wide range of opinions" about the Olympics left the impression that the Games were not necessarily a public good. The Olympics as controversy then set the stage for an intriguing drama. Second, the plebiscite made the Olympics a grassroots issue by giving every person an opportunity to "have your say." Rather than just accepting the Olympics as a policy decision made by those with governing authority, the plebiscite stirred public interest in the Games among individuals who were part of families, friendship, and work group networks where decisions about voting were discussed. In this context, it was harder to avoid the Olympics as just a bureaucratic high-level policy decision made in council or legislative chambers. The plebiscite, then, made citizens themselves part of the drama and not just observers in a much clearer way.

Third, the plebiscite campaign aroused emotions and elevated feelings about the Olympics that then carried on throughout the preparation period and even into the Games themselves. It was hard to discuss the Games in a dispassionate manner. People who were eager to support it (including the bid committee itself) found that the plebiscite raised their own anxieties, which motivated them into action. It made them confrontational with opponents of the bid. It motivated them to volunteer their time or make donations. It persuaded them to become ambassadors or advocates for the bid with passion and zeal. Ironically, the plebiscite had the same effect on those in opposition to the bid. It provided urgency and a stronger rationale for them to state their position and to convince others. It mobilized people and resources, creating solidarity among opposing groups, and provided opportunities to draw battle lines that were not erased on voting day. It was hard for people to be neutral because they were being asked to make their own decision, one that involved them personally, and it would be hard to make a dispassionate decision without there being intervening emotional forces (e.g., feelings about leaders proposing this idea, personal feelings about expenditures proposed and a person's own life conditions, personal feelings about sport, and personal feelings about civic pride).

The fourth reason why the plebiscite was significant was that it proved that there was indeed significant opposition to the bid. Bid boosters were quick to declare that the vote results demonstrated a solid victory for the "Yes" side. While in one sense this was true, it overlooked the fact that slightly more than one-third of city residents were opposed to hosting the Games. The majority may rule in a democracy and yet substantial minorities also have power. There may have been a tendency to write off opposition to the Games as being limited to a few extremists, but those who preferred to round off numbers pointed out that a 60–40 split was no grand victory and that the opposition was not limited to a few extremists. The plebiscite, then, demonstrated that there was significant opposition to hosting the Games within the city at the grassroots, which created an emotional tension throughout the preparation period.[10]

While the plebiscite could be considered an exercise in democracy, it was one in which the balance of power was tilted towards the Yes side. A whole range of well-known figures from the business world (Jim Pattison), political world (former NDP premier Mike Harcourt; former mayor Philip Owen), and sport community (Nancy Greene Raine, Rick Hansen, Lui Passaglia, Trevor Linden) became public advocates and therefore public symbols of the Olympic bid. Their endorsements were meant to communicate to city residents that voting "Yes" was in the city's best interests. One way of interpreting the entire exercise was that it was a "fabricated grassroots campaign" (Alexander 2005:59), for in reality it was the power of the Olympic bid organization – which included not only the bid committee but also its allied political, business, sport, and labor associations – that combined to convince voters that a "Yes" vote was appropriate. This power bloc had considerably more resources in money and personnel than the "No" forces. The entity that was established to promote a "Yes" vote was called "Team Yes 2010." The interesting thing about its campaign, Alexander has argued, was that it acknowledged that with the short time frame and limited resources it had available, the most effective way of convincing the electorate was not through a glitzy and expensive campaign but through face-to-face interaction, interaction in small groups, and through grassroots personal endorsements. Instead of flashy billboards and television ads, it utilized banners, lawn signs, bumper stickers, and buttons with slogans like "I'm Backing the Bid" or "It's Our Time to Shine" which could be placed by owners on their homes, places of business, automobiles, or on their shirts. These then became *personal* declarations of support by which, hopefully, to persuade others. In spite of the fact that these symbols were the product of organizational activity, the decision to appropriate these symbols as their own, particularly in a situation ripe with conflict, meant that such participation was essentially a personal decision. The decision to support the Olympic bid rather than be in opposition, apathetic, or uninvolved required residents to process the information at hand in order to make their own decision about the Olympic project.

The Bid Corporation had, of course, been attempting to get its message to the community for some time through open houses in communities, and this attempt intensified once the plebiscite was announced. The mayor held three community forums after the plebiscite was announced, and other forums were held as well, with strategic attendance by representatives from both sides to be sure that positions were heard, if not directly from speakers then also from people in the audience. Rather than look too polished and professional, Alexander (2005) showed how the goal of the "Yes" side was to demonstrate how ordinary people were behind the bid. For example, Team Yes 2010 used postcards with pictures of ordinary citizens (mothers, blue-collar workers, etc.) and short statements describing why they were supporting the bid, which were distributed at forums, gatherings, or just on the street. However, Alexander concluded that the most effective tool in the campaign was word of mouth:

> Whether it was key people in the Vancouver community telling their friends about the positive aspects of the Games, or the phone bank staff that called neighborhoods to encourage people to vote, or the everyday

conversations around water coolers, the Yes Team found their best tool was word of mouth.

(ibid.:67)

Employees and volunteers were taught to use their own social networks to encourage "Yes" votes, and union leaders and taxi drivers among others were armed with information that they could pass on to others. It was reported that grassroots enthusiasm was so strong in some instances that, for example, some condo owners spelled "Yes" with their Christmas lights on their condo balconies. People were encouraged to pick up their phones and talk to their friends and relatives about the Games. This is not to suggest that the "Yes" team did not have experts' support or advertisements, such as those provided by the *Vancouver Sun*, with ten full-page ads prior to the plebiscite (Alexander 2005), but what is clear is that whether by deliberate strategy or just through the nature of the process, the plebiscite provided an opportunity for people to interact with one another with the Olympics as the central topic. And while some of this interaction was clearly one-sided, people also argued, debated, and sometimes fought over this issue.

Word of mouth was also an effective mobilizer for the "No" side. Email lists and discussions in groups were ways in which a counter-position to the Olympic frame could be developed and people contacted. Tag lines such as "Healthcare before Olympics" and "If you are backing the bid you are spending my money. So back off" were created. A petition was organized to submit to the IOC prior to its decision for 2010 which urged that the IOC reject Vancouver's application "due to the extreme economic hardship that the Provincial Government has inflicted upon its citizens. The people of British Columbia do not choose to spend their tax dollars on the 2010 Winter Olympics." Chris Shaw (2008:37) became the primary spokesman for No Games 2010 and he noted that parties were organized to create anti-2010 buttons and bumper stickers. Sometimes referred to by the media as "Dr. No" because of his critical role in opposition to the Olympics, Shaw, a professor at the University of British Columbia, was a strident and articulate spokesman for the group. His book *Five Ring Circus: Myths and Realities of the Olympic Games* (2008) provides an intriguing road map of the interactionist encounters in the struggle for resistance against the Olympics in Vancouver.

Because No Games 2010 was a coalition of existing organizations and advocacy groups, it was possible to mobilize opposition through these ties. In most cases, such organizations consisted of a relatively small group of people who frequently interacted and who could mobilize others through word of mouth and email lists. But as Shaw himself points out, it was the discovery that several crown corporations such as BC Lottery Corporation and Insurance Corporation of British Columbia (ICBC) were using what he called "publicly derived money" to back the bid, and it was his decision to file a lawsuit against ICBC for using these funds for the purpose of the Olympic bid while automobile insurance rates were rising that captured public attention to opposition to the bid. This lawsuit drew the interest of others in opposition to the Olympic bid for a variety of reasons from anti-globalization, to the Green Party, and persons opposed to the support given to the Olympic project by native groups and labor unions. While No Games 2010 was the symbol of opposition to the Games, its membership or organizational presence was not nearly equivalent to the size of the "No" vote in the plebiscite. Thus, it is clear that either No Games 2010 articulated what many were thinking but were not publicly saying, or No Games 2010 was successful in raising issues that touched a nerve among those who were thinking through the logic of the Games bid and who then decided to vote "No." Thus, from an interactionist point of view the "No" side, as represented by No Games 2010, played a significant role in generating debate and proposing ideas which intensified the emotional climate around the Olympic bid.

A reporter for the *Vancouver Courier* (Tromp 2003) provided an illustration of how emotions were elevated through the plebiscite campaign. A sixty-two-year-old woman handed out leaflets against the bid in the lobby of Kerrisdale Community Centre, where the bid corporation had been hosting one of its open houses/information sessions in a rented room. The "Yes" side had its signs and material in the "public" lobby, so the woman assumed that the "No" side could do likewise. Apparently a "Yes" supporter approached the woman handing out "No" leaflets and tried to pull the leaflets out of her hand and exclaimed, "Give me one of those, let me see what lies you're spreading." A tussle between the two women ensued and the leaflet distributor was asked to leave the building on the grounds that political activity was not allowed in a public building. She then moved outside the building but continued to hand out her leaflets at the door. She was told to move again and this time handed out leaflets in the parking lot, which led to a request to move again. The woman then tried to leave her leaflets on a desk at the Kerrisdale Public Library but was told that that was not allowed. Eventually she complained to the Vancouver Parks Board and a policy change allowed her to hand out material at future meetings but outside the meeting rooms. The woman complained that in her experience "Yes" supporters tore down "No" side posters, and often security guards asked them to leave other places where she handed out "No" leaflets. The reporter concluded that few issues have ever raised such high contrary emotions of hope and fear in Vancouver, indicating that this plebiscite was not a dispassionate electoral decision.

The plebiscite, then, energized the Olympic issue into an urban controversy that drew citizens into both explicit confrontation and also less public but more interpersonal debate. Many families reported opposing opinions within their extended family unit on this issue, and people had to learn with which persons they could express their real opinions. The climate of controversy, divided opinion, opposing points of view, and indeed the clear acknowledgment that there were pros and cons to hosting the Olympics permeated the city. While supporters of the Olympics were firmly in control, an undercurrent of questioning and resistance was also firmly established.

The impact of the plebiscite on the continuation of debate about the appropriateness of spending any public funds on the Olympics was even expressed in the capital borrowing questions that were included in the city election two years later on November 19, 2005 (see the City of Vancouver Election Summary Report). Three questions were asked pertaining to borrowing money for public works, public safety and civic facilities, and parks and recreation facilities. Support for these items was in the 74–75 percent range. A fourth question was asked about borrowing funds for the city's share for community legacy projects related to the Olympics, and support dropped to 59 percent. The third question pertaining to parks and recreation was very similar to the fourth question, and yet 41 percent voted "No" to the question that involved the Olympics (and this was after Vancouver had been awarded the bid). This evidence suggests that costs associated with the Olympics were perceived very differently from other costs by taxpayers.

Conclusion

From the point of view of residents of the city of Vancouver, the bid phase acted as a mobilization factor for the Olympic project as an urban issue. The plebiscite in particular made the Olympics a matter of public debate, crystallized the difference between advocates and opposition, and enhanced the Olympic project as a drama. It aroused the public and involved them in a way that would not have occurred if there had been no opportunity to formally express personal opinions. While IOC president Jacques Rogge had stated the week before the plebiscite that a strong vote was necessary to convince the IOC of the viability of the bid, the clear majority support in the face of a significant opposition probably masked a lot of confusion among the electorate in that a simple "Yes"–"No" option could not account for uncertainties and hesitations which many felt while at the same time wanting to embrace the Games. The plebiscite in the bid phase ensured that the Games could not simply be viewed as a top-down initiative, and made the electorate much more aware of their involvement in the process. In that sense, the plebiscite enlisted them more clearly as participants in the drama.

The climax to the opening act of the drama was the announcement on July 2, 2003 in Prague that Vancouver had won the bid. Not only was there much jubilation expressed by Vancouver representatives in that European city, jubilation that was transmitted back to local citizens by the media, but there was also high drama at a rally at GM Place (now Rogers Arena). When IOC president Rogge announced "Vancouver," people jumped from their seats and cheered wildly, while fireworks exploded on the arena floor and red and silver streamers floated from the ceiling (Boei 2003). About 12,000 people attended the celebration, where people waved white towels with red maple leaves on them in response to the news (Mason 2003). This event represented the culmination of a process in which winning the bid was viewed by many residents as validation of the city's entrepreneurial competitiveness on the global stage. While the rally was both a staged and an authentic response, it did not obliterate the many undercurrents that prevailed within the city. But dramaturgically, it provided the color and the emotion that signaled the end of the first act of the urban Olympic performance.

3 Framing

Interpreting the Olympics project

How do host city residents interpret the Olympics as an event hosted by their community? One possibility is that they accept what they are told. A structural approach would point out how information is controlled and managed and how VANOC, for example, told people what to think about the Olympics. There is clearly a sense in which the management of information and the shaping of ideas about the Olympics is a top-down process. In fact, Olympic advocates and boosters attempt to shape public opinion by presenting their arguments as received and obvious truth. Statements such as "hosting the Olympics is an honor," "the Olympics will be good for business and strengthen the economy," and "the cost to the public will be minimal" are all frames of interpretation that advocates may propose to local citizens. In reality, while these messages may be touted by some government and business leaders, other leaders may emerge advocating their own frames or counter-frames of interpretation. Citizens also develop their own responses to the Olympics, and the battle for public opinion occurs as "issue entrepreneurs" (McCarthy and Zald 1977:1215) seek public endorsement for their own interpretive frames.

Framing refers to the principles and process whereby subjective meaning is given to what happens around us. As Goffman (1974) saw it, frames are interpretive lenses that people use in order to understand their everyday experiences and the world at large. Events and actions never speak for themselves but require that meaning be assigned to what occurs. How we define a situation is dependent on the frames we use to organize our experiences. Frames of interpretation can be controlled by those with power to impose their frame on others but it is also the case that people may question those frames, or even resist them. In either case, while there may be a dominant frame, there can be a myriad of frames that are the result of individual opinion and emerge from smaller interacting groups. There may be a desire to impose the dominant frame on everyone but it is also possible that counter-frames can develop, many of which are inconsistent and unstructured but some of which are structured enough by advocates who also attempt to impose their counter-frame on everyone else.[1] The claim that "the Olympics always mean debt" or "the Olympics will displace people and harm the poor" are also the result of an interpretive frame.

The decision by Olympic boosters to take on the challenge of mounting a bid to host the Games usually begins with the assumption that there either is or should be universal agreement about the Olympics as a sought-after event.[2] In reality, while there may be general public acknowledgment that the Olympics is a high-profile event of significant international stature, and that it would be a special or unique opportunity to host this event, it is quite another to assume that the emotions of pride and enthusiasm overwhelm all other attendant issues. For bid city residents, there is a public record of cities that have previously hosted the Olympics where indebtedness, disagreements about funding priorities, displacement of residents, political manipulations, and other issues create substantial doubts about the Games as an urban good. In one sense, bidding seems only like "playing with an idea" or "a preliminary exercise" because there is no guarantee that a bid will be successful. Yet the process does require the development of specific plans, which are often developed by the bid organization with little public input. There is tentativeness about the whole process because the Games are not coming, but they might come, and it is represented that this is what it might look like if they did come. On the other hand, from the IOC perspective bidding is taken very seriously and the bid book is considered a blueprint for the Games if they were to be awarded to that city. In the public mind, it is difficult to know how to deal with an idea for which people have inadequate information on which to make a firm judgment and which may never be more than an architectural model if the bid is not successful. Thus, from the local citizen's point of view the decision to bid as well as the formulation of the bid plan evoke a wide range of mixed emotion that cannot be simplified into just bipolar support or opposition. Instead, there is often confusion, apprehension, and uncertainty, as well as mixed and often inconsistent reactions to the idea of hosting the Olympics in spite of a wellspring of intrigue about such an ambitious possibility. So if on the surface hosting the Olympics is all about international recognition and pride, local residents become keenly aware that hosting such an event has direct as well as residual effects on them in that they have to deal with the consequences of such a decision. To the extent that urban residents become aware of these consequences and debate them, the idea of hosting the Olympics requires both interpretation and persuasion.

Master frames and competing frames

The process of becoming a host city is in many ways like participating in a social movement. The International Olympic Committee refers to itself as spearheading a movement that it calls "the Olympic Movement." Rule 1 of the Olympic Charter 2007 refers to all individuals and entities who want to build a better and more peaceful world through sport in accordance with the values of Olympism as being part of this movement. Participants in this movement are not only international federations, sport associations, and national Olympic committees, but also local organizing committees. By bidding, cities are acknowledging that they want to join and support this movement as governed by the International

Olympic Committee. All social movements are involved in what has been described as "meaning-work," in that they are "actively engaged in the production and maintenance of meaning for constituents, antagonists, and bystanders or observers" (Snow and Benford 1992:136). Meaning is transmitted through master frames which provide the overarching logic and values for becoming part of the movement. The master frame of Olympism is that it is a life philosophy harmoniously blending body, will, and mind as developed by its modern founder Pierre de Coubertin. Becoming a host city, then, means joining a movement with these principles, as organized by the International Olympic Committee.

If this is the master frame of the Olympics from a global perspective, it is also imperative that a host city develop frames of meaning whereby residents can interpret and support the Olympic project locally. As we have observed, framing is a dynamic negotiated process that allows people to interpret what is happening around them and to locate it in a larger system of meaning. There may be a dominant frame but there may also be a variety of other frames or competing frames that develop among people. Frames are developed as the result of interaction with others where meaning is negotiated rather than simply handed down through structures or ideologies. When frames not only interpret but are used to mobilize responses from others, they become collective action frames (Benford and Snow 2000). Collective action frames seek to restrict the impact of other interpretive frames and inspire and legitimate support for one frame. Olympic bid boosters, then, have a core framing task, which is to negotiate a shared understanding of how and why the Olympics should be supported. This is known as frame alignment, whereby it is attempted to make the interests of individuals and smaller groups congruent with the objectives of those seeking to enlist wider support (Snow *et al.* 1986).

In order to demonstrate the existence of widespread city support, a bid organization has to operate much as a social movement organization (SMO) in order to broaden its support. It seeks to successfully convince the public (frame alignment) of the Olympic frame, namely that Olympic values are congruent with their values and that being a part of the Olympic movement is an outstanding opportunity for the city. In the case of Vancouver, most of the leaders in the city and the province were supportive of the bid, which made this interpretation the master frame. But there was a need to convince others that they should accept this frame. While the logic of joining the movement as a host city implied the endorsement of the values of Olympism, local master frames had to be developed pointing out how the city would benefit through job creation, place promotion, tourism, and other economic benefits.

The logic of building interpretive frames revolves around developing a rationale that persuades others of the efficacy or value of a desired action. The articulation of a frame requires the social construction of a point of view known as claims-making. Claims-making is rhetorical activity because its goal is to persuade through marshaling an argument that appears logical (Best 1987). Because of the heavy financial commitments required by the Olympics, claims-making largely centers on economic benefits. Accounting studies are commissioned to estimate the contribution of hosting the Games to employment or to the GDP, for example, and a rationale is developed to show not only how businesses will benefit but also how the poor will benefit through employment, housing, or job training in order to make the claim to support the Olympics more compelling. By the same token, opponents also must be involved in claims-making by marshaling arguments and providing statistics that emphasize the costs of the Games rather than the benefits. Roche (1994) calls this process "situated rationality," but it is also subject to manipulation through the use of statistics that are imprecise, unverified, or approximations at best.[3]

Movements can only enlist supporters if there is a diagnosis of the context in a way that justifies their participation. Bid organizations often attempt to develop a diagnostic frame that explains how and why the Olympics are needed and what issues it will address. The Vancouver bid had considerable difficulty developing a diagnostic frame as a means to enlist support beyond the idea of securing the Games as an international honor (Black 2007). Vancouver already had a significant global reputation, partly as a result of its coastal location, its previous hosting of Expo 86, and its role as an international immigrant destination and Asian gateway. While there might be some employment and tourism benefits, there was no obvious and compelling reason why hosting the Olympics would improve the city or solve any of Vancouver's problems. If anything, the Olympics might exacerbate existing problems, such as increasing the already high costs of land and housing. Prognostic framing, or the ability to articulate solutions to urban issues, was also difficult to specify except in general terms such as how the Olympics would contribute to the economy. In contrast to other cities such as Barcelona or London, where urban redevelopment was a key part of the Olympic plan, there was no clear urban rationale for hosting the Games. Ultimately, the Inner City Inclusivity Commitment Statement adopted by the bid was one attempt to show how the Olympics could help contribute to resolving the problems of homelessness and the issues of the Downtown Eastside. But in general, establishing a convincing rationale and urgency for supporting the bid (known as motivational framing) did not lead to significant mobilization except through appealing to the uniqueness of the event and the desire to win the global competition to host it. When bid boosters approached the public, they did so by providing top-down information regarding plans that were being made. The weakness of the movement was reflected in the fact that the public was not asked to do anything but essentially endorse existing plans, which was not an effective mobilizing strategy. As we have seen, what changed the framing context considerably was the announcement that a plebiscite would be held, which provided a much stronger motivational tool for participation and did create a sense of urgency.

Those in the fledgling and somewhat uncoordinated opposition, on the other hand, began to let their voice be heard through a strong diagnostic frame that pointed out how the Olympic project was a wrong-headed priority and financial risk. They pointed out that Olympics everywhere were financial sinkholes, increased urban debt, marginalized the poor, and benefited elites – particularly land developers. The diagnosis was clear that corporations, elites, and real estate developers were the villains. The opposition articulated a cause or explanation that targeted boosters virtually as enemies of the people. This diagnostic frame was powerful in raising questions among those who had only considered hosting the Olympics as a badge of honor rather than an event with real consequences. The prognostic frame or the solution for the diagnosis, then, was very clear: oppose the Olympics and perhaps even disrupt plans or attack those who were promoting the Games. The motivation rationale came from pointing out how the public was being disadvantaged through education and healthcare cutbacks. Opposition to, and indeed rejection of, the Olympic project, it was argued, was the only way to save public services. The best-written description of this counter-frame is found in the book *Five Ring Circus: Myths and Realities of the Olympic Games* by Christopher Shaw (2008).[4]

The plebiscite forced the "Yes" side to address the issues raised by the "No" side, which meant that the prognostic frame, namely to win the vote, became the primary objective. The goal was to get people out to vote, and especially to vote "Yes." Thus, the plebiscite became a clash of frames crystallized into two positions: for and against. Each frame attempted to discount the other frame by marshaling evidence, statistics, testimonials by authorities, and logic to convince people of the fallacies of the other frame. The opposition frame was often extreme but was quite successful in vocalizing a counter-frame to which master frame promoters were forced to react. One of the most important ways of enlarging the support base of the "No" side was to link together with other groups who had different but potentially related frames. For example, opposition to the war in Afghanistan was very different from anti-poverty, and yet the two groups could come together in opposition to the Olympics because they both challenged the dominant frame in some way. Similarly, the Board of Trade and sport organizations had different frames and yet they could join together to support the Olympic frame. The clash was filled with socially constructed vocabularies and phrases labeling the other side's frame as unacceptable.

The problem of frame resonance

Viewing the plebiscite as two alternatives, "Yes" and "No," suggests that there were only two interpretive frames about the Olympics and that support of the two frames was continuous and consistent. This assumed a static view of frames that perhaps was best represented only among hard-core supporters on either side. In reality, reassessment and renegotiation occurred as the result of changing information, circumstances, and conditions that caused shifts in frames. Also, the substitution of one frame for another (frame transformation), which a simple yes–no response implied, did not adequately account for the frame confusion that many felt. There were some aspects of one frame (e.g., the honor of being chosen to host the Games) that might find resonance with many, but there were also aspects of the other frame (e.g., the fear of civic debt) that also might find resonance. The result was a significant portion of urban residents feeling torn, confused, and uncertain. So in reality, while being in favor or opposed to hosting the Games were the dichotomous choices, there were many positions in between, with some aspects of each frame resonating better than others. Just as it was found that utilizing the concept of "culture wars" as a framing device to describe the dichotomous value and ideological conflict in the United States was far too simplistic, given the diversity of attitudes that did not fit neatly into polar opposites (Kniss 1997), so the simple dichotomous options about hosting the Games did not allow for more nuanced views of the benefits and liabilities of hosting the Games.[5]

As has been noted, Vancouver was awarded the Games in Prague on July 2, 2003 on the second ballot with a come-from-behind narrow victory over Pyeongchang, Korea. Moving from being a candidate city to being a host city shifted the frame significantly. Now 2010 became a firm deadline around which all kinds of decisions would need to be made and expenditures undertaken to prepare the city for the Games. The Olympics provided an incentive to complete all kinds of projects, whether related to the Games directly or indirectly. Instead of opposition and controversy melting away in the face of the decision to host the Games, the number of new initiatives required in the preparation phase ensured that controversy dogged the project at almost every step.

Issues with competing frames

What were the issues that framed the Olympics as contentious during the preparation period and that generated competing frames? Ultimately, most of them had to do with finances and the use of public money, which included the appropriateness of Olympic projects as priorities for government spending. The problem was that any major civic projects undertaken after the Games were awarded in 2003 became intimately linked to the Olympics even when their relationship to the Games was in fact complex. There were three major construction projects that became the dominant symbols in the framing of the Olympics as problematic. The decision to build the Canada Line rapid transit system to the airport and the Sea-to-Sky Highway from Vancouver to Whistler came to be the major symbols in conflicts about the Olympics. However, the construction of a new costly Convention Centre also became a lightning rod for conflict about the Olympics. The framing struggle occurred over whether these projects were Olympic costs or not as a way of determining the "true costs" of the Games.

The RAV (Richmond–Airport–Vancouver) line, now called the Canada Line, was the third link in Vancouver's metro rapid transit system. It was approved in 2004 and completed in 2009 just prior to the opening of the Games. The relationship between federal funding for public transit infrastructural projects and the timing of the Olympics is unclear as it relates to Vancouver, but there is no question that Olympic leaders in Vancouver supported the idea of a rapid transit link to the airport. All advocates agreed that it would be most advantageous if it was completed in time for the Olympics. Some disagreement in the city was registered over whether other, unserved quadrants of the city should have priority, but linking an unserved community to the south (Richmond) with the downtown core (rather than just the airport) overcame these objections to a considerable extent. The line, then, could not be simply construed as serving Olympic visitors. But given the fact that the Canada Line was being built in time for the Olympics, the question was whether it should be considered a cost of the Olympics and/or a legacy of the Olympics. One answer, of course, was that the rapid transit line had nothing to do with the Olympics because congestion on the major arteries out of the downtown was already severe and a rapid transit line would be a green-friendly decision, particularly given that freeways into the core had been rejected years ago. Rail-based transit to the south would complement the existing SkyTrain routes to the east, which would underscore Vancouver's other green city initiatives. It could be expected that this decision would be non-controversial; yet that was not the case. While drawing simple battle lines is unfair, people opposed to the Olympics tended to see the cost of the Canada Line as a cost of the Olympics. People supportive of the Olympics tended to see the line as an infrastructural benefit to the city unrelated to the Games, which made it inappropriate to attach these costs to the Olympics. What helped to stir the controversy, however, was that Olympic organizers were often quick to list the Canada Line as a legacy of the Games even though the project was unrelated to their budget and not really required by the Games. The contradiction of viewing this rapid transit addition as not an Olympic-related cost but at the same time claiming it as an Olympic legacy created untold confusion and debate. Adding the final cost of over $2 billion for the train line to the total expenses of the Olympics made a huge difference in discussions about the real costs of the Games and played a major role in how the project was framed and interpreted.

The second project that became a huge symbol in the public debate generating significant controversy was the Sea-to-Sky highway from Vancouver to Whistler, a popular ski resort and the site of the downhill events. For many years, discussions had taken place about enlarging the winding two-lane highway along the coast.[6] Rock slides were a problem and many accidents occurred on what was often referred to as the "Highway of Death." If Whistler was to be the primary location for the downhill events (indeed, the bid was initially referred to as Vancouver–Whistler), it was obvious that improving the road could be part of the planning agenda. Jack Poole had already raised the issue as a potential deal-breaker in 2002. But when the IOC Evaluation Commission met in Vancouver in 2003, the chair, Gerhard Heiberg, went public by saying that the distance was too far and that something should be done to shorten the time. Therefore, whether an improved highway was something that was needed anyway became clouded by the need to provide safe and faster travel for the Olympics – and this made the highway an Olympic project in the minds of many. But whereas the rapid transit line had greater public benefit, the highway was quickly interpreted by opponents as "a roadway for the rich" to get to their ski chalets at public expense.

Both the Canada Line and the Sea-to-Sky Highway became critical symbols in the debate about the value and cost of the Olympics. Once each project came under attack, of course, there were many other reasons to oppose them as well. For example, the switch from tunnel bore to cut-and-cover meant that the underground portions of the track construction of the Canada Line disturbed communities along the route. Critics of the Olympics could also become champions of local businesses, whose revenues fell off sharply because of the protracted unsightly construction that was ruining the landscape and cutting off access for patrons. Disagreements over the routing of the tracks also tangentially reflected on the Olympics because of the need to forge ahead to complete the project in time for the Games. In other words, once a link was made between the project and the Olympics, all the debates about the project tended to draw out attitudes towards the Olympics.

The same could be said for the Highway – only with even more complexity. There were two issues that catalyzed opposition from other interest groups. One was the fact that instead of building a tunnel through Eagleridge Bluffs, it was decided to build a surface highway through an ecologically sensitive area of wetlands and arbutus forest, which provided justification for environmental opposition. This became an especially difficult matter given VANOC's commitment to a green Games emphasizing environmental sustainability. VANOC's response, however, was that roads were a provincial responsibility and outside its purview. The other issue about the highway was that it was to be built through native land. Some aboriginal people were prepared to take a public stand on that issue, which increased media coverage. Thus, while the highway was not an Olympic issue in a direct sense, there were all kinds of undertones that linked the road to the Olympics. The fact that the new road would also open up a previously secluded area for development, which environmentalists opposed, only accentuated the symbolic role of the highway as a way in which the Olympics were a catalyst for environmentally harmful change in the host region. The use for Olympic activity of the Callaghan Valley in the Whistler area, previously undisturbed public land, also awakened concern about the impact of the Games in Whistler.

The third project with Olympic links was the expansion of the Convention Centre, with its enormous cost overruns of $400 million. Whether Vancouver needed a larger, more magnificent and costly LEED Convention Centre at public expense was one issue, but the fact that it would be used as the Media Centre (International Broadcast Centre) for the Olympics and needed to be constructed in time to impress "the world" linked this controversial structure to the Games. With its spectacular location over land and water (Burrard Inlet), and looking towards the North Shore Mountains, the stunning vistas, in combination with its magnificent architecture, created an image of a huge public expenditure constructed to appeal to a wealthy visitor class. In addition, the desire to make this a LEED building using green technologies such as seawater heating and cooling, on-site water treatment, and a living roof with a variety of local flora ensured that all of these design innovations would add significantly to the costs. The decision to build the new Convention Centre was essentially a decision of the Liberal provincial government, which purchased the prime land from a development company in 2003. In view of the fact that the provincial government took the initiative with this project, criticism of this expenditure was primarily directed towards that level of government by those who thought public funds should be directed to other priorities. In fact, even though the Olympics were hosted by the city of Vancouver, all three of the projects mentioned here re-emphasized the link in people's minds between Olympic-related infrastructure projects and provincial government policy and funding. Therefore, any opposition to these projects became a criticism of provincial government policy decisions, thereby making them partisan issues.

Infrastructure needed for the Games themselves in the city of Vancouver was not controversial in any significant sense, largely because the biggest venues needed were already in place. The opening and closing ceremonies were held in BC Place, a 55,000-seat covered stadium, which ironically was not converted to a retractable roof stadium with other improvements until after the Games. The largest hockey and skating events were held in the existing GM Place (now Rogers Arena), seating 19,000 people, which was the home for the Vancouver Canucks National Hockey League team and a venue for many entertainment events. Another major venue was an existing arena called Pacific Coliseum on the grounds of the Pacific National Exhibition, which was updated, in addition to an updating of an existing arena on the campus of the University of British Columbia. Curling was held in a newly constructed facility in the Hillcrest area, which was reconfigured after the Games as a community recreational complex. While other communities may have wished that they had been chosen to have such an upgraded facility, there was little controversy about this project. The largest competition venue construction project was the speedskating oval built in Richmond and often referred to as "the crown jewel" of Vancouver's Games because of its design innovations. Initially it was hoped to build the oval on the campus of Simon Fraser University but ultimately the city of Richmond showed more interest in hosting this project. The Richmond Oval (as it was known during the Olympics) is a $170 million structure built along the Fraser River which became the kick-start for a mixed-use urban development project after the Games. The Oval itself was totally reconverted after the Games for community recreation purposes and would probably never again be used for speedskating competition.[7] In general, then, large structures needed as competition and celebration venues for the Olympics were not viewed as problematic by city residents.

The infrastructural project required by the IOC that initially was not viewed as problematic was the Athletes' Village. As the host city to the Games, the city of Vancouver was responsible for providing the Athletes' Village, and it decided to do so by building on a brownfield tract of city-owned land known as Southeast False Creek. The area had been used for a variety of industries over the years such as sawmills, rail yards, shipbuilders, foundries, and a variety of suppliers related to the fishing industry, especially in earlier days. Prior to Olympic

Village construction, the area housed dilapidated buildings, and from an urban revitalization perspective it was due for renewal. In some ways, it was ideal as a redevelopment site because it contained no housing and no one would be displaced. As prime waterfront land, the city anticipated that upscale housing there would maximize the return on the development and that the city would make a significant profit on the project. It appeared to be a project with minimal risk for the city. The city entered into a project development agreement with the Millennium Development Group, which obtained financing from a New York hedge fund that was deeply affected by the financial meltdown in 2008. The result was that Millennium needed an infusion of money, which the city was then obligated to provide in order to fulfill the requirement to provide an Athletes' Village. The city's charter did not allow for such borrowing without a city-wide referendum, and since time was of the essence, the British Columbia legislature passed Bill 47 in 2009, which allowed the loan to take place without the referendum but not without risk to city taxpayers. Slow sales of the housing units in the project in the post-Olympic period eventually led the developer to default on its repayments to the city, forcing the project into receivership in 2011. What appeared non-problematic thus became a crisis (Scherer 2011). However, the crisis did not become clear until the late stages of preparation for the Olympics, which meant that it did not play a central role in the framing battle in the pre-Games period.[8]

The framing debate primarily centered on Olympic costs and their relationship to what was appropriate as public expenditures. The fact that these costs required endorsement by government bodies then made them public and political issues. Cutbacks in any other sector (e.g., education, the arts, or health care) which might be required as the result of government fiscal problems exacerbated by the recession were then pitted against Olympic-related expenditures, which made framing so much more of an issue.

Counter-framing: organizations and protest

Protests and demonstrations became one of the ways in which opposition to the Olympics could contradict the dominant message being promoted as a counter-framing device.[9] Especially when covered by the media, protests provided the visual images for the opposition message. For example, a Coalition to Save Eagleridge Bluffs was formed to oppose and eventually to block construction on the Sea-to-Sky Highway. This coalition included a mix of West Vancouver residents, environmentalists, people associated with the Green Party and the Work Less Party, two aboriginal elders, and No Games 2010. Opponents filed a petition with the government in which the link to the Olympics was clear: "The provincial government plans to cut a highway through the bluffs in order to shave three minutes of driving time for people travelling between Vancouver and Whistler, primarily to accommodate the increased traffic during the 2010 Winter Games."[10] On April 10, 2006, a tent city was set up at the construction site at Eagleridge which lasted for thirty-nine days until May 26, when the police arrested twenty-three people. CBC News adopted the association with the Olympics as well, by framing its story with the headline "Vancouver Olympics Claim First Victims: Arrests at Eagleridge Bluffs." *Scientific American* headlined its piece somewhat later "Highway of Good Intentions? Vancouver Olympic Plans Bulldoze Rare Forest" (August 4, 2008). The media, then, also played a role in linking the highway with the Olympics in the counter-frame.

Three coalition groups emerged in the preparation period, though there was often considerable overlap between them. In reality, the No Games 2010 Coalition was already spearheading opposition in the bid period. While the motivations for participating in opposition were many, the coalition mobilized against the Olympic bid by promoting "the collective vision of a just, democratic society that uses public funds for public priorities." Clearly, the idea that the Olympics meant the misappropriation of funds was prominent. In many ways, that theme found resonance among many of the public when cutbacks were being imposed on critical human services such as health care or education. No Games 2010 was much more active and in some cases militant about its opposition. Its tolerance of whatever protest techniques someone wanted to choose, in addition to its desire to be an umbrella organization for a wide range of dissenters, tended to polarize its opposition towards extremism in the view of many members of the general public who otherwise agreed that public funds should be spent in other ways.

Related to No Games 2010 and 2010 Watch was a second group called the Olympics Resistance Network (ORN), whose members also thought of themselves as a "convergence of groups, issues, and sectors – anti capitalist, Indigenous, anti poverty, labour, migrant justice, housing, environmental justice, civil libertarian, anti war, and anti colonial." The ORN particularly wanted to identify with indigenous communities under the slogan "No Olympics on Stolen Native Land" and regarded the Olympics as taking place without their approval on Coast Salish Territories, considered unceded native land (O'Bonsawin 2010).[11] Their opposition was much broader, though, including issues such as concerns about homelessness and migrant labor issues as well as opposition to gentrification, privatization of public services, a ballooning public debt, police surveillance, criminalization of the poor, corporate profiteering, and repression of dissent. The ORN described itself as providing an "opportunity for all anti-capitalist, indigenous, anti-poverty, labour, migrant justice, environmental justice, anti-war, and anti-colonial activists to come together to confront this two-week circus and the oppression it represents." Its interpretive frame was anti-capitalist and anti-colonialist and shared solidarity with the oppressed.

A third organization that emerged in the Olympic preparation period was the Impact of the Olympics on Community Coalition (IOCC), which was composed of interested persons and organizations dedicated "to ensuring that environmental, social, transportation, housing, economics, and civil rights issues associated with the Vancouver/Whistler 2010 Olympic Games were addressed from a community perspective."[12] Member organizations included groups such as the Pivot Legal Society, the Building and Construction Trades Council, the

Tenant Resource and Advisory Council, and persons associated with links to civil liberties organizations and the University of British Columbia. The group was originally formed in 2002 prior to the awarding of the bid, with the goal of mitigating the impact of the Games on low-income residents, which made social sustainability specifically important. The goal was to ensure that "community based issues and concerns were turned into legacies." The original goal was to be neutral about the Olympics and just monitor or act as "watchdog" over VANOC and the government partnership's commitment to the Inner-City Inclusive Agreement. Yet it became clear that an interpretive frame with its own world-view and objectives dominated its action plan. An Olympic Oversight Interim Report Card was issued in 2007 which gave VANOC a grade of D-minus. The report acknowledged that there had been a loss of low-income housing in recent years, and the expectation was clear that the Olympics were to create a legacy of new low-income housing. There was a weak implicit causal connection to the Olympics rather than identifying the multiple causes of a broader process of gentrification ("gentrification pressures due to the Games") but it is clear that there was an expectation of "new legacy-related housing" even prior to 2010. Other aspects of the report dealt with environmental concerns, civil liberties in conjunction with protest ("attempts to limit legitimate protest opportunities to be seen and heard"), and the use of public space, particularly in the light of Mayor Sam Sullivan's Project Civil City, which aimed to reduce public disorder in time for the Games in what is sometimes called urban cleansing or the sanitizing of urban spaces.[13] The IOCC also identified a whole range of other issues such as true cost accounting by VANOC and open board meetings, more financial disclosure, and responses to public requests for information.

It is very hard to separate what IOCC considered a neutral position and being a watchdog from advocacy and criticism. In any case, its documents gave little sense of support for the Olympics. It was not surprising that early in 2008 (January 17), the *Vancouver Sun* reported that relations between the group and VANOC had broken down and that the group itself was losing control of its "radical element," which led to the prediction of a new wave of protests and boycotts. The IOCC experience also demonstrates how expectations about what the Olympics can accomplish can be frustrating. VANOC defined its responsibility as limited to those things that the Olympics itself impact, whereas other agencies wanted the Olympic legacy to address urban problems directly.[14] VANOC defined matters like homelessness as public issues that exceeded its authority or capacity to act, and the responsibility of its government partners. However, others saw these matters as directly connected to an Olympic social sustainability legacy. The report by the Inner-City Inclusive Housing Table in 2007 claimed that the legacy of the Games should be "the elimination of homelessness." This does not mean that VANOC was not interested in having a housing legacy for the homeless; rather, it considered minimizing negative social impacts of the Games as more central to its role than creating new social legacies.

The IOCC was somewhat different than other organizations but there was a similarity to all organizations that attacked the Olympics because the Olympic agenda interfered with their own perspectives and group goals. Some groups, like the Anti-Poverty Committee, were opposed to the Olympics from the start. Some groups were ideologically at odds with the Olympic agenda, and the goal was to attack the Olympics where they were most vulnerable. In other words, the Olympic frame was constantly opposed by alternative frames: an environmental frame, an anti-poverty frame, a housing advocacy frame, an anti-capitalist frame, or an anti-globalization frame. The goal of all these organizations was to seek public attention for their counter-frame, and this was done through media announcements or through a variety of forms of public protest. All of this contributed to a public awareness that the Olympics were in some sense controversial. It did not matter that these may have been small groups; from a media point of view their actions brought color and controversy to the Olympics as drama. Olympic boosters were the protagonists and Olympic opponents were the antagonists, at times a David challenging a Goliath, and it created an intriguing storyline (Benford and Hunt 1992). But what was more critical for the population at large was that the protest groups created a mood of uncertainty about whether hosting the Games was truly in the public interest.

The media and framing

The media play an enormous role in framing public perceptions of issues (Reese *et al.* 2001; McCombs *et al.* 2011). As was noted earlier, the local media, in particular, stimulated the sense of drama about the Olympic project and created and stirred emotions: apprehension–anticipation, fear–happiness, caution–determination, and suspicion–trust. The mixture of criticism and negativity in the media alongside constant highlighting and profiling of the Games and their issues put residents in a continuous state of suspense about what was happening and its consequences.

There is no question that the predominant issue kept before taxpayers in the media was the issue of costs and debt. Construction costs were usually portrayed as going beyond budget, which created images that the Games were a financial sinkhole. Headlines often screamed of ways in which the Olympics were costing much more than previously announced or expected. In June 2006, VANOC announced that it had increased its construction budget from $470 million to $580 million. The media carried this message in a way that sounded alarms and also pointed out that at the same time some other costs were downloaded to government agencies; for example, the road to the Nordic site was being built with provincial transportation money. Headlines announced that the cost of the sliding centre was underestimated or that there were cost overruns that were delaying the community legacy project in Killarney. In September 2006, the Auditor General of British Columbia issued a scathing report over the growing costs of the Games. One of the issues raised in this report was that there was no calculation of "true costs," as projects like the Sea-to-Sky Highway or some of the RAV line costs were not included. This report provided fuel to opponents of the Olympics, whose view was that some of the projects arguably not entirely related to the Olympics should be included, which of course would raise the total costs of the Games considerably. Headlines like "Auditor-General pegs Games cost at $2 billion" or "Government hides Olympic costs, says NDP" fueled the public debate about how much the Games were really costing. Calls for the firing of CEO John Furlong or speaking of the City of Vancouver as "a victim" around that time eroded public confidence in how the city would be impacted by the Games.

On January 23, 2009, the *Vancouver Sun* boldly proclaimed this front-page headline: "Add it all up, and you'll find **the Olympics is going to cost us $6 BILLION** (so far, anyway)." The argument was that it was not just construction costs but also contributions by various levels of government "who have shoveled taxpayer money to the event in a big way," from cash to payments in kind to the forgoing of revenues normally accruing. As one headline put it, "The running tab for the Olympics is running and running" (*Vancouver Sun*, January 13, 2009). The collapse of funding for the Athletes' Village, for which the city was responsible, intensified public worry. The discovery that the city council had secretly agreed to a $100 million loan agreement to the developer of the Village in 2008, which then turned into a provincial government rescue plan in 2009, created more public concern. Amending the city charter to allow the city to borrow $875 million without going to a public referendum led to references to the Games as "a big Owe," with parallels to the huge indebtedness in Montreal for the Olympics there.[15] The economic recession, the collapse of hedge fund support, and changing housing market conditions in Vancouver put the entire Athletes' Village project as a money-maker for the city not only at risk but at risk of substantial fiscal loss. And all of this was occurring as deadlines for completion stared organizers in the face, allowing no room for long delays. As one headline put it, "After the Olympics comes debt" (*Vancouver Sun*, January 14, 2009), which then raised panic among those who exclaimed that the city's AA+ credit rating was at risk, which could only mean that taxpayers would have even higher interest costs on the debt that would be incurred. By bringing these matters into public focus, the media contributed to the framing of the Games in a way that provided citizens with substantial questions about whether hosting the Olympics was a good decision.

The media and protest

Protest groups also used the media to keep criticism of the Olympics on the public agenda. Protests contribute action to the drama. They are also a form of staging that attract the media, for conflictual events are more likely to receive coverage because they involve drama. Protests move beyond words and give concreteness to them through colorful characters and direct confrontations. Oliver and Myers (1999) even point out how police and reporters form a type of improvisational troupe because there is a plan but not a script, meaning that how the drama will evolve is not known for certain. Most of the protests during the preparation period for the Olympics were still framed in the media in the manner of the plebiscite of dichotomous options of Yes–No. Even though the Olympics were indeed coming, the goal was to keep up the opposition to "the Olympic machine."[16]

Key commemorative events for the Olympic frame then became targets for the opposition. When the ceremonies for the Countdown Clock took place, on February 12, 2007, protesters grabbed the microphone on the stage and created general disruption. Something similar occurred at the Flag Illumination Ceremony at City Hall, but the experience with the clock at the Art Gallery had established the need for greater security and security fencing. About 100 protesters appeared but they were at least equally matched in numbers by police and other security people at this second event. The Olympic flag was later stolen from its location at City Hall by members of the Native Warrior Society (NWS), who claimed responsibility for the action:

> We claim this action in honour of Harriet Nahanee, our elder-warrior, who was given a death sentence by the BC courts for her courageous stand in defending Mother Earth.
> We stand in solidarity with all those fighting against the destruction caused by the 2010 Winter Olympic Games.
> No Olympics on Stolen Native Land!

Nahanee became ill with pneumonia while in jail for her actions during the Eagleridge Bluffs protest, but her death was apparently at least partly the result of a previously undiagnosed lung cancer. A picture was released showing three members wearing balaclavas and toques with their fists upraised and holding a Mohawk flag with a picture of Nahanee.[17]

On the supposition that the Olympics would lead to the displacement of the poor, some members of the Anti-Poverty Committee used more threatening procedures to "evict" leaders in support of the Olympics from their homes or offices. VANOC members were told by protesters, as a not-so-subtle threat, that they knew where they lived. Three activists who pretended to be delivering flowers to the office of the premier of British Columbia gained entry to his office in Vancouver, where their target was his assistant, who was playing a key role in the Olympic project. They overturned furniture, scattered documents, boxed up some belongings, and symbolically threw him out of his office. There were also threats to disrupt VANOC board meetings. In September 2008, when the Canadian Pacific Spirit Train began its ten-city tour across Canada in Port Moody (a suburb of Vancouver), what was supposed to be a family affair with exhibits and entertainment was marred by activities of protesters. They drowned out musicians and sought to disrupt the entire event. In November 2008, protesters attempted to provide a counter-frame to the Olympic frame by making their presence known at the World Press Briefing for the Games. About 200 media people attended, and members of the Olympic Resistance Network and native resistance groups handed out counter-messages about the harmful impacts of the Games. Of course, the actions of these protesters were covered by the media, though it was unclear whether they were to be understood as only "extremists" or "hooligans" as opposed to representing wider sentiments. It was also unclear whether these actions generated more sympathy or antagonism towards their point of view. What is clear is that these actions continued to cast the Olympic project into a drama with contested meanings.

There were also other issues that the media highlighted. Security remained an issue because the originally budgeted amount of $175 million was considered inadequate in the light of the need to plan for a "worst-case scenario." Fears about security costs were raised considerably before the Games themselves but reached a fever pitch just before the Games began, when costs were re-evaluated at $1 billion. But one headline caught another aspect of this issue, which was not only financial but the sense of the Olympics curtailing individual freedoms: "Fortress British Columbia: Huge sums are being spent on the creation of a vast and highly complex security shield to prevent a terrorist attack during the Olympic Games, one that may make BC seem a bit like a police state" (*Vancouver Sun*, August 4, 2007). For the average citizen, the Olympics began to appear hegemonic, an event in which security concerns would trump people's freedoms.[18] Fears of an increase in prostitution, human trafficking, and sex trafficking were also raised, and rumors flew about roads and bridges being closed. As early as 2006, one headline read "Brace yourself for disruptions, even if you are not attending the Games" (*Vancouver Sun*, July 8, 2006). A front-page story on November 26, 2008 referred to the fact that 650 city blocks would be affected by traffic restrictions during the Games, which was described as being part of "the price" the city had to pay for hosting the Games. Front-page headlines just a few months before the Games referred to "the inconvenience truth," and people were warned that gridlock could be widespread (*Vancouver Sun*, October 15, 2009). Advocates for elderly and disabled people used the media to convey their worries about accessibility during the Games.

Other issues supporting counter-frames

The media also made more visible other issues that supported counter-framing thinking. VANOC lobbied Parliament to protect Olympic marks from being used for profit from an unauthorized association with the Games. Bill C-47, which became the Olympic and Paralympic Act, was passed in 2007. In it, all kinds of words such as "Olympic," "Olympia," and "Olympiad" were protected, but also words like "Canada," "2010," "winter," "gold," "silver," and "bronze." Ultimately, even a phrase from the national anthem, "with glowing hearts," which was to be the theme of the Games, was protected. Not unexpectedly, these kinds of announcements did not create goodwill and often appeared to be high-handed or a form of bullying. While censorship in everyday usage was not the intent, protection from various forms of ambush marketing created an image of VANOC as a powerful organization that automatically created resistance in some.

It was also reported that the city obtained an amendment to the city charter which gave the city power to remove graffiti and illegal signs. People debated whether an anti-Olympic sign in a condominium unit downtown would lead to an arrest, and civil libertarians wondered whether wearing an anti-Olympic button would also lead to some form of punishment. Handing out leaflets was to be curbed because it would lead to litter, but others saw it as an attack on free speech. Fears were raised about security issues and terrorist threats that would be elevated because of the Games. Minor hockey teams were told that ice surfaces would not be available and that existing programs would have to be rearranged. The office of the Chief Judge announced that no criminal trials would be held in February because police officers as witnesses would need to be on duty. Some surgeries were being postponed because of the Olympics. For some, it was as though the city was being taken over by the Games.

A background issue that also created controversy was the absence of a ski-jumping competition for women in the Olympic program. Fifteen Canadian athletes took VANOC to court in 2009, arguing that this denial breached the Canadian Charter of Rights and Freedoms. The court action failed on the grounds that VANOC had no control over this decision because the IOC had supreme authority over the Games organization. But the issue provided a reason why some people who felt strongly about gender equality became irritated with the IOC and the apparent discrimination, which violated the principles of its own Charter, let alone the Charter of Rights and Freedoms of the host country.

There was controversy even within the Christian community. The *BC Christian News* had run an article in May 2007 pointing out how the Olympics could be a catalyst for church unity as Christians could be mobilized for a variety of service projects such as home stay and hospitality efforts as well as creative arts and cultural performances. This effort eventually became a multi-denominational program called "More Than Gold." However, the Olympics were not necessarily embraced by the Christian community as a whole. For example, the United Church countered "More Than Gold" with its theme of "Share the Gold" for addressing the issue of homelessness. Some opposed uncritical Christian support of the Games because "it mirrors the right wing's oblivion to the fallen nature of culture, and the de facto empire we live in" (*BC Christian News*, June 2007). They argued that Jesus related more to the poor than the wealthy, who are what the Olympics represent. Another group, called Streams of Justice, also criticized the Olympics from a Christian point of view in that the needy were ignored while urban culture bowed to fame and profit-making, which in their eyes is what the Olympics represented (*BC Christian News*, August 2009). It is no exaggeration to say that many churches were conflicted in terms of how to respond to the Olympics. Many wanted to support the Olympics as a community event but were also troubled by the framing of the opposition, which pointed out how the Olympics mobilized public financial resources at a time when other needs in society were so great.

Conclusion

The Olympic project provided the master frame but the existence of a strident counter-frame (some of its proponents being in radical opposition) to the

Games destabilized the master frame. Even though Vancouver had already been awarded the Games, the nature of the more public opposition was not to improve the Games in some way or to ensure that the city would benefit more from the Games, but to oppose the Olympics in their entirety. The nature of this opposition had two effects. First, it contributed to a "chilly climate" in the city about the Games and made them controversial rather than a triumph. It above all affected people who had doubts. For example, some teachers refused to participate in the Olympic education program in their schools because they embraced the rhetoric of the oppositional frame.[19] Employees of Olympic projects often found that they were sometimes hesitant to say what work they did at social gatherings. These examples reveal the extent to which counter-frames had made inroads into the thinking of many residents.

Second, almost conversely, the stridency of the opposition in engaging in various acts of civil disobedience marginalized their position as representative of extremists. Being uncertain over whether the city should host the Olympics was not the same as being disrespectful and in radical opposition. Thus, if in some senses the opposition dampened enthusiasm for the Games and pushed under-ground those who embraced the Games, it could be argued that there might eventually have to come a release of the supportive emotion. And ironically, if that occurred, would the media shift their emphasis from the agonizing parts of the Olympic drama evoking emotion surrounding the issues and problems to the more joyful and celebratory emotions during the Games period? The problem of contrasting the master frame with the oppositional frame, of course, is that it again implies two dichotomous choices. In reality, there was a plurality of frames present in the city that emerged from the groups into which people were con-nected. For example, people could decide in what way they might participate in the atmosphere of the Games. As we will see, participation in things like flash mobs required planning, showing hospitality to visiting guests required prepara-tion, and arranging time off work to take the family to visit pavilions required scheduling. As the Games came closer in time, interpretive frames could con-ceivably change. Issues and controversies might become less important, for perhaps in many ways they had repressed the positive aspects of what hosting the Games would mean. The opposite of the negative aspects of street closures might be the initiatives that were taken by groups to fill that space with fun. Or, the opposite of hearing how hotels were all reserved for the Olympic family was the requests from friends and relatives from near and far to be hosted in order to take in the Olympics. This issue will be explored in depth in Chapter 7.

It was argued at the beginning of this chapter that framing is a negotiated process. Interpretations of the Olympics within the host city cannot be taken for granted, for residents have a variety of frames to use to interpret the Games. What is important to understand is that the master frame is not monolithic or hegemonic in democratic societies, and the residents of each host city have to work through the meanings and interpretations of the Games as information becomes available and as those meanings and interpretations are relevant to their community or social networks. Given the fact that most members of the general public are relatively uninformed about the Olympics and their impact on a host city at the start of the Olympic cycle, it is not surprising that residents will bring their own personal perspectives to bear on events that occur and information they receive about the Games as the cycle evolves. The selection of any one frame may lack durability over time as interpretive frames change with the circumstances and the interactional inputs available. What this chapter has demonstrated is that local residents have much information to process in order to determine their own interpretive frame.

4   The public realm

Expectations of public responses to the games

The evidence discussed in Chapter 3 demonstrated that planning for the Olympics was moving forward but in a climate of considerable debate over both major and minor issues. It would not be surprising, then, if there was considerable ambivalence among host city residents. In two public opinion surveys conducted just prior to the Games, the negative undercurrent was clear.

In one national survey, completed in November 2009 (approximately three months prior to the Games), people from British Columbia, the host province, were more likely than other Canadians to state that they had "no interest at all" in the Vancouver Games. Twenty-one percent claimed that perspective, compared to the Canadian average of 16 percent.[1] When those with "no interest at all" were combined with those "not too interested," fully 37 percent of the population of the host province demonstrated little to no interest in the Olympics. Similarly, when people were asked whether the 2010 Games would have a positive or a negative effect on Vancouver, British Columbia residents were far more likely to declare that the impact would be negative (25 percent compared to 10 percent nationally) and far less likely to state that the impact would be positive (60 percent compared to 79 percent nationally). When another survey was completed two months later, in January 2010 (one month before the Games), the percentage of residents who thought the impact would be mostly negative had increased by an additional ten percentage points to 35 percent and the number who thought the impact would be positive had declined from 60 percent to 52 percent (77 percent nationally). Significantly, the percentage of respondents who said they were not at all interested in the Olympics had increased from 21 percent to 27 percent – again the highest of any region in Canada (the Canadian average was 17 percent).

It is somewhat unexpected that those living in the host province would reveal such a high level of lack of interest, or perhaps cynicism, just prior to the beginning of the Games in their own region. It was also unexpected that perceptions of a positive impact would drop. In general, there was more interest (combining "very interested" and "moderately interested") in the Olympics outside of British Columbia in the rest of Canada than in the host province itself. Whether these expressions of lack of interest or negative impact were symbolic of doubt, disillusionment, indifference, or resistance is not clear. What they do reflect is considerable confusion, pessimism, and trepidation about the Games. Since only half of the population thought that the impact would be positive for Vancouver, it might be possible to conclude that a rather low level of excitement and anticipation about the Games existed. If that were true, then public response to the actual Games themselves would be much lower than expected by those who viewed the Olympics as an international prize and once-in-a-lifetime opportunity.

Contrary to this perspective, the day the Games began, the city of Vancouver became a very different place. And indeed, as we will see more clearly in Chapter 7, attitudes about the Olympics began to change considerably. While it is difficult to explain complex matters like shifts in public opinion, the most compelling, visible, and dramatic form of public participation that took place in Vancouver during the Games occurred in the streets, or in what can be called the public realm. As has already been stated in the Introduction, President Rogge commented on the unusual nature of street life through the course of the Games, which suggests that this is indeed an important issue to assess and analyze (Kines 2010; Lee 2010). Consistent with our theme that the Olympics must be understood as much more than ticketed sport competitions, this chapter will focus on the role of urban public space in the transformation of the city during the Olympics.

Public space and private space

Before explaining what occurred in Vancouver, it is important to point out key characteristics of the contemporary city, especially as it relates to public spaces in the urban central core. Many metro residents avoid the downtown or have no reason to travel there because most of the services they need can be obtained elsewhere, and long commutes from suburbia are to be avoided. This means that being in the central core is more or less restricted to those who work there or live there, or to those who choose to go there for leisure commodification activities, particularly shopping, eating, sporting events, and concerts. Most of the places where people go in the downtown (office buildings, restaurants, retail shops and malls) are private spaces. In contrast, most of the space that is used by people to get to these destinations is public spaces – that is, roads and walkways that allow people to move from one location to another.

Urban space is fragmented by the privatization of space, since spaces have specialized uses that restrict access to those who belong in that space. One does not enter an office building or a restaurant and remain there without being questioned by security or servers who want to know whether they can help you do what that private space has been designed to do. Private spaces, then, have controls on who enters those spaces and what they do there, either through direct supervision or through electronic surveillance. On the one hand, this implies that there is a clear distinction between private space and public space.

But on the other hand, the boundaries between these spaces often overlap. For example, buildings that house retail outlets (such as malls) often have common spaces such as corridors, lobbies, seating and eating areas, and even parking lots that appear public but are actually private because they are owned by the mall. Privately owned public space also includes plazas, arcades, atriums, and other such spaces that are accessible to and usable by the public (Kayden 2000). Space that is public in the sense that it is the responsibility of government also operates according to fixed rules of entry and control. For example, libraries and transit stations operate with their own controls of public space, not unlike private space. Even public space-like streets and sidewalks are theoretically open to anyone, but they are organized to maximize the efficient movement of people and regulate what is considered appropriate behavior. Cafés are sometimes allowed to spill over onto pedestrian spaces in a way that integrates public with private (Blomley 2004). While public spaces often blend into private spaces, the role of doorways, various types of fencing, movable partitions, surveillance apparatus, and security charged with supervision of particular spaces gives the downtown a clear sense of order.

Interaction in private spaces is usually structured by the purpose for which the private space exists, but what is the nature of interaction in public spaces? Sidewalks are busy places of diversity where people encounter one another, but largely in anonymous ways. Most typical pedestrian behavior is goal oriented in attempting to reach a destination such as a place of employment, a service provider for which an appointment has been made, a retail shop, or a restaurant. Even strolling or window-shopping has its own objective, but seldom does that objective involve interacting with people along the way. Being cognizant of one another's presence, as Lofland (1973) has argued, is one thing, but actually speaking to or interacting with people seldom occurs because people who are visually available but personally unknown are considered strangers. Sennett (1976:14) noted that the increasing privatization of social relations has meant the decline of public life, with the consequence that public spaces have become places that people move through rather than be in. None of this contributes to the social fabric of a city. Thus, it is not surprising that there has been a renewed interest in the role of public space in cities as sites for "intersubjective presence" (Madanipour 2003:167).

The Olympics and resident participation modes

The organizational power of the Olympic industry, from the structure of the IOC, its policies, and its procedures, to the expectations and demands of sponsors and media, ensures that the Olympics are often viewed as dominant and hegemonic from the point of view of the host city. From the moment that the Games are awarded to a city, external requirements – the need for venues that meet international or federation standards, requirements and policies of the International Olympic Committee, the need to cater to the media, and the logistical issues of handling so many people from a security and efficiency point of view – define operational preparations for the Games. The organizers are in control and have mobilized leaders and managers to accomplish their task. We have already seen that this mobilization of everything, from money to personnel to venue control to hospitality and security, puts people into an organizational mode controlled by the organizational plan. How people interact with the dominant plan may vary in the planning phase, but is there something about the event itself that releases new energy or transforms the city at the grass roots? What has been observed, at least in some Olympic host cities, is that this new energy is expressed not in the confines of meeting rooms or in debates about Olympic policies and procedures, but in public spaces.

The pomp and ceremony of Olympic ritual, the magnificent and often extravagant nature of the opening and closing ceremonies, and the dramatic packaging of athletic performances into vignettes of television entertainment ensure that the Games become an impressive audio-visual mediated experience for more than just those in attendance. The fact that the Olympics captivate their audience, as evidenced by the demand for tickets to prime events, which leads to big crowds in attendance, or the ever-growing television audience for the Games, easily leads to the conclusion that the Olympics have become a spectacle. According to Debord (1994), a spectacle implies that people are passive recipients of images that are controlled by interests such as governments or corporations. A spectacle entertains and captures public interest but in essence is an instrument of power by disseminating images that shape the way people think (Harvey 1989). For example, the Olympics propagate images of peace, harmony, and fair play, when in reality often the opposite is the case. More so, the subliminal messages conveyed by the Olympics really mask capitalist interests or the instrumental purposes of governments that stand behind the Games. The spectacular nature of the Olympics creates enthralling appearances or images that result in expressions of "awe" and huge waves of public approval but hide perceptions of control or dominance. For this reason, it is argued, the spectacle should be resisted.

MacAloon (2006) has taken issue with this interpretation of the Olympics because it oversimplifies a much more complex matter. He acknowledges that the Olympics have moved in the direction of becoming a spectacle, largely because of the demands of television. Often, appearances or images do hide realities. On the other hand, he argues that the Olympics can evoke considerable reflection and action. MacAloon (1989) finds these human responses not on the inside of official Olympic events and structures but rather on "the margins, peripheries, and interstices of life in the Olympic city." He argues that the founder of the modern Olympics, Coubertin, conceived of the Olympics more as a festival than as a spectacle and that it is in the festival that one finds "spaces, activities and experiences" that reflect other cultural performances.[2] In contrast to the formal rituals of athletic participation and what happens inside stadiums among those with tickets or credentials, it is what happens in public spaces (streets, buses, restaurants, plazas) where social status and monetary entrance tickets are not important that festival takes place. If spectacle means that distinctions between performers and audiences are clear, in that performers act and audiences are passive, in festivals roles are more flexible, egalitarian, voluntary, spontaneous, transient, but united by mood or atmosphere. Mac-Aloon (1984) states that Coubertin would have seen joy as the dominant mood goal, and MacAloon himself links the mood to Durkheim's concept of "effervescence" or Simmel's "sociability." He acknowledges that spectacles can be tremendous recruiting devices, in that people may be drawn into action or participation which they had not expected.

These ideas are very important for an analysis of host city reaction to the Games. There is no question that the Olympics are a spectacle that dominates a host city. However, the response to this spectacle has many options, and while festival, with its implied emotion of joy, might be one form of participation, it is not the only one. One can be drawn into the event by being supportive but one can also be drawn in by being critical. One can be cynical and still buy tickets. It is possible to be enthusiastic and to become a formal volunteer suitably attired in the official uniform, with the status that brings. But it is also possible to react negatively to the hype that is part of the mood and to retreat or to actively oppose the event. There are many ways in which people respond. In that sense, it is not only what happens in the stadiums but also how people are responding outside these venues that is important.

Furthermore, from a host city point of view the Olympics are what is happening in other public and private places as much as what is happening at a competition site. The athletes are not the only performers; members of the public also perform in a variety of ways. They are not just passive. People who decide to serve as volunteers far outnumber the athletes, and more of them work outside venues than inside venues. Others provide paid support services, while still others are just selective consumers of the Olympic project. It is important, then, to look for the different ways in which the Olympics energizes and catalyzes a variety of forms of participation. And, perhaps because of their spectacular nature, the Olympics mobilize responses as few other events can do. This is why the argument needs to be made that the anticipation of the spectacle (the pre-Olympic period) and the memories of the spectacle (the post-Olympic period) are just as important as the spectacle itself. While the Olympics can be an instrument of alienation, they can also be an instrument of empowerment, from providing opportunities for dancers to perform their craft in a large production, to organizing anti-globalization activities, to stirring creative ideas about how the Games might help people accomplish other objectives (e.g., encouraging exercise and better nutrition). If spectacle stands for elitism, responses that challenge elitism, passivity, and social distance can be labeled anti-spectacle. MacAloon (2006) has argued that the torch relay is a good example of anti-spectacle because torchbearers and their entourage of local friends and acquaintances are a non-mediated person-to-person form of participation.[3] Again, there are far more torchbearers than there are athletes, and more people interact with the relay without paying anything than attend the Games as ticket-holders. Thus, in order to understand the Games in Vancouver it is important to understand the different ways in which people responded to the Olympics.[4]

Thousands of host city residents played formal, paid roles that served the Olympic event both directly and indirectly. Cooks and bartenders in pavilions, food inspectors and emergency hospital workers,[5] persons who emptied the specially designed trash bins in the downtown core, people who drove transit vehicles and traffic control personnel, clerks in retail stores, and servers in restaurants are just a small part of the cast that makes the Olympic event possible. Thousands more served as volunteers, such as the official Olympic volunteers (77,000 applied and 25,000 were selected). Four thousand five hundred volunteers participated in the opening and closing ceremonies, with twice-a-week rehearsals requiring about 100 hours. Tourism Vancouver advertised for 500 volunteers who knew the city and could roam the streets providing information for visitors and staff visitor centers; they were required to be available for at least seventy hours during the Games. Others volunteered to be part of the radical hospitality of "More Than Gold" and give free coffee to people on the streets. All residents were encouraged to participate with the "Top 10 Ways to be a Good Host," which included things like offering to help visitors, "share your love of the city," or using your language skills to make people feel welcome. Anti-Olympic organizers volunteered their time, and flash mob leaders spent considerable time organizing their unique street performances. The list of different ways in which people volunteered their time and participated in the Olympic project goes on and on. The list could be broadened even further to include those who entertained guests in their homes, those who went to neighborhood pubs to watch televised events with their friends, those who wore the famous red mittens, as well as those who joined the Paint the Town Red campaign by doing something public using red to celebrate the Olympics. But, as we have already observed, opponents and activists also participated in the Olympics as an event through organizing and participating in various forms of protest. Strategy meetings, letter-writing campaigns and blogs, and confrontational conversations were just some of the ways in which the Olympics also energized these activities. In a significant manner, then, the Olympics can be viewed as an emergent collective project with a variety of forms of participation/nonparticipation and with varying levels of energy.

The issue of street life during the Olympics

The form of participation that has been reported in some host cities and has achieved considerable media attention is the active street life that occurs during the Olympics, something which perhaps heightens the sense of the Games as a festival. Active street life with thousands of people milling around plazas, closed roadways, and consumption spaces has become of increasing importance to what is conceived of as a "successful" Olympics. The idea is that active street life is the strongest symbol of exuberant citizen participation and transforms the city from a container of Olympic events and a provider of Olympic services to a celebratory environment in which all can participate. This kind of environment transforms the experience of visitors from merely attending sporting events to participating in a giant festival. It is arguably the single most important factor in sending visitors home with a positive attitude towards the host city. But perhaps more importantly, it is active street life that transforms the Olympic experience for local residents. It is no exaggeration to say that it was active street life in Vancouver that played a huge role in heightening people's emotional connection with the 2010 Games and that arguably even served as the primary basis for collective memory. The reality of physical presence, individual participation with thousands of others, and a specific historical moment created a collective experience and a sense of "being there" (Rowe 2000) irrespective of attendance at ticketed Olympic events.

Street life refers to the gathering and mixing of visitors and host city residents, usually in the downtown core or a similar central area in public or semi-public places. This can occur on sidewalks, usually with vehicular traffic minimized, or on streets that have been turned into pedestrian corridors just for the Games through the banning of vehicular traffic. Street life can become more pronounced near bars and restaurants that enlarge their service from indoor to outdoor extensions. Street life can also be encouraged through planned activities, either announced (such as musical performances) or unplanned (such as buskers), that are free and available to the public in an open format. What characterizes street life the most is the sense of spontaneity and casual informal activity that occurs. People just show up and expect to be entertained by simply watching others or being with others. Individual performers (musical artists, jugglers, clowns) arrive to provide informal entertainment and people gather around them and then move on to see what else is going on. This is not to ignore the planned aspects of the use of public space, such as those organized by the Cultural Olympiad and especially CODE (Cultural Olympiad Digital Edition), for they provided important features to give life to urban space through things like the visual arts and light displays. However, it was the mixture of planned and spontaneous activity that attracted people to public spaces, with the informal performances being particularly accessible – less spectacular and more casual but often more amusing. It is not only the apparent spontaneity of street life that generates intrigue but also the casual and relaxed mood of people. Spontaneous acts of shouting, singing, or cheering can occur and there is a general feeling of exuberance and merriment. The variation of types of people almost always ensures that some will attract attention by their unique dress or appearances. With the myriad appeal to the senses, Whyte (2009) calls this the "sensory street."

Not all host Olympic cities have a thriving street life during the Games. MacAloon (1989) discovered this concept of festival at the Olympics first in Montreal at the 1976 Games, a city with a history of a festival atmosphere which he contrasted with Los Angeles (1984), where there was little notion of festival in the public realm. In Los Angeles, there was no central place where such activity could occur, and the dispersal of venues and the efforts needed to reach them and then return did not contribute to a festival atmosphere. The Athletes' Village was more or less self-contained, which did not encourage athletes to venture out and mingle with the public, and MacAloon notes that when celebration occurred, it was more likely to take place in private spaces. Public order was customary in Los Angeles, as opposed to open street life, which was associated with disorder – Los Angeles being a city with extremes of wealth and poverty. MacAloon notes that not all cities have a culture with a tradition of popular festivals or convivial street life, and so it is not surprising that Seoul (1988) and Beijing (2008) had less such activity. European cities with considerable open-air activities in public spaces, particularly in the summer, have fostered more active street life. MacAloon (1995:182) has argued that the sight of thousands of citizens strolling on the Montjuïc every night during the Games in Barcelona in 1992 "for no other reason than to be with everyone else" was unprecedented in his experience of the Summer Olympics.

The experience of two other cities hosting Winter Games is also noteworthy. Calgary (1988), with its history of the Calgary Stampede, and Turin (2006), with its European street ambience, had very active street life. My own work (Hiller 1990) on the Calgary Games discovered a very significant mood transformation and active street life downtown during the Olympics. The decision to hold the medal ceremonies downtown every night in a new plaza constructed in time for the Olympics (and adjacent to City Hall) in conjunction with a laser light show was a significant innovation for the Olympics and became a "must-do" experience for thousands who crammed into the area every night. In addition, a pedestrian mall became the center of much mingling throughout the day. There were other aspects of the festival-like atmosphere in the city, but the point was clear that much of the goodwill created by the Games arose from the interactive atmosphere that was present. A similar result has been reported for Turin, where mingling in the central plaza area was the result of thousands coming there every day during the Games. In both cases, in spite of traditions, the volume and nature of street life were unprecedented in those cities' histories.

Public spaces in Vancouver

From virtually the day that the Olympics began, vibrant street life played an important symbolic role in how the Games were perceived in Vancouver. It began with the recognition that thousands of visitors had descended upon the city and the awareness that the downtown had experienced a visual transformation through the placement of colorful banners, various forms of public art, gigantic building wraps on high-rise office and commercial structures, and the closure of selected streets. The streets were filled with people from everywhere; many people were dressed in various types of costuming, expressions of patriotism blossomed, and some would say that there was magic in the air in downtown Vancouver. For seventeen days, the city took on a character that was not typical of normal urban life. What happened? It was as though a new act in the drama had begun, with a completely different set and on a new stage. The new stage was the public realm. The Olympics were no longer an idea to be debated, a plan to be discussed, or an organization in an office building; they were a reality compelling action and collective participation. The preparation for the Olympic events had been the focus. What was less well known was the preparation that had taken place to prepare the public realm. Host city residents were expecting the focus to be on Olympic competitions. What was unexpected by many was that the public realm would draw them into the Olympics as an urban festival almost independent of the Games themselves.

The main stage of the public realm was the specially created pedestrian corridors in the downtown – thirty-two blocks of closed streets, including portions of Robson Street as the east–west spine, Granville, Hamilton, Mainland, and Beatty Streets running in a more north–south direction (see Figure 4.1). Key nodes were Robson Square (and the Art Gallery, where the Countdown Clock was located, and a traditional protest site as well), the Olympic Flame Cauldron, LiveCity Downtown and the adjacent Aboriginal Pavilion, and LiveCity Yaletown. Robson Square is in the heart of downtown and was the site of the evening laser light show, the zip line installed just for the Games, and GE Plaza (a skating and performance venue). LiveCity Downtown was the site of the Canadian Pavilion and a number of other pavilions and entertainment and, with strict capacity limits, averaged 12,000 people per day. LiveCity Yaletown averaged 24,000 people per day (most of the time at full capacity) because it was the location of the biggest entertainment acts and a 3D giant screen as well as the pavilions of TOP sponsors such as Coca-Cola and Panasonic. Adjacent to the Robson–Beatty intersection, pedestrian access continued to BC Place (the site of the opening and closing ceremonies and the nightly medal ceremonies), Canada Hockey Place (now Rogers Centre), and the False Creek pavilions

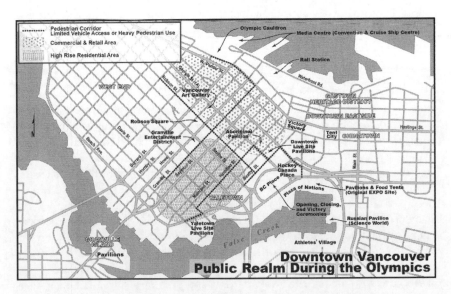

Figure 4.1 Map of downtown Vancouver public realm during the Olympics.

(sometimes referred to as Concord Place), linking to Science World, which served as the Russian Pavilion, and the food tents at the Plaza of Nations. Granville Island was also the location of important pavilions but they were not easily connected to the pedestrian corridors except by bridge or water taxi. Most of the large hotels were not located on these pedestrian corridors but were easily accessible from them, as well as the Media Centre and the International Broadcast Centre, which were adjacent to the Olympic Cauldron on the newly created Jack Poole Plaza, which drew thousands of people daily during the Games. Both the Canada Line and the SkyTrain had stops along the pedestrian corridor, ensuring easy access for those coming from the suburbs and other places outside the downtown.

With the exception of Robson Square, which was arguably the heart of street activity, businesses along the pedestrian corridor consisted of restaurants, coffee shops, pubs, takeaway food outlets, and small shops. Robson Street is well known as a shopping and entertainment destination for both tourists and locals, with direct entry from the sidewalk as opposed to being accessed through an interior mall. Part of Granville Street is known as the Granville Entertainment District, with nightclubs and the usual supporting fast-food outlets like pizza and hot dog establishments located on adjacent properties. Thus, there was an interesting unity of public space with private spaces that catered to leisure consumption as opposed to commercial activities such as insurance, real estate, banking, or big-box retailers (with the exception of Sears).[6] Customers could easily make the transition from private or semi-public spaces into the street or vice versa. The relationship between public and private spaces on the pedestrian corridor thus facilitated eating and drinking, browsing, strolling, and places for meeting. Office buildings, with their relatively blank walls and interior encapsulating activity, did not define the corridor. Indicative of the relationship between spaces for leisure consumption and the public realm was the fact that the dynamic scenes of streets filled with people were matched by the fact that restaurants in the area more than doubled their business, with some limited-service restaurants where seat limitations were not an issue reporting sales up 300–400 percent.[7]

There were three other factors that added to the vitality of the downtown. First, the pedestrian corridors were relatively close to high-rise residential towers.[8] Vancouver is known for the fact that the central city has a large residential population, most of whom live in condominiums (rather than rental apartment units) in the central city/downtown peninsula. The fact that the city has no freeways into the core and that high-density residential buildings are more numerous than office buildings meant that there was a large population to patronize leisure consumptive spaces. The population in the downtown peninsula had increased dramatically in recent years to approximately 100,000 residents, 89 percent of whom lived in buildings more than five stories tall and in which young adults between 25 and 40 years of age were over-represented (City of Vancouver, Information Sheet, City Facts 2006). Significant density was attested to by the fact that there were 15,188 people per square kilometer in this area, whereas the density for the city as a whole was 5,039 persons per square kilometer. The average household size was 1.6 persons per household in the downtown peninsula, suggesting that there were many people living alone, who may have been more amenable to experience the Olympics in a more publicly social context. The conclusion is that there was a substantial population immediately available for street activity.

Second, the Downtown Eastside (DTES), an area of considerable poverty, with its attendant issues of drug dealing, mental health problems, substandard housing, and homelessness, was within walking distance of the official pedestrian corridors and tourist areas like Gastown. As we will see, the DTES became the site (or stage following the dramaturgical model) of alternative activities in the public realm, and there was often considerable interchange between the two realms. The third factor that impinged on the public realm was the existence of Chinatown between the False Creek pavilions and the official Olympic stadiums (BC Place and Canada Hockey Place), and the Downtown Eastside. This thriving neighborhood was less directly implicated in the Olympic public realm, although the Chinese New Year parade during the Olympics drew more public and international media interest than usual. However, visitors using the pedestrian corridors often also visited Chinatown and it was interesting to see how merchants there also took on Olympic promotional ideas. While there were ancillary activities in other places of the downtown, or even elsewhere in the metro area, such as Surrey, Richmond, and North Vancouver, these pedestrian corridors were the nerve center of street activity.

Pavilions were either on pedestrian corridors or adjacent to them. They were always controlled spaces in the sense that they had entrances – some of which required security clearance. The LiveCity sites were secure, but other sites – particularly the southwest False Creek pavilions – were open and easily accessible. What added to the vibrancy of these spaces was big screens at which persons could stand and watch Olympic events, in addition to the free concerts, which attracted large numbers of people.[9] Important hockey games were of specific interest and attracted hundreds of, or several thousand, spectators at each screen.[10] Special events like the broadcasting of the American political satirist Stephen Colbert's television show from the False Creek site drew thousands of people. On the pedestrian corridors, it was also not unusual to see people milling around television sets placed at the windows of the establishment for easy public viewing, or even set up on the street.

Analyzing the public realm during the Olympics

There were four basic characteristics of the public realm on the pedestrian corridors during the Olympics that were of sociological significance. First, virtually no one was alone, even though there were crowds of people.[11] People came as families with children (often with babies in child carriers rather than strollers), as couples, and as friends, sometimes in clusters of three to eight people. There was no reliable means of counting the number of people who participated in these spaces, but some estimates were around 150,000 per day, with peak attend-ance in the evening. What was clear was that the pedestrian corridors were crowded with people, with lineups (often very lengthy ones) occurring outside live sites, pavilions, restaurants and pubs, and even at rapid transit stations (Figure 4.2). Lineups at bars and restaurants were also not unusual. If people were not strolling on the corridor, they were waiting in lines with the people they came with. The key, though, is that this crowd behavior was defined not by isolation and anonymity but by relationships that segmented the crowd into much smaller primary groups (Figure 4.3).[12]

Second, people often interacted with strangers – a behavior in which they would not normally engage in public space. The density of people milling in public spaces created a very different feel in the downtown core. Instead of the orderly movement of people on sidewalks, people wandered everywhere, calling out, interacting with others, laughing, and gazing. Other instances of people encountering each other on the streets meant that people who were previously unknown to each other would frequently engage in brief conversations that might include commentary on what was happening, exchanges of information, exchanges of biographical facts such as "where are you from and how long are you here?" and even on occasion invitations to share food and drink. Lineups

Figure 4.2 The Olympics promoted prosocial behavior. Here, people are lining up in large numbers to visit the Russian Pavilion and engaging in interaction with others while waiting.

UNIVERSITY OF WINCHESTER
LIBRARY

Figure 4.3 More evidence of prosocial behavior. Here, people are watching Olympic events outside on a large screen, and doing so with other people.

were particularly conducive to this kind of interaction, but so was the kind of exuberance that was expressed on the street. Persons enthusiastic about a medal win or a hockey win, or just expressing hospitality or patriotic feeling, were often swept up in expressions of connection that included physical touching such as shaking hands, high-fives, and even hugs with complete strangers – actions not typical in urban public space. Watching a Sikh male wearing a turban being hugged by an unknown non-Sikh male on the street, all in the name of celebration, was one of the strongest experiences of this kind of behavior. Reports were often received of residents meeting visitors and even Olympic athletes on the street and engaging in conversation with them – even if it amounted to nothing more than small talk. Torch carriers would often bring their torches on the street and people would have their picture taken with the carrier even when they wouldn't know who the person was (Figure 4.4). A more specialized form of conversation occurred among those wanting to trade pins or obtain pins from people who they thought might have them. For example, athletes who finished their competitions would enter into the spirit of the occasion by joining others on the corridor, and if they wore any marks of identification on them such as team jackets, people would enter into conversations with them, hoping to obtain one of their pins. Certain pubs and restaurants were known to

Figure 4.4 Citizen torchbearers sometimes wore their uniforms and carried their personal torch in the public realm. Even though they were not known by name, they were treated like mini-celebrities and provided many photo-opportunities for the general public.

be places where members of specific national teams would hang out after hours when their competitions were over, and people often went to these places to interact with them.

Third, the atmosphere was totally relaxed, as people had no particular destination in mind except to enjoy whatever was going on. If a juggler or musician was performing, people could elect to stop and listen (Figure 4.5). Laughing and clapping when the performance was finished signaled personal interaction with what was occurring. Street performers included unicycle acrobats, ventriloquists, magicians, a junkyard symphony using metal pails, pots and pans, and plates, and all kinds of musical groups from jazz to bluegrass, a takeoff of Atlantic folk music (using a bass fiddle, banjo, violin, and Spanish guitar), a carnival band, and a mariachi band among others. Almost all of these performances were spontaneously presented by one to four people. A singer would use a portable sound system to sing popular songs karaoke-style and people would gather around to listen. Where did these groups come from? A drum group was said to have come from France, but in general there was little sense of who these people were. They were willing to perform and knew that they would find an audience. What

Figure 4.5 Various types of street performers from jugglers to musicians to theater provided informal entertainment in the public realm, often combining skill and
talent with humor and intriguing costuming.

they did do was contribute to a relaxed and cheerful atmosphere. Of course,
some people on the street may have had a few drinks, which would have relaxed
them even more. In general, however, most people interpreted what was occurring on the street as family-friendly behavior. There was no program and no
agenda; everything just happened. In comparison to the normal goal-directed
behavior of people in the downtown core, people were much more relaxed and
in a festive mood. Being surrounded with people in that context made the
Olympics an urban experience.

Perhaps most important of all was the fact that everything that took place on
the street was free. Even the pavilions and the live sites were free. Interestingly
enough, no one on the street was trying to sell anything. Food and drink were
readily available for purchase inside buildings or in the temporary structures of
the pavilions, but not on the street. In fact, some manufacturers even gave away
product samples on the streets, which added to the atmosphere. No tickets were
needed for anything, and in contrast to the public demand for tickets to popular
Olympic events and the significant purchase price of these tickets, the street
became a place where purchasing power did not matter. In that sense, the public
realm became an egalitarian space. People from the Downtown Eastside could

enjoy the atmosphere as well as members of the International Olympic Committee. The street, then, became a social leveler.

The street as a performance stage

The downtown core is physically an everyday performance stage in which buildings and structures are a backdrop or setting. Buildings and their arrangement also reflect social relations and have social meanings. Banks, gleaming office towers, and even hotels operate with social codes that are reflected in their appearance, codes that suggest their institutional power and clientele. While anyone could walk into the Fairmont Hotel Vancouver, the combination of the décor and surveillance by hotel personnel would lead people to feel "out of place" if they did not belong there. In a similar way, banks and office buildings have social codes that prevent lingering unless there is business to perform. Thus, performance on the everyday urban stage is highly structured: people move about according to the roles they play and the established rules. Leisure in public space in the downtown is discouraged unless it is connected to consumption, for otherwise it is assumed to be loitering. So, if downtown is a stage, normal daily life is filled with actors following clearly scripted roles as shoppers, office workers moving about in business dress, or bustling activity focused around people having clear destinations in mind, whether as tourists or clients. The stage, then, is predictable and the drama is ordered, and kept that way by police, security personnel, and convention.

During the Olympic period, the stage of the drama was remade. In Olympic terms, this is referred to as overlay. The concreteness of urban space was given new flexibility, and barricades and traffic cones were props that announced the borders of transformed urban spaces. Existing buildings were transformed by multistory building wraps that altered their appearance. Huge banners or signage such as "Welcome Olympic Visitors" or "Go Canada Go" were placed either in prominent places on the exterior of buildings or in windows. Temporary structures such as tents were erected on plazas as building occupants extended their presence to more public view (e.g., BC Hydro's temporary demonstration Power Smart Village, or an arts or sports film showing in a shipping container called ContainR which attracted 18,000 people). The local CTV station moved its broadcasts from the studio inside the building to a tent and platform outside the building right on Robson Street, which made its activity much more visible. The creation of exhibits and pavilions in buildings traditionally more closed and used for other purposes also helped to change the meaning of urban space (e.g., the Royal Canadian Mint Pavilion, Canada's Northern House). The Olympic Superstore in the Bay Department store transformed a place with normal retail functions into a lively place for Olympic merchandising, with long lines (serving 10,000 customers per day) where people would not normally have gone during the Olympics. Some restaurants were taken over by corporations that put their names on the front, changing the look of the street (e.g., the Bell Ice Cube), and one restaurant on the Beatty corridor, the Atlantic Trap and Gill, was totally made over with temporary structures attached to it and turned into a meeting place and restaurant/entertainment place called Alberta House. Parking lots, which are normally "dead spaces" from an urban point of view, were also transformed by temporary structures and the activities that they hosted. The Downtown Live site brought new life to a whole block, ordinarily a parking lot, with its tents, displays, and entertainment. The vast asphalt surface on the southwest corner of False Creek became a veritable entertainment zone with pavilions and entertainment. Giving unoccupied spaces new uses and having them throbbing with people gave the downtown new energy. German Fan Fest, as another example, took place in a tent in a smaller parking lot between the downtown commuter station and Gastown. Robson Square, in particular, was redefined as an entertainment zone. A newly refurbished skating rink known as GE Plaza during the Olympics, the installation of a zip line only for the Olympics, and a laser light show every evening provided new meaning for this location as urban space. Six thousand banners extolling the Olympic theme, "With Glowing Hearts," were installed on light posts along the street, and the general effect was that the Olympic overlay contributed to a visual transformation of the streetscape. The implication was clear that these were not normal business days downtown. The stage had physically been altered.

As has already been suggested, behavior also was transformed. New activity took place in spaces previously restricted to traditional uses. Normally busy streets such as Robson Street were closed to vehicles, and streets took on new functions, such as spaces for performances by jugglers, musical groups, or speakers on a soapbox. One of the more unusual genres of performance was flash mobs, and especially the flash mob on Robson Street on February 13. Suddenly, hundreds of people in ordinary dress began a choreographed dance routine in the middle of the street, to the surprise of onlookers. In other cases, people were observed wearing distinctive apparel or colorful costumes such as shirts or hats that emphasized their role as performers. But there were many other actions that could also be considered performances. For example, an obviously planned street hockey match took place on Granville Street one evening, with the players on the opposing teams representing Canada and the United States and dressed in unusual patriotic costumes representing each country (Figure 4.6), which made it a much more interesting experience to watch and cheer. Families or friends would sometimes all be dressed in unique full body costumes that had obviously been obtained from a costume store (one store advertised, "We've got your gear to cheer"). In fact, it appeared that some people almost considered street life as a costume party of sorts, as every kind of dress imaginable could be found at various times. Even foreign visitors came with costumes, such as a couple from Sweden dressed in colors of the national flag and wearing Viking helmets, or people from the Netherlands wearing orange costumes.[13] Face painting was also frequently observed. These casual small-group actions can be considered "performances" and occurred in many places throughout the central core, and streets provided new spaces for such activity. Sprinkled around the streets also were policemen wearing their costumes (uniforms) playing their important role as well. It was interesting to see how street life even affected how police at times reinterpreted their roles away from strict and stern security to what they called "meet and greet." For example, police were observed playing street hockey even while working, or they volunteered to take pictures for people. Street life was clearly a drama in which there were many characters rather than just a few dominant "official" characters, and there were many platforms on which to perform. While things like costuming and face painting were not a majority activity, there was enough readily visible that it made the streets an interesting place to be. As evidence that people wanted to capture the scenes of this drama, many used digital cameras or cell phones to record in video format the sights and sounds of what was occurring. The street, then, became a stage or platform in which all who attended became part of the drama in some way.

Nowhere was the theatricality of the Olympics as an urban performance clearer than at Olympic venues which required significant security. The two major urban venues for Olympic activities in the central core in Vancouver were the neighboring BC Place, where the opening and closing ceremonies were held, as well as the nightly medal ceremonies, and Canada Hockey Place as the arena for most of the hockey games. Both of these facilities utilized the same

Figure 4.6 Among the various forms of costuming observable in the streets were humorous parodies of Olympic events, such as this hilarious street hockey game between the United States and Canada, with the players dressed in exaggerated patriotic clothing.

security operations, which included a perimeter zone with controlled access only to those with tickets and involved mag-and-bag searches and hand wands. Surveillance cameras surrounded the secure zone, creating a very different space than usually found at these locations. The Athletes' Village located nearby had similar security measures, although access was limited to athletes and officials. LiveCity sites were also places where the security performance was part of the drama as people were classified, monitored, and sorted to ensure that the Olympics as urban theater proceeded. The precautionary principle (Toohey and Taylor 2008) required a public demonstration of safety that was visible and communicated dramaturgically. The process of qualification to enter these spaces was strictly controlled by a regimen of performances by those who desired access as well as by those controlling access. Thousands of security guards, suitably attired, played their roles of impression management to convey the feeling that these spaces were safe and resistant to terrorism. In comparison to other aspects of the Olympic cycle, the Games themselves were carefully scripted, and the planned narrative must unfold on the city as stage as scripted. Security and surveillance were the guardians of social order in the face of potential disorder, and the security ritual was a visible element of the drama.[14]

Alternative street events

It would have been possible to participate in the street life identified above without being particularly supportive of the Olympics. However, for those who opposed the Olympics, alternative street life was also available. The Olympic Resistance Network announced an Anti-Olympic Convergence beginning two days before the Olympics began, and continuing through the first weekend in Vancouver, on what it called "Coast Salish Territories" (rather than British Columbia) to imply solidarity with aboriginal resistance groups (Figure 4.7, left). The first two days involved a conference and workshops on topics such as creative resistance and medics training. On Friday, the opening day of the Olympics, a mass demonstration included a rally at the Art Gallery, a typical protest site in Vancouver and the location of the Olympic Countdown Clock. This location was on the opposite side of Robson Square – in other words, adjacent to the street corridors. With the theme "Take Back Our City," a festival and parade were organized by what was billed as the 2010 Welcoming Committee. After speeches and other activities, a protest parade involving approximately 2,000 people took place down Robson Street to BC Place, the site of the opening ceremonies for the Olympics.[15] Dozens of police on foot and on horseback met them at the stadium, where protesting continued in order to evoke a public response that could be recorded by the media.[16] On the Saturday morning, another march took place involving around 200 people down Georgia Street. This march ultimately turned violent and led to the smashing of windows of the Bay Department Store, which led to several arrests.[17] This march had been labeled the "Heart Attack March" because its goal was to use the streets "to clog the arteries of capitalism" (Figure 4.7, right), and the Bay, as official supplier of Olympic merchandise, became the

Figure 4.7 Opponents to the Olympics were also active in the public realm. These posters describe various marches and demonstrations that were planned. Note that the poster on the left identifies the city of Vancouver as being located on aboriginal land, "Coast Salish Territories," signaling solidarity with native peoples. Ironically, four aboriginal groups served officially as host nations for the Games.

target. There were other, smaller street marches and rallies such as at the Art Gallery and at Pigeon Park in the DTES.[18]

The Downtown Eastside, however, became the locus of most of the anti-Olympic activity throughout the Games.[19] Even before the Games began, Olympic opposition countered the Olympic frame in a public way through parodies of the Olympics. For example, the 2010 Poverty Olympics created their own mascots ("Itchy the Bedbug," "Creepy the Cockroach," and "Chewy the Rat") as a way of protesting homelessness and poverty. A mock torch relay was organized just prior to the opening of the Games, and their opening ceremony included many people dressed in costumes making fun of the mayor or dressed as characters such as Mr. Con Dough, pointing out how low-cost housing was being gentrified by "condo"miniums for the wealthy by the "money-grubbing developers." A satirical version of "O Canada" was sung by the opening ceremony choir, and humorous skits were presented, such as a curling match between Team VANOC and Team Poverty organized by Streams of Justice. In general, it was a light-hearted event in a festival atmosphere that made the point about why the Olympics represented a different point of view or frame from the concerns of those participating in the DTES (Ryan 2009).

Once the Games began, rallies were held at Pigeon Park, a very small concrete space with benches in the heart of the DTES, and an Olympic Tent Village was set up overnight across the street in squatter style on a vacant lot owned by a developer. This tent village was meant to draw attention to the need for housing for the poor, and attracted visitors and media representatives, who strolled by or interacted with residents. But it also served as an urban space to bring together diverse groups who were part of the anti-Olympics resistance (Boykoff 2011:54). Many home-made signs were visible, with phrases like "People Not Profit, Homes Not Games," "BC Olympic Gold!!! #1 in Child Poverty 6 Years Running," "Housing Before Olympics," "Resist the 2010 Corporate Circus," "End the Vanoccupation," "Homes Before Hockey," and "Olympics = Class War" (Figures 4.8 and 4.9). One of the issues in the Downtown Eastside was that old buildings and old single-room-occupancy hotels were threatened by gentrification. One multistory banner hanging from a ten-story building read "Homes Now. End Homelessness, Gentrification, Criminalization

Figure 4.8 At a rally held at Pigeon Park in the Downtown Eastside during the Olympics, it was clear that the Games provided an opportunity to protest other issues such as the increasing gentrification of the area and the loss of affordable housing as well as the criminalization of poverty.

Figure 4.9 The framing of the critique of the Olympics in this sign links the Games to capitalism and opposition to class warfare.

of Poverty." Adding critical humor, a counter-banner hanging from a gentrified condominium next to the tent village said "Build Resumes Not Tents." A "Share the Gold" action took place in the late afternoon during the Games in what was billed as a "Half Hour of Solidarity" in which people were to stand three meters apart on Hastings Street for three blocks. Participants wore yellow and claimed that just as the Olympics had shown what the city could do in mobilizing resources, so homelessness should be addressed in the same way by "sharing the gold" and "connecting the worlds in our own city." In any case, opposition to the Olympics also had public visibility, and those who wanted to use the Olympics to advocate for those with housing needs succeeded in doing so in the public realm as well.

The meaning of the public realm

Urban spaces, then, were transformed through actions in the public realm during the Olympics. Instead of rigid and predictable behavior typical of normal urban life in which there was a more or less wooden relationship between people and structures, the meaning of structures and the meaning of behavior were altered. Instead of viewing themselves as individuals with mutually exclusive identities, people using the sidewalks and streets during the Games actually began to encounter one another as people with a common focus. McPhail (1991) prefers to use the term "gatherings" rather than "crowd" to describe such collections of people, for each group of persons present engage in different behaviors simultaneously but in shared space. He calls this collective-behavior-in-concert rather than collective-behavior-in-common, which implies doing the same thing. The space produced by planners and builders (Lefebvre 1991) who created buildings, canopies, sidewalks, streets, and all the regulations that control them was suddenly transformed into lived space in which city dwellers filled these spaces with their own spontaneous activities. Whyte (1980:19) calls this desire to be with other people in public spaces "self-congestion." It is true that by making pedestrian corridors out of streets, regulations had been relaxed to allow human action to bring new life to those streets, but it is the way that human behavior transformed these streets from their typical uses that made the Olympics such a dynamic urban experience for their users. Liggett (2007), following Lefebvre, speaks about the need for unplanned but situated connections between city dwellers called "urban encounters" as necessary for the humanizing of cities, whereby residents cross paths with people different from themselves. Liggett calls these "dialogic occasions" because they create momentary hybrid spaces.

Marches, demonstrations, protests, and riots are often part of the history of cities. So also is celebratory activity related to annual festivals, commemorative occasions, and political, military, or sport victories. In the case of the Olympics, it is unclear why active street life of a celebratory nature can become such a defining aspect of the Games for the host city. What are people actually celebrating? Is it appropriate to call it just a party? Is it the release of tensions that are part of the pre-Games conflicts and anxieties and are now channeled into something more joyful? Is it the desire to be part of something unique to the city? Is it a form of participation in the Olympics that is available to anyone regardless of status or finances? It is probably all of these and more.

Perhaps part of the answer is to be found in the fact that the Olympics are one of a genre of unique events in which the interruption of normal routines is tolerated. Coronations, royal marriages, or state funerals, for example, have a way of transfixing a population that justifies the suspension of customary behavior even though only a few attend the actual event. The point is that there is general acceptance of the fact that what is occurring is of sufficient importance to a city to warrant the rescheduling of daily activity. Rothenbuhler's (1989b) research on the 1984 Los Angeles Olympics found that in spite of all the controversies in which the Olympics were embroiled, there was widespread agreement that the Olympics ultimately stood for values in principle that people embraced: international ties through friendly competition, good sportsmanship, personal sacrifice, and skill in performance. Whether or not the Games always lived up to these expectations was another matter, but his study concluded that the values and symbols of Olympism were ideals with widespread acceptance. Rothenbuhler also found that the television audience for the Olympics was much broader and less socially structured than sport audiences or audiences for regular television programs. Olympic audiences were less gender-divided and drew in members of social groupings that the normal television schedule could not do. In that sense, the Olympic time period may be one of the "high holidays" of television, with both broadcasters and the public recognizing the Olympics as an event worthy of the disruption of normal scheduling.[20]

The television audience probably mirrors what happens in a host city. For many, hosting the Olympics justifies the suspension of normal activities because the symbolic capital of the Games is embraced at least in some sense. The pageantry of the Games and its production for mass consumption also clearly plays a part in legitimizing support. Nevertheless, the Olympics are an intrusion in the normal life of the city, although of limited public duration. The Games start, people shift into a different genre, street life begins. The Games end, people shift back into the normal genre, street life ends. The temporary structures are taken down, visitors leave, and regular routines are embraced. Victor Turner (1969, 1982) refers to a period of transition where normal behavior and thinking are relaxed and people are more open as a state of liminality. This is not a permanent condition but is a transitional state, something a person or community passes through. Experiences in that process are liminoid in that they are more playful and less structured. Furthermore, Turner argues that during liminality, hierarchical differences are de-emphasized or ignored in deference to a common human condition. Again this is not a permanent condition and does not replace social structure but provides a temporary alteration of the constraints of structure.

The street life that occurred during the Olympics represents such a liminal experience. The street provided a place where hierarchy and status were set aside and people entered into a playful mood, even if only for seventeen days. Liminality did not change life before or after the Olympics but it suspended the nature of that life by creating a temporary zone of exuberance and joy, where people either enjoyed each other or encountered each other in new ways. The crush of people all milling about contained its own energy because people were relaxed and had no other agenda than to take in the atmosphere. Instead of the anger that is typical of protests, or the goal-directness which is the hallmark of business days, people were generally smiling and laughing at the unique costuming they observed, enjoying buskers who sought audiences, or were caught up in cheering and chanting. Part of the intrigue of the street as a place to be was that it confused the normal appearential and locational coding and ordering of public space (Lofland 1973). People became characters on the city stage and took on roles in places where such activity would not normally occur. Perhaps most unusual was the fact that the relaxed atmosphere and the proximity of people to each other in crowds or waiting lines allowed people to talk to each other even as strangers.

The fact that athletes, members of the Olympic family, international visitors, and local residents co-mingled in an anonymous yet interactive way on the street played a key role in the transformation of attitudes about the Olympics among Vancouver residents.[21] Whyte (1980:94) would call this a triangulation event in that the Olympics as festival provided an external stimulus that prompted people to talk to others as if they knew them. Residents discovered that a break from normal routines, enhanced face-to-face relationships, and collective enjoyment were a part of being urban that was neglected in the face of the typical segmentation of urban life. In a curious sort of way, this atmosphere helped to humanize the city in a new way, however short-term it may have been. Perhaps more than the actual Olympic competitions, these interactions and experiences on the street created the strongest affective bonds for local residents about the Games and play a central role in their memories about the event.[22]

Conclusion

After seven years of planning, the Olympics as an event do not just happen in a city; they remake the city in important ways. Urban spaces are categorized in terms of their relation to the Olympic plan. Some spaces are transformed functionally and even visually on a temporary basis. Olympic infrastructure may also permanently transform some urban spaces. Other spaces, on the other hand, are considered irrelevant to the plan. Barriers are put in place, signage changes, traffic flows are altered, routines change, Olympic overlays change appearances, and security zones with surveillance and police presence reorganize urban spaces. The Olympics re-territorialize previously functioning space into their own image, and when the Games are over, that space is de-territorialized in some ways as though the event had never happened (Dansero et al. 2006). The Olympics, then, serve as a temporary interlude in the normal functioning of a city. However, there can also be makeover effects as cities use the occasion of the Olympics to make significant structural changes to segments of the city. Thus, the transformation of urban spaces, whether permanent or transitory, ensures that the city must be seen as more than merely the site for the Games.

The Olympics qualitatively changed Vancouver, and particularly the central city, for a short period, and they did so primarily in the public realm. Residents came to redefine their city in a way that allowed them to view crowded streets more positively as giving vitality to urban space rather than in a negative manner as competition for scarce urban space. Street life during the Olympics rearranged the order of the city in spite of the fact that security and planning sounded repressive. If evenings were normally times when downtowns were quiet, then during the Olympics thousands gathered in confined spaces and encountered each other, turning the normal rhythm of the city on its head. It was in public spaces that people could experience other people's presence in spite of the fact that they did not enter their private worlds (Madanipour 2003). City streets were transformed from automobile congestion to pedestrian congestion, but, ironically, they were places where people could encounter one another. MacAloon (1989:6–23) describes exchange as the idiom of festival. Among the many performances that took place on the street, the most basic form of exchange or "free-form performances were looks and conversation." If the Olympics are one of those events that cross-recruit interest from a diversity of subgroups once the event begins, it is especially because in the street, local residents come to participate and experience their city in a new way. Interaction is a powerful mood-changer. Ironically, this is the exact opposite of Lofland's (1998) observation that it is the public realm that has historically bred anti-urbanism because of the fleeting mixture of diverse people.

Instead of creating new urban spaces, Vancouver transformed existing spaces into sites for collective consumption and collective interaction. Urban order was maintained and yet also turned on its head by social controls that were not restrictive but supportive of a different kind of atmosphere. For example, a policeman allowed a police dog to play tug-of-war with a little girl rather than working the street. Police officers were observed pouring out containers of alcohol on the street rather than arresting people for public intoxication.[23] The police presence was more observatory and participatory rather than invasive, except when violence took place.[24] Security fences were covered with Olympic images to appear less restrictive and enhance the visual appeal of urban spaces. The Olympics of the streets were an important part of the Games for city residents. But so also were the Olympics of small spaces, the homes and community centers where people encountered one another on this occasion.

This chapter has demonstrated that a major and neglected factor in understanding the Olympics is its symbolic inversion of the meaning of urban public space. Just as fiestas, parades, and carnivals have the potential to temporarily invert everyday social structure and the hegemonic meaning of public space (Low 2000), so too the Olympics, and perhaps even to a greater extent, can set aside existing order and structure and replace it with new representations of space. While it might be suggested that all of this activity in the public realm was a form of resistance to typical meanings of space, it was more like a mutually collaborative action of order-keepers and order-transformers creating a new temporary order of mingling celebrative interaction. It was sanctioned acting out-of-place in a manner that transformed the meaning of space.

In a curious sort of way, crowds on the streets were also a form of empowerment. The Olympics may have been all about organization and structure and tickets and Olympic accreditation, but the bodily compression of crowds represented a new form of expressivity that had liberating and transformative qualities (Borch 2009). If spontaneous action and the expressivity of crowds are a response by those who lack institutional power (Drury and Reicher 2009), then the active public realm during the Olympics may represent the grassroots reaction to the exclusive control that the Olympics, as an orchestrated performance, demanded. It may not be a form of resistance but it is a way in which local residents make the Games their own. It is also a form of "being there" open to all city residents, and one that becomes part of collective memory.

5   The host city as a symbolic field

The word "Olympics" is a symbol. In previous chapters, the Olympics were interpreted as prompting a drama on a stage. In this chapter, the Olympics are a symbol generating dynamic energies (MacAloon 1981). Symbols are important for interactionists because they are created by human beings to abstractly represent something else. The meaning of a symbol is not inherent but emerges from interaction with others. It is the search for common interpretations of symbols that makes society possible. Language is one way in which we use symbols to communicate personal and cultural meanings. When we use the word "Olympics," there is usually general agreement that it is a symbol for sport competitions between elite athletes representing countries in the global community. However, symbols are of sociological significance because the meaning of a symbol depends on how it is interpreted, who interprets it, and often even where it is interpreted. This process is akin to our discussion of framing in Chapter 3.

While we may agree on the base meaning of the Olympics as an international sport competition, different groups of people will develop their own interpretive systems of shared knowledge, sentiments, or beliefs (called idioculture) about that symbol that will serve as a basis for interaction among their group members.[1] For some, the Olympics may mean huge expenditures for sport which crowd out expenditures for other cultural activities or needed human services. For others, the Olympics may symbolize corporate marketing, the IOC as a closed institution, the use of illegal substances to win at all costs, or political manipulation. The base meaning of the Olympics as sport, then, is crowded out by other meanings and evaluations that are related to individual life perspectives and the interacting groups that sustain those perspectives. The Olympics as a symbol are polysemic in that their avowed meaning is layered with other meanings and interpretations quite different from those of someone else, who only thinks of the Olympics as pageantry and personal achievement in thrilling competitions. It is clear, then, that while there may be some general agreement about the meaning of the symbol represented by the word "Olympics," there is an overlay of meanings that vary among different groups of people and influence how the symbol is evaluated. All of these different meanings are wrapped up in the word "Olympics," and which meanings a person chooses or emphasizes is a consequence of reflection and interaction with others where similar or other meanings are encountered.

The official symbolic meanings of Olympism are contained in the Olympic Charter. Here, values are specified that link sport to far more than competition. Instead, Olympism is related to "a way of life based on joy of effort, the educational value of good example and respect for universal fundamental ethical principles." The objective of Olympism is to use sport to promote a "peaceful society concerned with the preservation of human dignity." The charter sets out a set of values that legitimates the Olympics in a manner that in principle can obtain universal support. The concept of global peace through sport as an instrument of international relations, for example, is an ideal that generates widespread acceptance and for many people is what the Olympics symbolize. On the other hand, the charter also sets out ideals against which the Olympics themselves can be judged. The ethical principles of the charter have frequently been compromised by doping and various scandals and improprieties that have been the object of much criticism. The Olympics have also exhibited the opposite of cordial international relations through national boycotts and even terrorist activity. For example, the United States (and quite a number of other nations) boycotted the 1980 Moscow Olympics in protest against Soviet involvement in Afghanistan. The Soviet Union boycotted the Los Angeles Games in 1984. And at the 1972 Munich Games, eleven Israeli athletes were murdered by the Palestinian terrorist group Black September. Yet while the symbolism of the Olympics has often failed (Tomlinson and Young 2005), there is clearly a sense in which its ideals continue to serve as an important framing device for people's perceptions of the Games. These examples illustrate how public events such as the Olympics are important in the production and modeling of symbols that mirror the existing social order and its conflicts (Handelman 1990).

The symbolic power of the Olympics

At least partially because of the ideals which the Olympics represent in promoting an international public culture based on sport, the Games' role in the world has a particular air of legitimacy. In that sense, its status as an international phenomenon is arguably unrivaled. Therefore, it is not surprising that people in power roles (whether economic power or political power) will be attracted to such a symbol. The universal familiarity with the symbol also means that it has general appeal, for example, among those who might be impressed with the "honor" of having won the bidding competition to host the Games (or even, in some instances, being selected for the shortlist to host the Games). Other interest groups, in recognizing the power of the symbol, will also want to associate with the symbol. As Leavy (2007) notes, iconic events are often co-opted for a variety of purposes, whether to spin ideology, sell products, or further the purposes of special interest groups. What is critical here is that the Olympics are not just a symbol that is passively received; the nature of the symbol is such that others want to use it or manipulate it for their own purposes. The power of the symbol is shared by those representing the Olympics, and especially the president of the IOC, who is often greeted in countries around the world as though he were a global leader or head of state. Heads of state will meet with him when he visits and heads of state attend Olympic events or even appear before the IOC, such as when bidding for the Games. News from the IOC or about the IOC and the Olympics in general is continually broadcast. There is always news about cities bidding or thinking of bidding, news about the personal lives of athletes, the politics and controversies of the Olympics, or difficult issues facing host cities. With the Winter and Summer Games alternating every two years, the Olympics are never far from public awareness through the media. The Olympics as a symbol is indeed pervasive and powerful, and often contested.

Because of the influence and authority of the Olympics as a symbol, it is not surprising that governments want to connect the symbol with images that they want to convey to their own citizens as well as the rest of the world. In some cases, governments use bidding, or even talking about bidding, as a way to signal to their own citizens as well as the global community their emergent ambitions or present capabilities. Hosting the Olympics often leads to the construction of iconic buildings that have immense symbolic value to host cities as well as nation-states. Buildings hosting key Olympic events may be expected to be grand and glorious in the same way that another genre of mega-events, World's Fairs, produced structures of symbolic value such as the Eiffel Tower in Paris and the Crystal Palace in London. Along with the cauldron for the flame that remains at all Olympic competition sites, splendid stadiums in particular are hallmarks of having hosted the Olympics. The Bird's Nest and Water Cube in Beijing are two examples from the Summer Games, but Winter Games as well have often produced signature structures (e.g., the Olympic Saddledome or Olympic Oval in Calgary) that play an important visual role in the urban landscape. These symbols serve as enduring reminders of the Games and in that sense convey a sense of their power and legacy to the city.

The Olympics as a powerful symbol can also be used to mobilize people and resources. Politicians can use the Olympics to justify unusually large expenditures for projects that might otherwise be questionable. Governments can use the Olympics to build support for the state or inculcate national pride or to set aside normal operational procedures (such as fast-tracking projects without scrutinizing their full impact). Governments can use the symbolic power of the Olympics to justify plans and projects, and people can agree to the disruption of their normal routines, the suspension of their civil rights, or the adoption of new codes of conduct (such as the campaign against spitting in Beijing) because of the symbolic power of the Games. Corporations can agree to the contribution of large sums of money to Olympic or sport bodies preparing for the Olympics to an extent without parallel. These mobilizing actions are all possible because of the symbolic power of the Olympics.

Local promoters of the Olympics use the Games' symbolic power to generate public support and to push ahead with their plans, assuming the public will follow as a taken-for-granted assumption just because a project is for the

Olympics. The symbol is so influential that it usually transforms the urban agenda of the host city, because everything must be ready. The global symbolism of the Olympics encourages the host city to make decisions that support a global image, and urban elites and urban citizens become conscious that their global reputation is at stake, which again both justifies and mobilizes action. The symbolic power of the Olympics provides synergy in the host city that probably was not there before. Budgets are rearranged and manipulated to accommodate the Games. The Olympics become shorthand for urgency, timelines, deadlines, exceptions, and priorities. They are all-inclusive and comprehensive in that they mobilize people from all walks of life, from security and safety to health care and education, from entertainment and food services to construction and telecommunications. The Games require planning by management in each of these sectors, and also implementation by employees. All of this happens because there is considerable recognition in the host city of the power of the symbol.

The transfer of the Olympic flag from Turin to Vancouver at the closing ceremonies in Turin in 2006, and the raising of the flag at Vancouver City Hall, were staging moments that symbolized the centrality of the Olympics in the city's life. The Countdown Clock at the Art Gallery also was an important symbol of how resources in the city were being mobilized towards a particular goal with a specific timeline. The Olympic Torch Relay across Canada, involving 12,000 torchbearers, was not just promotion for the Games but symbolic of the deference given to the Olympic project, and even its preeminence as a national objective. In particular, the final days of the torch relay in Vancouver were an extremely vivid portrayal of the mobilization capabilities of Olympic symbols as hundreds of people lined the streets, school classes watched, waving Canadian flags, and people talked about the passing of the torch as an emotional moment. As we have seen, it was not surprising that those opposed to the Olympics would attempt to use these symbolic moments for their own purposes or create their own staging moments that were designed to elicit public support to challenge the symbol. The symbolic power of the Olympics was demonstrated in all of these performances (both in support and in opposition) that were meant to communicate interpretations of the symbol. Understood in that framework, the Olympics are a contested symbol, as we have already seen.

To the extent that the Olympics possess symbolic power and can serve as a mobilizing agent, it is possible to identify the ways in which the Games can serve as a symbolic platform for interests beyond sport – both economic and non-economic. While economic interests are often most typically associated with the Olympics, among the non-economic interests that can be related to the Games are the interests of the state and national collectivities, not only as top-down initiatives but also as spontaneous outbursts of patriotism. A third element to be discussed in this chapter is how the Olympics as a symbol system can play an important role for residents in stimulating a range of emotions.

The Olympics as a symbolic platform

Given the power of the Olympic symbol, persons or groups may come to see how associating with the symbol relates to their own interests. When the Olympics as an event and their symbolic meanings are interpreted from the point of view of the interests of a specific group or entity, and this interpretation leads to specific actions to align themselves with the Olympics or respond to it in some way, the Games serve as a symbolic platform. The term "symbolic platform" is used because the Olympics as a symbol are used as a platform or launching point for objectives other than their primary intent as a sporting competition, and by other groups not normally part of the IOC and sport federations. There are four ways in which this occurs. First, when an explicit relationship is formed with the IOC or a local organizing committee, that entity is officially allowed to use the symbols of the Olympics for its own purpose, usually for a fee in a role identified as a sponsor. Second, there are others that do not or cannot officially associate themselves with the symbol but who recognize the symbolic power of the event and want to benefit from it. In both of the situations discussed so far, economic interests serve as the primary driver. Third, still others recognize the symbolic power of the Olympics as a public focus and visualize this as an opportunity to bring their own preferences and group objectives into the public domain. Fourth, there are others that recognize the dynamic presence of the Olympics as a public event and want to participate in it in some way as a community organization but without capturing it for narrower purposes. In all of these cases, the symbolic power of the Olympics provides a platform for a multitude of groups with other interests, whether for marketing, advocacy, or community presence, to use the Games for their own objectives.

1 The symbolic power of the Olympic brand and corporate marketing

Perhaps the interest group that receives the most discussion is the corporate sector, which understands the global reach of the Games as parallel to its own interests. While the IOC understands this commercialization as a means to give financial stability to the Olympic movement,[2] multinational corporate interests use the Olympic symbol as a way of enhancing their public image internationally as well as a product marketing strategy. Claiming to reach "billions of people in over 200 countries and territories" of the world, TOP sponsors (the highest level of sponsorship) pay millions of dollars to the IOC for exclusive global marketing rights within their designated product or service category. The principle of exclusivity is important because it denies access to competitors. It is for this reason that Olympic administrators and organizers are vigilant in preventing what is called ambush marketing: use of the symbolic value (i.e., its popularity or reputation) of the Games by corporate entities that have created an association with the Olympics without authorization and for which they have paid nothing (Schmitz 2005; Pitt *et al.* 2010). It is also the reason why the

IOC has come to understand its reputation as a "brand" that can be commodi-fied and generate revenue. The IOC seeks to protect the integrity of its brand so that the public sees it as a values-driven operation (e.g., concerned with world peace and friendly competition between countries) rather than a commercial venture (MacRury 2009). This symbolic capital is necessary in order to obtain and retain the support of the corporate sector, but there is a dialogic tension between the Olympics as a set of ideals and also as a property with commercial value (Barney *et al.* 2004). Perhaps the most coveted reward for being a sponsor is to be considered part of the "Olympic family," with the access that such a status implies, and the ability to use the Olympic rings: five rings, representing five continents of the world, often referred to as the world's most recognized trademark. The Olympic rings are a very important symbol of the Olympics, not only a symbol representing the IOC but also a symbol to be sold. Companies like Coca-Cola, McDonald's, Visa, and Omega have a long history of associ-ation with the Olympics, and the Games provide a platform that fits their inter-national marketing objectives. Other companies more relevant to the country hosting the Games are called premier national partners and for Vancouver they included companies such as Hudson's Bay Company, RBC, Bell, and Chevrolet. There are other companies that become official suppliers and official licensees; they supply services and products but pay a fee to do so. It is indisputable that the Olympics have become a symbol with international marketing value, which means that it is not surprising that multinational corporations would want to be aligned with the Olympic symbol. Clearly, the Olympics provide a platform for entities with economic interests.

2 Symbolic power and economic leveraging

The symbolic power of the Olympics is also useful for those who want to use the event for economic leveraging. While some may have an official association with an Olympic Games, the interests of the media[3] in general can be intimately connected to the Olympics. The symbiotic relationship between media and sport generates considerable profit (Whannel 2009), and, as was noted earlier, the Olympics produce significant audiences beyond the traditional sports crowd. While one role of the media is the dissemination of news, the ownership of the mass media by private interests implies that the media need to make a profit. This can only be done if there is an eager audience that advertisers are willing to reach with their advertising dollars. Therefore, the existing audience needs to be retained and hopefully also enlarged. Controversy and provocative headlines and stories arouse that interest – especially in the host city. This was the case for the largest newspapers in Vancouver such as the *Vancouver Sun* and *Vancou-ver Province*, but also for many of the smaller Vancouver newspapers like *24 Hours*, or alternative papers.[4] The same could be said for radio and television, where the Olympics became a major topic for talk shows and newscasts and where opposition to the Games provided considerable color and fuel for public debate. An Olympics without controversy would give newspaper reporters little to do and would not captivate their audiences. The privately owned television broadcaster in Canada, the CTV network, was the official national network for the Olympics. It developed a campaign to heighten public interest in the Games around the theme "I Believe," which included a specially written song that had strong emotional overtones. With words such as "I believe in the power that comes / From a world brought together as one, / I believe together we'll find, / I believe in the power of you and I. / This is the moment we have dreamed of all our lives…", and sung by an emergent sixteen-year-old jazz singer, the message was clear that the Olympics stood for higher values at the same time that broadcasters could understand that pulling in big audiences was what their high financial bid to be the official broadcaster required. Local media (in fact all commercial media), then, understood how making the Olympics controversial as well as celebratory news among the public supported their own interests.

The symbolic value of the Olympics in relation to the media can be understood from other perspectives as well. Just as the 10,000 accredited media personnel played a role in translating the Games to their audiences, which also generated revenue for their news and entertainment products, so local tourism officials wanted to use the media in Vancouver for the Olympics to represent the city in such a way that it would reflect favorably on the city and thereby encourage inward investment and tourism.

It is now commonplace that host governments and economic development authorities want to use the Olympics as a means of attracting new business to the host region. O'Brien (2006) refers to the Games as providing seed capital for networking. The British Columbia government and the city's economic development office held seminars and workshops in advance of the Olympics to help local businesses use the Olympics to promote themselves to the international business community and not just to benefit from business opportunities directly related to the Games. During the Games, a business hosting program sponsored by the government and Metro Vancouver municipalities was targeted towards international companies that had been screened for relevance, and their executives (as well as others identified as global economic leaders, such as Richard Branson of the Virgin Group) were hosted. The Games, then, were to be used to leverage other economic opportunities. Local businesses also prepared for additional trade anticipated by the Games by creating special promotions or products that might appeal to Olympic visitors. For example, Lululemon, a Vancouver-based supplier of athletic clothing, produced a special line of hooded sweatshirts with the words "Cool Sporting Event That Takes Place in British Columbia Between 2009 & 2011 Edition." The objective was to gain media attention and stir marketing interest in the company during the Olympics but without using wordmarks or trademarks from the Olympics, which required a license from VANOC. Bars were permitted to stay open longer than usual, and some coffee shops and restaurants even decided to open twenty-four hours during the Games. Having promotional signs in the window implying endorsement of the Olympics was a way of showing affinity with the Olympic spirit. That spirit of course was easily allied to their economic interests, although some merchants benefited much more than others, and some businesses even suffered during the Games as the result of their location or product offerings, which were less relevant to the Games atmosphere.[5]

3 Advocacy and symbolic manipulation

One of the neglected elements of Olympic analyses is how the Olympics can also serve as a symbolic platform for advocacy for other interest groups unrelated to sports.[6] As we have already seen in the case of Vancouver, opposition to the Olympics was often based on the contention that hosting the Games represented a misplaced priority as a public expenditure. Behind that conclusion stood other preferred alternatives, particularly that of housing for the poor. Existing advocacy groups for low-income housing viewed the Olympics as an opportunity to make their case public, given the obvious fact that resources were being marshaled to provide housing for elite athletes while little was being done for the poor. Using statistics and evidence about population displacement from other cities that had previously hosted the Games (COHRE 2007), these groups could use the Olympics to sound the alarm and elevate housing as a key issue that should be addressed by either Games organizers or the government. This was clearly one of the objectives of the Impact of the Olympics on Community Coalition, which included such groups as the Tenant Resource Advisory Centre and the Pivot Legal Society, for which housing for the poor was of primary concern. Monitoring the loss of low-income housing units due to building disrepair, building destruction, or building conversion, the Pivot Legal Society in particular had both a national and a local objective of creating more adequate housing policies for the homeless as well as those of low income. The Olympics provided a very public occasion ("the best opportunity in a generation") to promote its Red Tent campaign, which sought to draw attention to "Canada's housing crisis" and "homelessness epidemic." Red Tents became the symbol of this campaign, and the Olympics provided a high-profile opportunity to make it known. For example, a squatter village of red tents was set up overnight in the green space along False Creek called Creekside Park, right next to the Russian Pavilion (Telus World of Science) on one side and the Hockey Canada Pavilion on the other side. As we have already seen, other expressions of advocacy that emerged from the Downtown Eastside aimed at using the Games to enhance public awareness of other issues facing the poor.

There were many other causes that also viewed the Olympics as an opportunity for advocacy of their interests.[7] For example, persons concerned about global warming and the melting of polar ice created a two-person costume in the form of a gigantic polar bear that appeared in public places during the Games as a way of drawing attention to that issue. Others used the Olympics to declare support for the Kyoto Accord and to pressure the Canadian government to support it. Opposition to the war in Afghanistan ("War No More," "Stopwar," "Yes we can! Get out of Afghanistan") was also an issue expressed during the Games. A large banner on the fence at the Tent Village exclaimed, "Welcome to Vancouver, City of Peace. Enjoy your Stay and Please say No to War and Occupation." One campaign that considered sport being given priority over the arts came out with a slogan using the Olympic theme ("With glowing hearts, Olympics kills the arts") as a way of advocating for the arts community. An anti-prostitution group, REED (Resist Exploitation, Embrace Dignity), using the theme "buying sex is not a sport," considered the Olympics as a paid sex bonanza which they opposed because of its role in human trafficking. Some religious groups also saw this as an opportunity for proselytization or the promotion of Christian goals (e.g., the Olympic Bible project or members of local Slavic churches singing songs at the SkyTrain station by the Russian Pavilion). Nutrition and fitness groups such as the BC Healthy Living Alliance took the Olympics as an occasion to promote daily exercise and healthy living. The LGBT (lesbian, gay, bisexual, and trans-identified) community established PRIDE celebration sites to celebrate the achievements of their favorite athletes and to raise awareness of the need to eliminate homophobia. First Nations chiefs planned a twenty-nine-hour hunger strike prior to the Canada–Norway hockey game to protest Norwegian-owned fish farms in the Broughton Archipelago. People for the Ethical Treatment of Animals (PETA) created its own "seal slaughter Olympic logo" using the inukshuk (stone landmark) logo from VANOC but stylizing it so that it held a club which was used to beat a baby seal on the bloodied ice. The Olympic rings were also on the logo but with one of the rings dripping blood. This logo was also made into a lapel pin. The idea was to capture the global focus on Canada created by the Olympics by showing how Canada was also linked with this kind of treatment of animals. These are just examples of the way many interest groups with no clear link to sports used the Games as an occasion for advocacy.

The globally recognized symbol of the Olympics is the interlocking five rings. As noted with PETA, it is interesting how advocacy groups manipulated this symbol to make their own points. Three other illustrations come from opposition to the Games in Vancouver, primarily in the Downtown Eastside. In one stylized rings creation, four rings had sad faces and only one had a happy face (Figure 5.1). In another one, the rings were made into hearts in an urban garden in the DTES with the sign "Hearts of the DTES." Another had pictures of the premier of British Columbia, Gordon Campbell, within the rings and was entitled "Gord the Clown's Five Ring Circus. Watch Your Tax Dollars Disappear. See Politicians Party on Your Buck." None of these parodies had widespread circulation, so VANOC did not take legal action, but they showed how symbols could be manipulated to present a contrary point of view.

4 Event symbolism and community participation

The last group in the host city that understood the symbolic power of the Olympics was made up of those who had no official place in the Olympics and who were not protesting or advocating alternative ideas but who viewed the Olympics as a high-profile community-wide event in which there would likely be

Figure 5.1 Much of the protest aimed at the Olympics within the city was focused on the fact that the Games became a financial priority while other issues considered more pressing were being neglected. This graffiti in the Downtown Eastside used the Olympic rings to convey that message in a graphic way.

considerable community participation and in which they wanted to play a role. A charity called Imagine-1-Day organized a flash mob on Robson Street on the first Saturday of the Olympics, with about 2,000 participating. Imagine's primary focus as a non-profit organization was working with communities in Ethiopia, but the flash mob had nothing to do with those objectives. Participants were recruited via Facebook, and the dance was posted in advance so people could learn it. Dancing to the song "Dancing in the Street," the goal was just to provide an opportunity for civic participation in the Olympics at the grass roots in a fun way. Another example was a cross-denominational Christian initiative called "More Than Gold" involving both evangelical Protestant groups and the Catholic archdiocese that promoted the idea of "radical hospitality" during the Games.[8] Volunteers roamed the streets providing free coffee for Olympic crowds, churches in the downtown were open as "quiet sanctuaries" or as viewing places with large screens, and "Aha" concerts were organized which included visiting and local musical groups. Still another example was the Ukrainian Catholic Church, which offered its facilities at Ukraine House as the hospitality arm of the Ukraine delegation to the Olympics. For these kind of endeavors, there was a perception that the Olympics were an important community festival or landmark event in the history of the city, and they wanted to be part of it without necessarily committing themselves to taking a position on the Games themselves.

The Olympics and patriotism

Just as we have seen that there are strong institutional linkages between the Olympics and the media, so there are also strong linkages between nation-states and the Olympics because of the Games' symbolic value. Theoretically, the Olympics transcend politics because they promote universalist principles that serve as the ideal of a global civil society (Tomlinson and Young 2005). Yet athletes compete as representatives of nation-states, are often funded by government agencies either directly or indirectly, and are treated as national heroes when they win. Athletes enter the stadium at the opening ceremonies marching behind their own national flag, and their national anthems are played when they win a gold medal. Their participation in the Olympics is done under the auspices of National Olympic Committees. Coubertin had embraced patriotism as love of one's country in such a way that national differences were to be celebrated as different ways of being human (MacAloon 1984:266). The Olympics were to result in friendliness and respect between nations, and yet it is clear that patriotism also can mean the manipulation of nationalist feelings. Political leaders understand how the Olympics can be a diversion from internal problems and they also know that the Olympics can potentially consolidate support behind their own government. The Olympics have been used to promote political ideologies (Espy 1979; Senn 1999), in that successful Games have been said to reflect the superiority of a people and their way of life as well as their leadership. The medals count (how many medals each nation has won) is often considered to be a proxy for national merit and even international power (van Hilvoorde *et al.* 2010).

Because Canada has historically been a linguistically divided nation between French and English speakers, national unity and patriotism have always been an issue. To a relatively young country with a high immigrant population, the Olympics provided an opportunity to promote greater cohesion, and one of the ways to do so was through sporting success in this international forum. The failure of Canada to have won gold medals on its own soil in spite of having already hosted the Olympics twice was a clear pressure point for the Games in Vancouver and presumably a form of international embarrassment. Canada therefore established a program targeted to winning more medals called "Own the Podium" for these Games, which was clearly predicated on this notion that winning medals was a badge of national standing, and that winning few medals reflected poorly on the nation (Knight *et al.* 2005). To the extent that winning medals can be considered a symbol of national prowess, the Olympics can play a role in nation-building. However, even though government provided funding to assist with hosting the Games, it was primarily the retail sector that made

Figure 5.2 The Olympics clearly can be a merchandising bonanza – even twenty-four hours a day. Much of the focus was on patriotic clothing rather than just VANOC-licensed items such as miniature mascots.

symbols of patriotism more publicly visible (Figure 5.2). In addition, patriotic activity appeared in the form of spontaneous acts of enthusiasm.

Symbols of patriotism in the public realm

One of the striking things about the Vancouver Games was an unusual expression of Canadian patriotism at the grassroots level that occurred in micro-interactions but in public spaces. Canadians have historically been very low-key about expressing their national loyalties (especially in contrast to their neighboring American cousins). One would expect that since Canada was the hosting nation, there would have been expressions of patriotism at competitions. The waving of Canadian flags at competitions would not be unusual, but the use of Canadian flags by businesses and at residences during the Games would be a declaration of participation in the event. Canadian flags were observed on display in the windows of single-room occupancy inexpensive hotels and rooming houses as well as gigantic flags created on the front walls on stores. Yet what surprised even most Canadians was the expression of patriotism in the streets and public places. In short, the symbolic meaning of the Olympics became tightly entwined with national symbols – and especially the national anthem and the maple leaf. It was most unusual to hear people on the streets breaking out into the singing of "O Canada" at the slightest provocation. It happened at transit stations, in lineups waiting to enter pavilions, or just anywhere on the street. It was particularly more boisterous after Canada had had particular success in the competitions (especially hockey), but it occurred anytime. Groups of individuals began to sing and others would join in. This was spontaneous behavior in which two or three persons or a small group would sing – sometimes only the first few lines of the song, but it made the point.

In contrast to singing the national anthem, the decision to wear apparel with the maple leaf on it and/or the stylized word "Canada" on it was a consumer choice. Individuals eagerly bought what was called "Canada gear," meaning shirts, jackets, toques, and any other apparel that had "Canada" on it. It virtually became a symbol of lay participation in the Olympic atmosphere, certainly within the city but also beyond. Such consumer choices could easily be viewed as the result of a successful marketing program carried out by the Hudson's Bay Company and its multiple affiliated stores. Yet the link between marketing and consumer choice is a complex one.[9] Creating products that might be successful is dependent on consumers being open to purchasing that product. For some reason, the demand for the popular red mittens with the maple leaf on them (Figure 5.3) was almost insatiable. Over 3.5 million pairs of mittens were sold,

Figure 5.3 Among the most popular items of merchandising were the mittens, which quickly sold out.

and stores had sold out long before the Olympics were over. Obviously the media played a major role in making the public aware of these items, but they were very popular and became a badge of being part of the Olympic spirit in the city. For example, one Catholic priest even gave the final blessing on the first Olympic Sunday in his church by holding up his hands with the red mittens on. Flags of all sizes were also available for purchase, such as hand flags for waving or large flags that could be carried on the street or worn around the body as capes. Stickers, hats of various types, washable tattoos, and different paraphernalia with maple leaves on them were available for purchase and taken into the public realm. Again, following our earlier observations, such patriotic behavior was particularly likely when people were in small groups with others who also decided to do something similar. A count at the corner of Robson and Granville one evening during a thirty-minute period estimated that of the thousands on the street, more than half were wearing something that could be called patriotic clothing.

Two other types of items should also be mentioned because they were also symbols of identification with the Olympic spirit in the city. One was lapel pins (or stick pins) and the other was the plush mascots (which came in several sizes). About fifteen million pins were made by the licensee, and included everything from sponsor pins to committee pins to pins for retail sale. This of course did not include pins brought to Vancouver from other countries which were available for trading. Pin trading might be viewed by some as merely dealing in a marketable gimmick, but what should not be forgotten is that the pins were an important element in interaction between people – often again especially with strangers. About three million plush mascots were sold, primarily to be given to children by adults. While children may not fully understand their relationship to the Olympics, they easily became attached to them, and adults who purchased the mascots considered this a personal way to relate to the Games. Rather than emphasize the popularity of these items as merely evidence of successful marketing, my interpretive perspective considers these items as symbolic ways in which people became part of the Olympics as a festival. The fact that the hype over these items virtually disappeared when the Games were over suggests that there was something about the event itself that generated these forms of participation.

Patriotism as consumer behavior

An explanation for the purchase of these consumer items is undoubtedly complex. At one level, it might just symbolize people with disposable income making trivial purchases. But at another level, it may also represent urban residents anticipating or assessing the context and meaning of an event and adjusting their consumer behavior accordingly. It has often been observed that people buy things not just because of their functional importance but because of their symbolic significance. One possibility is that the Olympics represented a limited purchase opportunity for what many considered a once-in-a-lifetime event

UNIVERSITY OF WINCHESTER
LIBRARY

(Abendroth and Diehl 2006). Related to this point is the idea that people usually associate their possessions with memories important to them (Richins 1994), and these consumer purchases may have been seen as symbols of the pur-chasers' own Olympic experience. It is likely that these two points can be blended, in that because people perceived the Olympics as a special local occa-sion, these items did become a representation of their stored memories. However, since most items were purchased just before or during the Olympics, it is likely that the social context played a major role in people's decision to buy. The public realm during the Olympics could be defined as an opportunity for identity signaling (Berger and Heath 2007). Identity domains or the social group which shape a particular product choice can influence the decision of whether to choose to wear sweatshirts as something more conventional, for example, or face decorations as something more unusual. Nobody told people to wear patriotic clothing, or even (except for retail marketers) encouraged them to do so. Canada gear took on significance because of the public realm, where it could be worn rather than being stored in a closet. Attaching patriotic items to the body in the public realm during the Olympics reflected both a personal choice and a declaration of self-identity (Figure 5.4). The decision to wear sticker tattoos on the face, or a maroon hoodie with "Canada" emblazoned on

Figure 5.4 One of the surprising things about the Olympics in Vancouver was the rampant expression of Canadian patriotism in the public realm. Identity signaling was expressed in a variety of creative ways.

the front, or a top hat with a maple leaf on it was both a personal form of costuming and a form of national identity or expression of solidarity with Canadians as a collectivity that became relevant to a specific event. In contrast to viewing identity signaling as a way of distinguishing oneself from the majority, what was observed in Vancouver during the Olympics had some elements of personal uniqueness but otherwise signaled a desire to relate to the people of Canada as a collectivity. The fact that this was temporary behavior expressed with short-term enthusiasm during the period of the Games suggests a strong similarity with fads or fan behavior.

Explaining patriotic behavior

In some ways, this outburst of patriotic activity is difficult to explain with any degree of confidence. It is true that in Canadian cities where National Hockey League teams (e.g., the Vancouver Canucks) operate, local residents are accustomed to wearing apparel in the public realm that indicates their team loyalties at the time of important games. But wearing "Canada" items is less typical. The "backpack Canadian" is a well-known phenomenon: Canadians who travel abroad having the maple leaf symbol on their backpacks in order to differentiate themselves from Americans. There is also some history of Canada engaging in international competitions (particularly hockey) that have stirred national sentiments. The 1972 hockey series between Canada and Russia is often viewed as a high-water mark in prompting national exuberance and pride. Canada is also annually represented in international hockey tournaments that also cause people to think in national terms. But in general, Canadians have not been boisterously patriotic, although it has been argued that they are becoming more so (Millard *et al.* 2002). There have been a variety of arguments made for why Canadians have been less patriotic (Hiller 2006a:273–308). Most of these arguments have to do with historical and structural factors such as Canada's relatively short history and its colonial relationship to Great Britain (the mother country), which delayed the development of its own distinctive symbols. For example, Canada did not officially have its own flag until 1965 or its own Constitution until 1980. The weak Canadian identity has also been tied to Canada's subordinate relationship to its more powerful neighbor the United States. Other factors usually discussed include the English/French linguistic divide, powerful regionalist sentiments, and different waves of immigration from different source countries. The conception of Canada as a British-oriented country with its attendant symbolism (for example, the British monarchy is still represented on Canadian currency) has been increasingly strained by immigration from other parts of the world. In short, there are many reasons why the shared identity of Canadians as a collectivity has been fragile.

Perhaps the most important demographic factor of recent significance has been the transformation of Canada's largest cities through international migration. According to the 2006 census, 20 percent of Canada's population was foreign-born – the highest percentage of foreign-born residents in the country in seventy-five years (Statistics Canada 2006). Most of this immigration was destined for Canada's three largest metropolitan areas, Toronto, Montreal, and Vancouver. Vancouver (40 percent) was second only to Toronto (45 percent) as the metropolitan areas with the largest percentage of immigrants, and fully half of those immigrants in Vancouver had been in Canada for less than fifteen years. In contrast to earlier years, when most of the immigrants were from Europe, the more recent wave of immigration has been primarily from Asia, with China, India, and Hong Kong being the largest source countries. The foreign-born population of the Vancouver metropolitan area more than doubled since 1981, and between 2001 and 2006 it had increased five times faster than the Canadian-born population. When the municipalities making up the Vancouver metropolitan area are considered separately,[10] it is noteworthy that foreign-born persons made up almost half (46 percent) of the municipality of Vancouver and 57 percent of the municipality of Richmond (the site of the Olympic Oval and the Richmond Ozone Celebration site). Richmond was the municipality with the highest percentage of foreign-born in all of Canada. What is of further relevance to this analysis is that a high percentage of these immigrants to the Vancouver metropolitan area had become Canadian citizens. Only 21 percent of those who had arrived in Canada between 1991 and 2002 had not as yet become Canadian citizens. While some still retained their citizenship of another country as well, it is very clear that there were many residents of Vancouver who were relatively recent arrivals to the city and had only recently become Canadian citizens. Vancouver was, then, a unique setting as a city in which there were large numbers of foreign-born residents and a large number of "new Canadians" as determined by citizenship. The implication for patriotic celebrations during the Olympics is clear in that a significant proportion of participants were offered an opportunity to express their newfound national identity in public for the first time. Wearing "Canada gear" and joining thousands of others on the streets expressing their patriotism became a critically symbolic way of expressing that personal identity. It is not that immigrants were the only people celebrating their patriotism on the street but rather that they provided an important local base for such activity. Moreover, in a country now composed of many visible minorities, and in a city where foreign-born visible minorities combined were on the cusp of being a majority, the Olympics provided an opportunity for people to encounter one another with common patriotic symbols as though race and immigration status did not matter.

This outburst of patriotic behavior also needs to be understood as a form of tension release. Seeking and appropriating common symbols in a country with so many divisions – as demonstrated, for example, by the fact that Canada was being governed by a minority government that almost lost its ability to govern just prior to the Olympics – meant that there was an opportunity to celebrate national unity on at least one level, even if only for a short time. It could be argued that there have been few shared moments in Canadian society, as even the annual Canada Day celebrations are fragmented by the Saint-Jean-Baptiste Day celebrations in Quebec around the same time. Most patriotic events are structured and planned, in comparison to the spontaneity of the street patriot-ism that occurred during the Olympics. The fact that the Olympics linked patri-otism with sport also added more exuberance to its expression. Within the city of Vancouver itself, as we have seen, the Olympics had been a controversial project. National symbols could be mixed with Olympic symbols in the creation of a patriotic performance in the eyes of the world. Expressions of patriotism showed how the Olympics did indeed serve a higher good in spite of the local debates.

The relationship between patriotism and consumer items as observed during the Olympics is not totally new. For example, Molson's brewery had earlier created a brand called "Canadian" and marketed it through an advertising cam-paign called "I am Canadian." One commercial theme in particular used a char-acter named "Joe Canada" who poked fun at stereotypical images of Canada in a light-hearted way (Millard *et al.* 2002). Molson was very visible during the Olympics with its pavilion called Molson Canadian Hockey House, which pro-moted its new "made from Canada" theme. A clothing company called Roots had also made use of the maple leaf and other national symbols in its product designs, including providing the uniforms for Canadian athletes at the 1998 Games in Nagano. Therefore, the decision by the Hudson Bay Company to build its own stable of merchandise utilizing patriotic symbols was not new. What is critical, however, is that the marketing of a product requires an amen-able consumer and an appropriate context. This is where the Olympics served as an important catalyst for patriotic behavior.

National symbols provided the threads of connectivity in the midst of a diverse and heterogeneous society. The Olympics, as an iconic event, provided the occasion for a shared experience. In contrast to the limitations of the Olym-pics as an experience for which a ticket was required in order to obtain special access to events, or the Olympics as a mediated experience via the quasi-personal electronic media, the Olympics of the streets became the place where identities could be encountered in an interactive sense with broad public partic-ipation. The symbols of a nation provided an opportunity for people to share that which united them rather than emphasizing that which divided them. In that vein, it is interesting that VANOC decided to use a phrase from the national anthem ("With Glowing Hearts") as its theme. If the Olympic project had previously meant controversy and debate, the leveling nature of the street and the celebratory mood of street-goers found its unity in the symbols of a nation which provided a superficial yet emotional gloss of unity. No one was asked to celebrate a particular historical or ideological version of the Canadian polity. It was not a Canada as defined by a political party or by some ethno-racial group. In fact, it was patriotism as form without content, rooting for the nation as a fan would cheer for a team (Schrag 2011).[11] Moss (2009) calls this strategic nationalism, as it is a focused pride rather than an uncritical celebra-tion of all things Canadian. It was a celebration of the symbols of Canada as an imagined community that allowed people to find a brief interlude among the things that divided them that provided such emotional power to the patriotism which was supported by the Olympics as a festival. It was in the public realm that Canadians rediscovered one another and it was through the symbols of a nation that a common identity, however fleeting, could be found.[12]

Symbols and emotion

The Olympics also became a powerful symbol in evoking emotion. The most frequent commentary by residents of Vancouver about the Games was that during the Olympic period the mood of the city changed dramatically. Mood and emotion are critical aspects of interactionist theory. Collins (2004) points out that when people feel bodily co-present, and when there is a mutual focus of attention and a shared mood, there is likely to be a greater sense of group solidarity, emotional energy, and an attachment to shared symbols. These ingredients and outcomes feed back upon each other, although they are only the result of successful interaction rituals in comparison to what he calls faded, mediocre, empty, or forced rituals. In other words, when mutual focus and intersubjectivity are intensified through interaction, the successful interaction ritual will leave the participants feeling energized and enthusiastic. While interaction is based on face-to-face encounters in the first instance, overlapping networks and co-present networks create larger groups, especially when they have a common focus.

The Olympics provided the common focus for Vancouver residents, and the mood was manipulated at least partially by events involving athletes, which heightened public interest and evoked emotional responses. The media played the critical role in disseminating information and interpretations of these events, often through frequent repetition, that created a roller coaster of emotion which intensified affectivity.[13] Rather than the urban context being a factor in resident response, in this instance the athletes and the competitions of the Games themselves became a human drama that evoked a range of emotions from sorrow, sadness, and sympathy to happiness, anticipation, and exuberance. These emotions quickly spread through the host population through interlocking networks.

Competitions and negative emotions

The emotional entrainment began already on the first day of the Olympics when it was announced that Nodar Kumaritashvili, a luge competitor from Georgia, had died on a training run at Whistler. The message of the crash and then the announcement of his death followed by video replays of the crash in the media ensured that this tragedy became a major topic of conversation among Vancouver residents. In fact, it served as a clear demonstration of interactionist theory in that it drew many more people into discussions about the Olympics as the news spread from one person to another (e.g., Did you hear …? Wasn't that awful? What do you think …?). The sadness of this tragedy meant the needless loss of a life, but the debate about what could have been done to prevent it made the Olympics controversial in a totally different sense. For some residents, this tragedy not only meant sympathy for the family but in some ways was interpreted as reflecting negatively on the city and/or casting a pall on the Vancouver Games. In any case, the glitz and pageantry of the opening ceremony later that day and the awe and wonder and festive atmosphere that they evoked were emotionally counterbalanced by the moment of silence, the Olympic flag flying at half-mast, and the Georgian team parading with black armbands at the opening ceremonies in which an undercurrent of sadness and sorrow was also present. When the local media reminded residents of the protest outside BC Place, which has already been discussed, the cauldron pillar malfunction, and the criticism that initially came from the British press, it was not surprising that countervailing mixed emotions created at least some affective confusion. The sadness of a death, the dramatic excitement of the opening ceremonies, and the anger of protest represented a roller coaster of emotions for host city residents concerning activities happening in their own city all in one day.

Host city residents have more at stake in what happens in their Olympic city than non-residents, so they are more likely to become emotionally involved. Resident emotions were further manipulated by dashed expectations in competition performances. As the first week of competition went by, there was significant disappointment with the performance of Canadian athletes. In fact, the failure of well-known athletes expected to do well led to media labels of the results as the "Hard Luck Games," or "Black Saturday" when a triple medal threat failed. The Canadian Olympic Committee even admitted at a press conference that its goal for total medals was probably unrealistic and in that sense virtually admitted defeat regarding its medal goals. Given the prominence of hockey in Canadian culture, much was expected of the hockey teams. The women's team performed as expected, but the expectations were much higher for the men's team, though the competition much stronger, and when the team almost lost to Switzerland, not considered a serious threat, in a game that went to an overtime shootout, panic began to set in. When the men's hockey team did indeed lose to the United States two days later, there was little to celebrate. The media, however, did make much about the first gold medal ever to be won on Canadian soil (Alexandre Bilodeau in freestyle skiing), which seemed to be a form of relief since that achievement had been elusive in the two previously hosted Games.

Athletes as human stories and emotions

Whereas medal success had been somewhat elusive for Canadian athletes during the first seven to ten days of competition and was the source of considerable disappointment and perhaps even sadness, there were still other ways in which people became emotionally connected to the Games. The media understand that public interest in the Games is not just dependent on who wins or loses but can be found in the dramas of personal stories related to the competitors. In that sense, competitors are actors whose personal lives can be useful for media consumption because they increase interest. Under the right conditions, the personal lives of athletes can become "stories" that make them more human and easier to commoditize. These human stories, even more than athletic performance, support interaction with other people where the stories of personal achievement amidst difficulties or tragedy are recounted over and over again with others, sometimes to empathize and sometimes to inspire. In fact, it is possible that the narratives or stories behind the medals provide more emotional power than the medals themselves (van Hilvoorde *et al.* 2010). There were several Canadian athletes whose personal stories were particularly compelling. The first gold medalist, Alexandre Bilodeau, received considerable media attention because of his personal story, in which he identified his brother Frederic, who has cerebral palsy, as his hero. He was frequently photographed with him and pointed out how he was inspired by his brother's determination to walk when that was not expected. Another athlete whose personal life had considerable emotional traction was the tragedy of Canadian figure skater Joannie Rochette, whose mother died of a heart attack upon arrival in Vancouver to watch her daughter skate. This misfortune was compelling enough but the question then was whether Joannie would still skate. Two days after her mother died, she did skate and ultimately won a bronze medal. Every time she skated, of course, her story brought increased public interest in the outcome as well as media interest in more in-depth personal information. A good indication of this public interest was the fact that her site at the CTVOlympics.ca website was the most visited site for days during the Olympics (Bell Media, Day 10). There were also lots of other "stories" behind success and failure of Canadian athletes such as the failures of previously successful speed skater Jeremy Wotherspoon or the missed final takeout that lost gold for the women's curling team, the dramatic finish of the dance pairs Tessa Virtue and Scott Moir, or the story of blind cross-country skier Brian McKeever, who was not allowed to compete. Each of these athletes had personal stories that made their performance an object of interpersonal intrigue and discussion, largely because the media presented personal details with numerous close-up shots that provided a sense of intimate knowing. Athletes were transformed from impersonal actors on the competitive stage to real people on the runway of life, thereby creating emotional ties of identification.

Competitions and positive emotions

In the second week of the Games, after the disappointments of the first week, Canada's success in the medal count became much better. The men's hockey team won a game it had to win against Germany in order to move ahead in the competition. The women's hockey team won the gold medal game against the United States (a gold medal win against any other team would not have meant quite as much) and restored some of Canada's confidence. But ultimately the stage was set for what most Canadians considered the most important event of the Games, which was the men's gold medal game against the United States on the last day of the Olympics. Given the unequal yet symbiotic relationship between Canada and the United States in so many respects, the stage could not have been set better for a more concluding drama, and Canada beat the United States 3–2 in overtime.[14] Needless to say, then, as far as men's hockey was concerned, the emotional intensity of the buildup for this final game was immense and its outcome contributed significantly to the exuberance expressed in the city on the final day of the Games. Indeed, it could be argued that this gold medal may even have played a primary role in residents' final evaluation of the success of the Games for the city, let alone for the nation.

The picture, then, is clear: the Games themselves played a major role in stimulating the emotions of city residents and broadening interest in the Games.[15] This was done through making athletes actors in human dramas as well as the dramas of competition. To put it bluntly, you did not have to know much about freestyle skiing or figure skating as sports to identify with athletes who have been challenged by disability or death, and whose stories were available everywhere. In spite of the emotional lows of the first week, Canada eventually won more gold medals (fourteen) than any other nation and placed third in total medals awarded (behind the United States and Germany), and its overall medal performance was considered an outstanding success. These results of course contributed to the sense that the Games were a success for the city. What is significant from our perspective is that there were elements in the competitions that had an emotional impact on residents and drew them into the Games as performance. From sadness and disappointment to exhilaration and enthusiasm, it was difficult to be apathetic about the Games because all segments of the media reported these stories. These elements helped to transform residents from passive observers of the Games to people who not only interacted with the Games but also interacted more with each other. It was not only wins and successes that provided incentives to interact on the streets, in homes, or in third places; failures and tragedies, too, provided occasions for heightened interaction. The anxiety over how the Games would be evaluated by non-residents amidst problems and issues (even the weather) created one set of emotional issues which were juxtaposed next to tragedies and triumphs – all shared emotionally and not just factually by the metropolitan community as a common focus.

Symbols and the public realm

The bodily co-presence of people in the public realm who themselves were part of interaction rituals found a sense of unity through national symbols. These symbols pre-existed the gathering of people and in that sense were not the product of interaction. But the clustering on the streets heightened the role that symbols played in providing visual and oral confirmation of a commonality which Collins calls temporary situational solidarity. Collins's (2004:42) point is that when there is a high degree of mutual focus of attention, intersubjectivity, bodily synchronization, and mutual stimulation, there is greater attachment to cognitive symbols and more emotional energy not only for groups but for individual lives. These moments of ritual intensity are high points that people remember and that give meaning to their personal biographies. When people in a crowd move from being passive observers to actively taking part, Collins calls this a focused crowd, whether they clap their hands simultaneously or chant a refrain or sing a song. Because the people participating do not know each other personally, these are secondary group identities. Nevertheless, when these inter-actions reach this level of intensity, they have a profound influence on people, unlike most other interactions.

In Vancouver, it was interaction in the public realm (whether experienced personally or vicariously) that had the greatest impact on city residents. The Olympics became a focus of attention with intense emotional overtones, at least partly because of the human dramas interpreted and repeated by the media, but also because of the way the narratives linked to other forms of participation, whether on the street or utilizing the symbolic value of the Olympics for other causes. Patriotic activity provided the symbols that served as the basis for a sense of temporary common focus (or solidarity) in a heterogeneous city. The density of people on the streets who were active performers themselves rather than just passive provided the context of mutual stimulation, which was reinforced by the uniting power of national symbols that also stirred emotions. Given the fact that such interaction is not normal or typical of daily life in Vancouver, the result was that residents often experienced euphoric feelings that have become part of their memory about the Games, and which may have swept aside at least some of the controversy. Unexpectedly, the Olympics could thus become an emotional experience.

Conclusion

The insertion of the Olympics into the evolutionary history of a city involves the incorporation of a powerful symbol into that city's collective identity and its residents' personal experiences.[16] The power of the symbol is felt in the way the Olympics become a priority on the city agenda but also in the way they mobilize other forces that want to be associated with that symbol or utilize the symbol for their own purposes. If the Olympics has become a symbolic platform for a variety of interests, so also has the host city come to serve as a symbolic field for the expression of these interests. While VANOC's takeover of all public billboards in the city for the use of Olympic corporate sponsors represents one side of the presence of this symbolic field, the use of the Olympics by advocacy groups to promote issues about which they feel passionate represents another way in which the city becomes a symbolic field and the symbolic power of the Olympics is experienced. The dominant presence of patriotic symbols in the city during the Games also illustrates how the alignment of national symbols and Olympic symbols may occur. The fact that the symbolic power of the Games themselves was also experienced emotionally by residents helped to solidify the Games as an experience and not just a hosted event. And because the public realm became the primary domain of the symbolic field, the Olympics had an inescapable presence that captured the attention of city residents. The Olympics, then, made the city not only a symbolic field but also an interactional field in which interpersonal encounters increased around a common focus.

6 The social media and urban interaction

Interactionist theory stresses the importance of bodily co-presence as a critical micro factor on which meaningful relationships and ultimately society can build. But is bodily co-presence always necessary for meaningful interaction to occur, given the mediated communication age in which we live? The digitization and mobility of communication change the way people relate to each other in important ways, but also open up new possibilities. Miah (2010:15) has pointed out that the Vancouver Olympics were unique in that they were the "first genuinely digital and mobile Olympic Games." This chapter examines how interaction occurred through the social media during the Games.

Mobile communication has changed our ability to interact with others. Communication is no longer directly connected to a place through landlines but is transportable to virtually anywhere in a city where a signal can be obtained. Mobile phones, and especially internet-capable phones such as the Blackberry and the iPhone, provide powerful ways to allow people to communicate with others who are not physically present. Using interactionist theory, Ling (2008) has demonstrated that while new bonds can be created through the social media, people with existing bonds can maintain and nurture their relationships through mediated interaction even when physically separated. He showed how mediated interaction enhances co-present forms of interaction through the use of symbols and communication strategies that support the relationship even when people are not bodily sharing the same space. He refers to the mobile phone as a "connecting presence" strengthening relationships in what he calls "bounded solidarity." This suggests that mobile forms of communication must also be examined if we are to understand the Olympics from an interactionist perspective.

Social media are distinctive in that they are a decentralized, easily accessible, and virtually immediate form of communication via the internet. They are media for interaction because of their user-generated content and their support of dialogue. One of the primary ways in which this interaction occurs is through websites and blogs. Whatever is posted represents the poster's ideas or creations, but at the same time there is room for comment or reaction and response. Instead of information being presented as final, social media allow for discussion, debate, correction, and new information. In relation to the Olympics, any person with a camera could paste pictures on their website or post articles or discussions about what they observed. The key thing about social media is that they work outside the boundaries of traditional publications and news dissemination outlets. People who like using the internet for this purpose and do not receive pay for doing so are referred to as citizen journalists. Sometimes, existing media outlets may incorporate links from their own sites to the sites of citizen journalists, and sometimes the media outlets get story ideas from citizen journalist posts. During the Olympics in Vancouver, an entity called True North Media House attempted to provide a coordinated outlet for citizen journalists and was quite successful in doing so.[1] Many people who took the social media seriously and devoted huge amounts of time towards them (e.g., Kris Krug) posted large amounts of material or photographs and blogged daily on their own website about the Olympics. Blogs and web postings have the advantage of making pictures, ideas, and information available immediately. Another form of citizen journalism is online newspapers like the *Vancouver Observer*, which posts stories and pictures from contributors but does so in a more structured way.

Acknowledging the role of unaccredited media, a Media House was created by the British Columbia government at Robson Square for persons who lacked the accreditation to obtain entry into Olympic sites but who were interested in recording what was happening in communities and on the streets and at places less likely to be covered by the accredited media. Because spaces were limited, True North Media House was created by volunteers to encourage and facilitate coverage by those not officially recognized as accredited media – even through the provision of self-accreditation badges. The Vancouver Media Cooperative (VMC), in opposition to the Olympics, was another vehicle available for grassroots input via the internet to what the public came to know about the Games. VMC's goal was to reverse the nature of news production by talking to people affected by government policies first, thereby being both independent and progressive in reporting about the Olympics and how they affected communities. These can all be called "alternative" media in that they represent ways in which information and audio-visual images were collected and transmitted beyond what was available through the usual media outlets. As more and more people use internet platforms to communicate as well as to obtain information, it is clear that sources of information can be bottom-up rather than just top-down. Miah (2010) calls this "new media activism" because it represents a voluntaristic, instrumental, and fervent use of the internet to communicate news and interpretation of events as the result of private individual initiative rather than institutional programs. It has also been referred to as citizen journalism because of the wide variety of ways members of the public participate in defining and interpreting the news.[2]

The internet and new media

It is widely recognized that television has changed the Olympics not only from the perspective of the global audience reach of the Games but also from the perspective of how the Games are marketed and utilized for commercial purposes (Whannel 2009).[3] Real (1996) points out that television, and especially television rights, have contributed to the post-modernizing of the Games in that the Olympics have become focused on commodity values. The goal of reaching the widest possible audience heightens the commodity value of the Games. Not only has television made athletes a marketable commodity, but the opening and closing ceremonies have taken on the qualities of show business in order to attract and retain a global audience. Similarly, the customization of Olympic events by the broadcast media for many different audiences (known as designer broadcasting) creates many different versions of the Games. While television is still the largest and most traditional form of media consumption of the Olympics, other forms of media are gaining in importance (Marshall *et al.* 2010; Hutchins and Mikosza 2010; Tang and Cooper 2011). Broadcaster websites that provide live streaming and video views are gaining in popularity. However, new forms of interactive communication have emerged through the social media that not only link people to events but also link people to each other. Facebook, Twitter, YouTube, and personal blogs provide channels whereby information, commentary, photos, and videos can be shared in relation to what is happening in the Olympics. These platforms are not mutually exclusive, in that watching television or live videos can occur simultaneously with participation through the social media. But the variety of media platforms available to the Olympic consumer is what adds a new dimension to our understanding of the Games from an interaction point of view, and nowhere is this clearer than for people in the host city, who are at ground zero to what is happening. Mobile phones and other mobile or smart devices transform the way in which urban residents encounter the Games.

The Vancouver Games have been described as a "defining moment" in Olympic broadcasting history because they were the first to fully utilize new media platforms.[4] Digital coverage accounted for about half of the overall broadcast output from Vancouver. For example, broadcast coverage was available not only on free-to-air terrestrial channels but also on more than 100 websites worldwide which augmented traditional coverage. Online video views were 785 percent higher for Vancouver 2010 than for Turin 2006. What is perhaps most remarkable is the fact that people have a variety of ways in which they can use the internet to interact with the Games. The Vancouver 2010 website attracted 275 million visitors – more than double the Beijing 2008 site. The IOC Facebook page was launched just before the Games and attracted more than 1.5 million visitors in a short time. Users can post their comments on Facebook or Twitter as events evolve, whether they are at the event in person or are experiencing something on television or through live streaming. Over 6,000 hours of broadcast hours were available on mobile phone platforms. Communications about the Olympics are now increasingly occurring on the internet rather than just the traditional news outlets of radio, television, and the print media.

In order to understand the role of the internet in relation to the Games within the more local and national Canadian context, two formats can be highlighted: websites and Twitter. The websites of interest are those established by information providers and broadcasters that have an official role in relation to the event. In the case of Vancouver, this obviously meant the VANOC website and also the websites of the Broadcast Consortium. Both of these websites had as their goal the provision of information that would help people experience the Olympics. People looked to the VANOC site, especially in the pre-Games period, to find information on ticketing and other logistical issues. The Broadcast Consortium as news providers supplied reports, video, and photos that were especially valuable during the Games themselves. Newspaper websites were also relevant but are not discussed here. The websites of the Consortium and VANOC also provided blogs and links to Facebook and Twitter that allowed people to interact with what was happening. Photo galleries on these sites were also popular as the Games progressed.

The second internet platform discussed here to indicate how people experienced the Olympics is Twitter. By using specific hashtags, it was possible to provide a more localized interaction analysis of how people communicated in real time in relation to Olympic-related activity. Both sources provide a sense of the interaction that the Olympics supported, although Twitter gives us a more city-specific personal encounter expression of that interaction. The internet of course does not restrict participation to people from one country, but it is probable that more Canadians would go to the Canadian Broadcast Consortium for their information than people from other countries.[5]

Websites

The primary source of information about the Olympics within Canada before the Games, as already noted, was the VANOC website. People would naturally look to it for information during the Games as well. As an indicator of how important this website was, Vancouver2010.com was visited by 275 million visitors in total. Seventy-six percent of Canadians with internet access visited the website during the month of the Olympics.[6] The mobile spectator guide that VANOC produced had more than 1.25 million downloads, which generated 8.7 million visits and illustrates how important the site was for those with smartphones. VANOC also had 1.1 million Facebook followers and 14,000 followers on Twitter. Vancouver2010.com provided news about events and their results, which made the website an important source of information during the Games.

Perhaps the primary place where the public would go online to find current information about the Games – and particularly up-to-the minute results of the Games – was to the producers of the electronic forms of news. Newspaper websites also played that role, but television broadcasters had the advantage of being able to provide more video feeds and not primarily photographs or news stories in print. The websites of Canada's Olympic Broadcast Media Consortium (particularly CTVOlympics.ca and RDSolympiques.ca) not only were important sources of information but also provided the opportunity to experience events all over again through video replays. In addition, broadcasters in the Consortium maintained their own blogs and Facebook and Twitter links. The Consortium was made up of eleven Canadian television networks (e.g., CTV, APTN, TSN, Sportsnet, Omni) broadcasting "every second" of the Games with unprecedented coverage in multiple languages. The saturation was so strong and the interest so great that the opening ceremony became the most-watched television event in Canadian history at the time it occurred (later to be superseded), with 69 percent of Canadians watching at least part of it.[7] The websites of the Consortium generated almost one million video views during the Opening Ceremonies alone (Bell Media, Day 1). Page views of CTVOlympics.ca reached 9.4 million on the first day of the Games, and 50,000 Canadians participated in a live chat during the ceremonies at the same website. By Day 14, there were three successive days of page views over fifteen million and video views over two million per day. When the Games reached their concluding day (Day 17), overall television viewing in Canada had increased by 22 percent over the preceding five weeks, and 30.5 million people (91 percent of the Canadian population) watched at least some part of the coverage of that final day. Peak concurrent streams reached 133,000 for the closing ceremony. By the time they were over, the Olympics had generated the top five largest television audiences ever in Canadian history (Bell Media, Day 17): the gold medal men's hockey game (16.6 million), the closing ceremony (14.3 million), the opening ceremony (13.5 million), the Canada vs. United States men's hockey match (10.6 million), and the Canada vs. Russia men's hockey match (10.5 million). Nearly half of all internet users in Canada had visited at least one of the two dominant broadcaster websites during the Games. Total page views throughout the Games exceeded 215 million and averaged 12.7 million page views per day. These statistics show how television broadcasting saturated the Canadian market but that online viewing was also important. The use of computers for online viewing also meant that computers were available for other kinds of online Olympic-related activity.

While these figures do not tell us anything specific about the host city, it is clear that the Olympics were a major media event for Canada. If this was the case for the country as a whole, it can be assumed that interest in the host city would be even more intense. This was indeed the case, as Vancouver had 25 percent higher ratings in audience size than Toronto, Calgary, and the national average over the first three days of the Games (Bell Media, Day 3). By Day 13, Vancouverites were watching more Games coverage than the inhabitants of any other Canadian city. The Vancouver average was 32.3 hours per week, in comparison to 29.3 hours per week for Calgary and twenty-six hours per week for Toronto. Perhaps of greater interest from an interactionist perspective was that watching the Olympics on television was something shared with others rather than being an isolating behavior. As of Day 5, more than half of the Canadian population had watched the Olympics on a television outside their own homes. For Vancouverites, the number was even higher, as 77 percent of Vancouverites had watched at least some of the games outside their homes (Bell Media, Day 7). This undoubtedly means that television sets were turned on at workplaces so that people could watch together (rather than just watching on their computer screens, which of course also occurred), as well as in retail establishments, in bars and restaurants,

UNIVERSITY OF WINCHESTER
LIBRARY

on sidewalks, in churches, as well as community centers (called Community Living Rooms) for the purpose of watching collectively with others.

The Media Consortium also reported that interaction on its social media sites also increased dramatically as the Games progressed. For example, the number of Facebook fans at the site increased quickly and more than doubled from the first to the second day. Facebook interactions totaled more than 10,000 in the first full week (Bell Media, Day 10). During the opening ceremony on the first day, about 1,000 people used Twitter to see virtually immediately the words used by slam poet Shane Koyczan in his instantly popular presentation called "We Are More." Viewers did not know this was coming but were so moved by his soliloquy on Canadians as a people that they immediately sought to examine the words more carefully. Of course, others present at the ceremonies recorded it and made it available on YouTube. By Day 5, the Consortium had 8,000 followers on Twitter and 20,000 friends on Facebook, and the numbers continued to grow from virtually nothing to a huge following of people looking for interactive opportunities during the Games. The two major broadcast media sites reported that thousands of referrals to their sites came via the social media. For example, the Broadcast Consortium reported on Day 10 that there were 31,000 referrals and on Day 14 that there were 35,000 referrals through the social media to its site, indicating that the social media played a major role in directing people to where they could join the interaction.

Whenever something especially interesting, dramatic, or emotionally moving occurred at the Olympics, there was usually a flurry of comments on these websites. For example, when Bilodeau won his gold medal (and the first gold medal for Canada on home soil) on Day 3, there was a flurry of comments on CTV's Facebook site. And when Joannie Rochette (see Chapter 5) and the women's hockey team won their medals, there were thousands of messages on their Twitter accounts. Their live blogs also generated public response: even when, for example, the Canadian women's hockey team played Slovakia, 5,000 people participated online (Bell Media, Day 2). It is impossible to determine to what extent these postings were the result of being at an event in person, watching TV or video, or just hearing the news from others via the social media. It is clear, though, that people were interacting with what was occurring and not just consuming it passively. What is also important is that people were not tied to a physical location to experience the Olympics. The Consortium reported that page views via smartphones and mobile devices surpassed 5.7 million by Day 14.

Web searches

As the most prominent search engine, Google Trends reported that, worldwide, searches involving the word "Olympics" spiked during the Games itself, just as similarly happened during the World Cup. It can be assumed, then, that internet usage increases during any major event such as the Olympics as users search for information as well as opportunities to interact with that event. It is noteworthy, however, that Canada as host country was the major source of such searches worldwide. Even within Canada, more searches took place in Vancouver than within any other city. The point here is that it is clear that the host country, and the host city in particular, generate more internet activity pertaining to the Olympics than any other location. Another measure of the role of the internet during the Olympics is how many people attempted searches pertaining to medal winners. The American snowboard gold medal winner Shaun White had a large number of searches from the United States, Canada, and elsewhere in the world – possibly because of the attraction of snowboarding to young internet surfers. Joannie Rochette, on the other hand, the Canadian bronze medal winner in figure skating whose mother died on arrival in Vancouver, obtained almost all of her searches within Canada, and especially from her hometown region of Montreal. Her compelling story, even though she did not win gold, was particularly of interest to surfers in Canada. The conclusion, then, is that people use the internet to obtain information on those athletes who particularly attract their attention, and the more local the athlete or the place of the competition, the more people initiate searches for that person.

Twitter

Twitter was launched in 2006 as a form of micro-blogging that is limited to 140 characters. Its primary advantages are that posts are shorter, the time and content investment is much smaller, and updates can then be done more often. It is very suitable to mobile devices with wireless connections, which means that posts can be made virtually anytime and anywhere. These characteristics allow users to share daily experiences, opinions, and commentary on any topic considered relevant (Java *et al.* 2007). Twitter also allows users to have followers through the use of hashtags, which enable users to focus on the posts of particular people or particular topics. Tweets can be directed to specific persons but they can also be available to anybody (Huberman *et al.* 2009). Twitter, then, can be used to obtain information, to share information or news, to tell others what a user is thinking or experiencing as a form of daily chatter, or to sustain relationships. Users may post themselves but they may also be content to just read the posts of others.[8]

Twitter use exploded in 2009, which, of course, was just prior to the 2010 Games. The Pew Internet Project (Fox *et al.* 2009) found that internet users who already used social networking sites such as Facebook or MySpace were more likely to use Twitter. Younger people were more likely to tweet than utilize any other status update, and staying in touch with people or topics they care about was their primary reason for being a user. Twitter is especially useful for posting real-time reaction to events or experiences as they occur, including links to images and videos or textual material. It is a form of instant messaging that uses an "economy of words" to broadcast to many people immediately (Zhao and Rosson 2009). In comparison to email, which produces cognitive overload, Twitter has a voluntary readership in which there are no obligations either to read a post or to respond to it. It is "always-on" communication with "ready-at-hand" digital production available for photos and messages (Ito

2008:3). Instead of the one-to-many (O2M) format of traditional communication, Twitter provides both peer-to-peer (P2P) and many-to-many (M2M) communication. Ito calls this phenomenon "networked publics" in which the audiences are not passive or consumptive but are active participants, makers, and redistributors of information. Twitter, then, is current and literally up to the minute with direct input that is often also monitored by institutional news organizations as people on the ground can report quickly what is occurring – a very decentralized and non-hierarchical form of communication. Whereas texting is directed to specific persons, Twitter reaches a much wider audience in which sharing occurs between people who are often relative strangers.

Messages are sent on Twitter by using hashtags starting with # which identify conversation groups. These hashtags are created by users but are not part of a lexicon of established names. Instead, users make them up or discover them and pass them on to others. A variety of hashtags were examined that were used during the Olympic period to determine which ones might be particularly helpful. Some hashtags, such as #yvr, #olympics, or #2010, were too generic to produce interesting results. There were many possible hashtags but several will be discussed here to illustrate how Twitter was used by city residents.[9] These hashtags all demonstrated strength during the Olympic period only.

The hashtag #van2010 generated considerable activity and was a hashtag that was frequently passed on through other tweets as well. Figure 6.1 illustrates

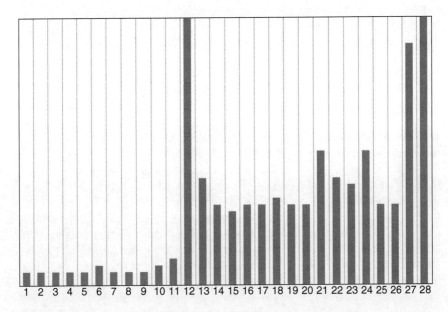

Figure 6.1 Volume of tweets using the hashtag #van2010, February 2010.

Note
This and subsequent graphs in this chapter are representations of the relative volume and frequency of Twitter search terms derived from the Twitter API.

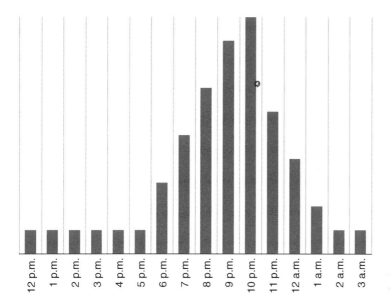

Figure 6.2 Volume of tweets using the hashtag #van2010, February 12, 2010.

the variation in volume and frequency of tweets over the course of the Olympics and for the month of February 2010.[10] It is clear that there was little activity until the Olympics began and then there was a huge spike on opening day. That day there was a protest at Victoria Square in the morning when the torch passed by, a protest down Robson Street in the late afternoon prior to the Opening Ceremonies, and of course the Opening Ceremonies in the evening, which might have played the most important roles in prompting tweets. Yet Figure 6.2 illustrates that the heaviest volume of tweeting using this hashtag was after 6 p.m. and the volume increased as the opening ceremony proceeded. Here are some samples of how people in Vancouver used Twitter to share their reactions and emotions about what they were observing.

"I've never seen Vancouver like this. Kind of incredible."
"Here we go! Can I just say how much I 'love' the Olympics?"
"Ahhhh!! I am so excited for the Opening Ceremonies! – all right Vancouver lets show the world how great we are!!!!"
"At the opening ceremonies … Its [sic] electric. Congrats Vancouver. Go Canada!"
"Choking up already."
"Absolute sucker I am … tears already forming."

This hashtag provides no comment at all on the protest activities earlier in the day. It does illustrate how people shared their excitement, emotions, and feelings through Twitter. They felt compelled to tell others physically distant rather than just those with whom they physically shared space how they were reacting.

Tweeting peeked at 10 p.m., after the opening ceremonies were over, and continued until midnight. Three things can be said about these tweets. One is that users did interact with the Opening Ceremonies and did use Twitter to offer their comments, whether they were present at the stadium or were watching on television. The second thing is that once it was over, tweets were used to comment on the overall performance and impact. Third, at the conclusion of the ceremonies the flame was taken by well-known former hockey player Wayne Gretzky unexpectedly through the public streets to an unknown destination where it would remain on public display during the Games (next to the Broadcast Media Center on a specially constructed plaza). Tweeters provided commentary along the way, providing news about its route and eventual final destination. It is clear, then, that most comments on that day using this hashtag were about the opening ceremony. Another huge spike in tweets occurred on the last two days of the Games, which of course were related to the finals of the men's hockey games and the closing ceremony. But this hashtag was used with considerable regularity throughout the duration of the Games as well – the bulk of which were focused on street life and the public realm.

A second hashtag of interest was #no2010. If the hashtag #van2010 provided little evidence of response to protest, it was thought that perhaps this hashtag would pick up that topic. Figure 6.3 illustrates that the volume of tweets using

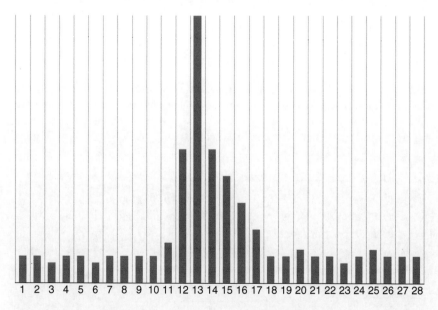

Figure 6.3 Volume of tweets using the hashtag #no2010, February 2010.

this hashtag was strong for the first few days of the Olympics but then tailed off. It particularly peaked on the first Saturday of the Games. It picked up some of the protest on the opening day and some after the protest march on Saturday but then lost its relevance, which may have been an indication that protest was no longer a major factor in the public realm. Figure 6.4 points out that tweeting using this hashtag peeked on the Saturday during and after the Heart Attack March, which produced the violence discussed earlier. In the sample of tweets listed below, notice how some tweets were observations by those who were there and some at the end were commentary. CTV even put out a call on Twitter for someone to report to it what was happening at the protest, acknowledging that tweeters might have access to more up-to-the-minute information.

"Police have circled a group of protesters in a marching band and are refusing to let them disperse."
"Riot police have broken up the demo. Many arrests."
"At the protest in Vancouver? CTV wants to talk to you."
"50 people arrested surrounded by riot cops in Vancouver."
"Georgia and Jarvis lots of cops … anarchists holding line."
"Morning demonstration has left and is making its way down Hastings Street taking both lanes."
"Watching the protest march past our house/neighborhood."
"I hear drums, whistles, shouting."
"am on the ground checking out the protest moving up Robson."
"These protests disturb me because I'm sure half of them aren't old enough to understand exactly what they are protesting."
"I'm so disappointed in the protesters. Peaceful protest is one thing but this is simply wrong."

By the next day, links, pictures (such as riot police in battle gear), and videos of this protest were being tweeted. It is interesting that in the afternoon a flash mob took place at the other end of Robson Street with around 2,000 dancers. The flash mob produced fewer tweets than the protest, but more of the tweets were from people who were there and reporting what was happening, although the event produced little commentary. However, as time passed, tweets about the protest increasingly were from people who were apparently not there and were critical of it. In large measure, however, tweeters clearly were citizen journalists in making the public aware of what was happening right at ground level.

Street protests may be particularly newsworthy items in that they are much more dramatic, are meant to obtain public attention, and thus result in many postings. The first protest on the first day of the Games was a human barricade that was set up at Victory Square to prevent the torch from being brought into the Downtown Eastside. When #torch was used as the hashtag, all postings

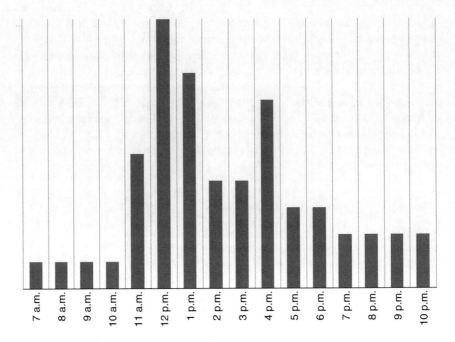

Figure 6.4 Volume of tweets using the hashtag #no2010, February 13, 2010.

between 10:24 a.m. and 11:36 a.m. were carefully examined. At 10:21, a posting indicates that an observer was waiting at Victory Square among protesters. Another post foreshadowed the potential implications of the conflict ("protesters disrupting the torch relay. Reroute?"). The first picture of the protesters appeared at 10:23 with the comment "Pipers, protesters, vets, firemen, and fans! Waiting for the torch! I love Canada!"[11] At 10:24, six posts announced that the torch had been rerouted. One of the posts was by a television commentator who had 40,000-plus followers. The first pictures of the blockade were posted at 10:25 and almost immediately comments were posted critical of the protesters – perhaps by at least some people who were not there. However, most tweets were just passing on information. Re-tweets of the television commentator's tweet were made virtually immediately as the news expanded. By 10:32, the tweet density was averaging ten tweets per minute. Most tweets announced what was happening but also included the occasional comment. "Odd scene. Veterans who fought for democracy near protesters testing democracy at Victory Square torch relay standoff in Vancouver." "I will be SO angry if the protesters stop the veterans from having their time at Victory Square during the torch run." In the first fifteen minutes from the initial post, more than eighty different people had participated in the "torch" hashtag for a total of ninety-nine tweets. Once the torch had been rerouted, tweeters announced its new route and that it was moving again. From 10:21 to 10:40 a.m., there were 122 tweets, an average of six tweets per minute. Counting the number of followers that each tweeter had, the estimated audience for these tweets was in excess of 100,000 persons. While it is not possible to determine precisely how many of these tweets were written by people present or people in Vancouver, the content of the reporting tweets suggested that many of the tweeters were present and a high percentage of the other tweeters were in Vancouver where the action was actually happening.

Athlete performances also produced Twitter action, and these posts demonstrated how Twitter can be used to vent emotional feeling. Just before Joannie Rochette skated, two sample tweets illustrate how users communicated: "I'm really tired, I have a headache but I have to see her skate." "gonna make me cry … full on waterworks this week." During her performance, others commented, "loved your hand slap with your coach. We're with you." "I'm getting so scared watching." "Her performance is giving me goosebumps." And after she skated, users tweeted their reaction: "a true inspiration. Bronze medal for Canada I believe." "amazing performance" "The courage and strength showed through." "What a story." "JR's medal could be made of tinfoil and her country would be just as proud." "She's my hero right now." "Your courage and strength just inspired the world." There were literally hundreds of tweets at five-second intervals, suggesting that the combination of Joannie's personal circumstances along with the pressure of the performance stirred considerable public interest. Again, while it is possible that at least some of these tweets originated somewhere other than Vancouver, it is likely that many of them were Vancouver based, including some from persons actually present at the arena.

Street activity also was something to Twitter. When "Robson,Van2010" was a combined hashtag, there were lots of reports of people's experiences, including the posting of pictures reflecting the jubilation at what was happening. On the first day of the Games, here are some samples of the Twitter reports that were being posted all day.

8:05 a.m.	"Robson Street is buzzing."
8:25 a.m.	"holy crap. Look at the crowd on Robson."
11:01 a.m.	"wow, never seen ziplining in the city! Check out Robson Square."
11:50 a.m.	"all I can hear is shouting and screaming from the 19th floor."
2:00 p.m.	"awesome busy vibe around Robson today."
3:30 p.m.	"swarms of people around Art Gallery."
4:46 p.m.	"protesters on Robson Street are deafening."
6:10 p.m.	"opening ceremonies projected on the big 'screen' in Robson Square. Massive, electric crowds. Glowing!"
10:25 p.m.	"the crowds on the streets outside VAG and at Robson Square are still cheering and hollering."

These tweets helped to publicize what was happening on the streets in the downtown core and also served as a recruitment device to encourage recipients to attend. On the last day of the Olympics, similar reports were tweeted as there was an air of celebration on the streets prompted by Canada winning gold in the men's hockey. "We can't move! Complete mayhem." "Walking up Robson. Love hearing everyone cheer." "So loud. People flooding the streets of Vancouver." "Never seen so many ppl on the street! So much fun!" "Robson and Granville a sea of red and white humanity." "This city has never been alive like this." Many people were observed texting friends as well to tell them individually what was going on in the streets and to confirm meeting places where they could rendezvous with their friends among the masses of people.

Street hockey turned out to be another activity that was tweeted using the hashtag "Granville, van2010." "There is a road hockey game broken out on Granville." "Yes this is awesome. Gotta love Olympics." "This is POSITIVE." "Can see the Granville street hockey game from my apartment. The crowd is going crazy." "Granville needs to be like this all the time year round." There were particular spikes in volume of tweets on February 16 and February 28. What appears to have prompted such communication on the 16th was a very popular hockey game between two sides. As was mentioned previously, one side dressed as American, with appropriate apparel such as stars and stripes in red, white, and blue. The other side represented Canada, with players dressed in red and white, often also including the maple leaf. This was only a pickup game on the street with no official meaning, but the crowd got into it in a big way.

The spike in tweets on the 28th was clearly related to the crowning end of the Olympics and the celebration of the performances of Canadian athletes, which brought many people onto the streets. There were many pictures posted from these street activities and some videos as well, taken with cell phone cameras.

The social media and public space

Castells (1989) developed the concept of the space of flows as a contrast to space of places because geographic proximity has been transformed by electronic links that connect people and their activities in spite of their different geographic contexts. This also means that multiple social realities can occur in one place. Shared information is more important than shared physical space because of the mediating power of new technologies. It is now possible to interact with others sharing the same space at the same time that it is possible to switch back and forth with others in other physical spaces while an individual remains in the same space. Interaction is fluid and not dependent on spatial references. Cities, then, will consist of "performative physical spaces" as well as transitory social spaces. Or, from our perspective, it is not just what happens in the public realm as physical space but how those events are part of the process of increasing connectivity between people wherever they are in the city that is important in understanding interaction.

While people were on the streets during the Olympics, they were able to report what was occurring or their reactions to what was occurring to their friends, followers and others who were not physically present. In many ways, this kind of networking technology redefined the meaning of public space because it facilitated interaction with others who were not co-present and created private spaces even for those surrounded by others. This phenomenon is often referred to as "telecocooning" (Varnelis and Friedberg 2008). The distinction between public space and private space, face-to-face interaction and mediated interaction, and urban space as a world of strangers is significantly blurred. Word of mouth is not verbal but primarily textual, loaded with personal comment and illustrative material (pictures, videos, links) as it spreads through the electronic universe. Tweets, then, are an electronic word of mouth that spreads information and ideas through a variety of online social networks (Jansen *et al.* 2009). The power of Twitter is not so much that it creates online communities but rather that it creates online social networks. It is difficult to prove with absolute certainty the extent of the impact that Twitter had on Vancouver residents and how it affected their participation in the public realm. At the very least, there was clearly an interaction between persons in attendance at Olympic-related activities and online participants. But it is also highly likely that this interaction facilitated more visible real-time behavior that contributed in a new way to the overall experience of the Olympics in the city.

Conclusion

The social media played a very significant role during the Olympics in Vancouver in a number of ways. First, they allowed users to interact with the Games subjectively and emotionally and to share those reactions with others. They enabled residents to respond to what was occurring even if these reactions were incomplete thoughts or quick judgments, which micro-blogging particularly encourages. Statements of enthusiasm, praise, or celebration were typical, but so also were words of criticism, cynicism, and even mocking. The social media provided a platform or soapbox for the airing of opinion or emotion and allowed users to learn of the feelings and opinions of others. They transformed the Games from something about which users felt detached or peripheral to an activity in which they became a participant. This conclusion is also supported by the work of Gruzd *et al.* (2011), whose analysis of the content of all tweets during the Vancouver Olympics found that there were more tweets with positive messages than with negative messages, and that positive messages were more than three times likely to be re-tweeted. Negative users were more prolific posters as individuals but their messages were less likely to be re-tweeted. The researchers concluded that Twitter users during the Games used the service primarily for social reasons such as keeping in touch and having fun, whereby they could share their own thoughts and experiences, rather than primarily to obtain information. The social interactionist role of Twitter, then, is clear.

Second, the social media provided an opportunity for city residents to participate vicariously in the Games and their atmosphere without actually being physically present at everything that happened. Traditional media and social media supported one another, but so also did citizen reports from people who were physically present. This may not have been active participation in the traditional sense but it was using "technologies of the self" and linking them to a "universe of social orbits" in which they were a player as a detached individual but yet as part of something much bigger than themselves (Song 2009:115). Rather than feeling part of the Olympics as a community in a bounded sense, the social media provided an opportunity for participation through shifting networks online rather than interaction dependent on shared physical space. The fact that this participation could be multi-mediated (Panteli 2009) through audio, video, photos, blogging, and text made participation both intriguing and compelling.

Third, the social media served as a mobilization tool by arousing and intensifying interest and announcing ways to participate in Olympic-related activities. McPhail's (2006) research on crowd behavior demonstrated that those who were able to gain information through social networks about activities were more likely to participate than those who did not gain information in that way. The social media provided a mechanism whereby collaborative activity or collective action could take place outside the framework of traditional organizations and in more informal ways. Flash mobs and protests were coordinated much more easily through the social media during the Olympics, but so also were reports of activities on the streets that were occurring, which encouraged others to be there. Merely reporting what was happening on Granville or Robson provided news that encouraged others to go to that location either around the same time or on another day. In that sense, social media created a sense of things happening and excitement, which encouraged others to be a part of it. The ability of the social media to assist in self-assembly of otherwise dispersed individuals or groups has been recognized (Shirky 2008; Rheingold 2002) and appears to be relevant to understanding public responses in the city of Vancouver during the Games.

There is no question that the social media played an enormous role in creating a lively public realm in Vancouver during the Olympics. News about what was happening, the atmosphere, and reactions to it aroused even more interest. The social media also provided a means of coordination that allowed people to identify locations, places to meet, and contacts with friends to enable them to meet there too. This mobilizing capacity was more likely to occur because the social media made it possible for people to interact with people previously known as well as persons previously unknown in either virtual time or real time. In particular, it supported interaction among people with similar topic interests such as interests in protests, street performances, or particular athletes. Social bookmarking or collaborative tagging occurred as groups were formed on the basis of common interests or identifiers. Whereas the mass media may in theory contribute to more homogenization of attitudes about the Olympics, the internet demonstrated the wide range of ways in which people experience the Games, and that these experiences were constantly in flux and changing in response to what was happening as well as through learning of the opinions and experiences of others. With Twitter, for example, as tweets were posted, they were subject to re-tweeting, which produced a cascading influence as ideas were spread through the internet. But they were also subject to modifications or counter-tweets in reposting or as users responded. The Olympics demonstrates how an event can serve as a catalyst in connectivity between people through the social media by serving as a common focus. The social media, on the other hand, played a pivotal role in escalating the interpersonal responses, which intensified the event as an unusual experience for city dwellers.

7   The consequences of interaction
Public opinion and the Olympics

One of the key arguments of this book is that from the host city's perspective, the Olympics cannot just be understood as a sporting event or as an event restricted to those with sporting interests. Since one of the pillars of Olympism is culture, there has always been some emphasis on other aspects of culture than sport. However, in recent years there has been a further broadening of the role of culture in the Games through the Cultural Olympiad. This aspect of the Games has been expanding and has become more complex, thereby making the Games more inclusive of those without sporting interests (Gold and Revill 2011). The new millennium brought still another focus, on environmentalism, sustainability, and legacy, which has resulted in a multiplicity of new initiatives that also have demonstrated that the Games were much more than sport. For example, the construction of Olympic-related facilities has raised issues of the displacement of existing populations, who are typically poor, and the themes of "sustainability" and "legacy" have come to be understood to mean that the Olympics should leave a legacy that contributes to the remediation of poverty and homelessness with the provision of affordable housing (Hayes and Horne 2011). The IOC now requires that Olympic planning be connected to urban planning so that sport facilities built to accommodate the Games have a post-Olympic usage in order to ensure that there shall be "no more white elephants," as President Rogge has put it (see also Mangan 2008). But legacy, interpreted as outcomes that benefit the host city, means that a whole range of urban issues are now being addressed by Olympic organizers, issues that go far beyond sport and the seventeen days of the Games themselves. All of these developments and initiatives mean that more and more residents outside the sporting world see themselves as stakeholders in the Olympic project.

The recognition by the IOC that the Games involve more than sport for the host city parallels perceptions by host cities themselves that the Olympics provide an opportunity to accomplish much more than merely planning for the Games. The Olympics can serve as a catalyst for new initiatives to improve the city (such as better transportation infrastructure or urban renewal and regeneration), can mobilize capital from higher levels of government for these projects, and can provide a powerful tool for place marketing (Hiller 2000b). In fact, in a curious sort of way the Olympics can serve as a convenient pretext for a host

city to embark on a variety of projects to alter its urban form and create operational improvements in which the Games themselves are merely an ally along
the way in this process. There are clearly differences between cities in this
regard, but Barcelona provides a particularly strong example. One member of
the organizing committee in that city described the Games as conceived from
the beginning as a great pretext to subordinate what was useful to the Games to
what was useful to the city and to accomplish in five or six years what had not
been done in fifty years (Abad 1995:11–14).[1] While such an emphasis has often
served as a convenient legitimation or rationalization to be used by those promoting the hosting of the Olympic Games in the past, the urban transformation
argument has now virtually become an imperative for any city wishing to host
the Games and is represented by the code word "legacy," meaning "What will
remain once the Games are over?"[2]

The preceding chapters have demonstrated that the Olympics generate a
public response from host city residents far beyond what is typical of most urban
projects. The fact that preparing for the Olympics drives the urban agenda,
crowding out other issues, the fact that externally imposed requirements on a
fixed timeline impose controls on the city's response, and the fact that the
Olympics require the mobilization of people in a variety of supporting roles,
from a growing paid employee group in the offices of the organizing committee
to the planning efforts required by supporting organizations such as police, fire,
food services, transportation officials, as well as the recruiting and training of
thousands of volunteers, all broaden the scope of direct and indirect participation by urban residents in the Olympics. In contrast to other civic projects that
are only local in nature, the international character of the Olympics alters the
meaning of the project, since decisions that are made are much more open to
global scrutiny and are related to global marketing objectives. It is this same
international character that also heightens the importance of the Olympic
project in the public mind and catalyzes greater local interest. When the Games
actually take place, it has been shown that participation by local residents is
broadened still further. Planned activities, temporary land use alterations, and
various forms of urban overlay combined with an assortment of spontaneous and
informal activities and the interactions which they represent typically make the
Olympics a unique type of community-wide event. Local media communicate
the color and drama of local celebrations and participation, which, combined
with word of mouth, helps to transform the Games into an urban festival (Hiller
1990). In short, the actual occurrence of the Olympics in the host city transforms the Games from something external to the city to something residents
appropriate and interact with through their own social networks. In short, as
has been argued, host city residents experience the Olympics in a variety of ways
that visitors to the Games and observers from afar do not.

We have also seen that the Olympics as a civic project are fraught with multiple controversies. Initially, the controversy is the appropriateness of the
Olympic project as a fiscal and agenda-dominating priority for the city. While
this argument might be more typical of the bid stage, it often does not disappear

and has lingering effects during the preparation period and, as we have seen, into the Games period itself. The Olympics as a project represent government policy in important ways and stir opposition arguments from political opponents who prefer other project priorities. But there are many other ways in which the Olympics become controversial for host city residents, such as decisions about where to locate Olympic facilities, which communities or property owners benefit from urban transformations, or which groups of people are negatively affected by Olympic planning. Displacement of the disadvantaged by new Olympic construction often related to regeneration efforts is a repeated issue in many host cities (COHRE 2007). Other controversies erupt over budget over-runs, changed plans and broken promises, statements by officials deemed inflam-matory, political criticism, and even debates over ticket distribution. Local residents may worry over how the Olympics will interfere with their daily rou-tines, and some even threaten to leave town to escape the bedlam. The local media thrive on the debate of these kinds of issues, and the Olympic project is in the news virtually daily, which ensures that the Games are a repeated topic of discussion among urban residents.

Interaction and public opinion

These three factors (the fact that the Games are more than sport events, the fact that the Olympics mobilize widespread participation in a variety of roles, and the fact that the Games are a continuous source of discussion and often controversy) ensure that local residents personally encounter the Olympics, although in a variety of different ways and to different degrees. The important thing, however, is that the Games are encountered not primarily as a cerebral exercise but rather through social interaction in which ideas, opinions, emo-tions, and argumentation are shared with other people. The Olympics serve as a catalyst for discussion and often for debate, which connects residents with each other. New information and new perspectives are processed through interaction. People are influenced not only by what happens around them but also by the actions, attitudes, and decisions of other people, and especially by those with whom they have close ties. This would suggest that attitudes towards the Olym-pics are dynamic and not necessarily fixed.

While the Games may be encountered at first as merely an idea or concept, as the time for the Games approaches it is likely that the possibilities for involvement and participation will grow, which again may impact attitudes because of the mediation of interaction. While this may be the case for those with more direct involvement such as in advocacy, planning, or opposition, there are many who still remain at some distance or at the margins of the whole process but who can be affected by changing social contexts. The biggest question, especially after all the debate and discussion in the pre-Games period have occurred, is how urban residents-at-large will embrace the Games, and whether this response will be visible or clearly evident in some way. The evidence presented in earlier chapters suggests that something demonstrative did occur in Vancouver, although no statistical proof has as yet been provided to explain what happened or show that this impact reached beyond what was visible in the streets. It was established in Chapter 4 that preceding the commencement of the Games in Vancouver, there was considerable apprehension, lack of interest, and outright criticism among citizens. Was there any significant shift in public opinion when the Games began or were these expressions of enthusiasm in the public realm reported earlier either limited to one segment of the citizenry or unrelated to general attitudes towards the Olympics?

Measuring host city public opinion

In order to explore these questions, an online survey was conducted by Angus Reid Public Opinion in six waves (roughly every three to four days) throughout the Games. The six points in time included just prior to the start of the Games, roughly the middle of the first week, the end of the first week, the middle of the second week, the end of the second week, and a final survey three days after the Games concluded. The sample size of each survey consisted of approximately 500 residents of the Vancouver metropolitan area. The sampling took into consideration a weighting process for age, gender, and region, clustering by postal code, and response rates for different groups.[3] The result is a database that allows us to see whether public opinion about the Olympics remained as divided as it was prior to the Olympics and whether there were any changes in public opinion as a result of experiencing the Games.

Surveys of public opinion about the Olympics among host city residents have usually been tied to the bid phase, when the bid organization attempts to convince the IOC that there is public support in the city for hosting the Games. The IOC also commissions its own survey during that time in order to determine the strength of support for the bid. After the Games have been awarded to a city, the IOC and the organizing committee are less interested in the degree of public support, as all energies are engaged in the task of readying the city for the Games. The scholarly and scientific community has expressed some interest in public opinion in host cities, usually as annual surveys primarily before the Games but also usually one survey after the Games. Calgary (Ritchie and Lyons 1990), Atlanta (Mihalik 2001), and Turin (Scamuzzi 2006; Guala 2009) are the host cities where such surveys have been undertaken. These studies demonstrated strong support for the Olympics over time, although some reticence was often expressed about debt, costs, and fears of inconvenience before the Games. However, overall, and including in retrospect, city residents reacted positively to having hosted the Olympics. None of these studies measured shifting attitudes throughout the Games themselves, nor did they include explanatory variables such as age, gender, income, or voting preferences in their analysis. The survey data presented here, in contrast, provide evidence of public opinion shifts as the Games evolved and utilize demographic and other variables to understand these changes.

Evidence from the polling of public opinion

Figure 7.1 indicates that on the eve of the beginning of the Games (February 11) there was already a noticeable shift in interest in the Olympics as measured by the question "How closely are you following the Vancouver Winter Olympics?" In comparison to the survey done one month earlier, there was a significant increase in the percentage of those who were following the Olympics "very closely" (from 23 percent to 38 percent). Much of this gain probably came from those who had previously followed the Olympics only "moderately closely." But there was also a significant drop in those who earlier had said that they were following the Olympics "not closely at all," who now became much more interested in the Games. These data make it clear that for many urban residents, interest in the Olympics was heightened considerably by the event actually happening, which might be expected. It is significant, however, that interest in the Olympics continued to increase as the Games progressed. In fact, the two categories of minimal interest in the Games ("not closely at all" and "not too closely") declined over the period of the Games from a combined 32 percent to 15 percent. By the end of the Games, the percentage of people who followed the Games either "very closely" or "moderately closely" reached a striking 85 percent of metropolitan residents. In contrast, the percentage of those who followed the Games "not too closely" declined to 9 percent and "not closely at all" to a minimal 5 percent. What is noteworthy is that declared interest in the Olympics grew as the Games progressed, and by the time the Games had concluded there had been a massive shift towards interest in the Games, indicating that the Olympics had truly captivated the city. This evidence unequivocally demonstrates that the Olympics as an event presently occurring and not necessarily the Olympics as a concept aroused unusual interest in the city. But it also shows that the Games created a sequence of events

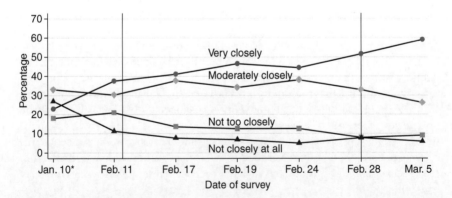

Figure 7.1 Responses to "How closely are you following the Vancouver Winter Olympics this month?" by survey date, Vancouver Metropolitan Area 2010.

Note
*   The January 10 item was phrased "How interested are you in the Vancouver Winter Olympics?" and was asked of a British Columbia sample.

on which to focus, and an experience that was very different from perceiving the Olympics as merely a plan or an organization, such as represented locally by VANOC in the pre-Games period.

It was suspected that one of the reasons why residents may have been alienated by the Games before they even began was the way in which people were told to change their normal routines as VANOC laid out its plans and told people what was expected of them, such as dealing with road and lane closures, the anticipated crush of people using public transit, punishment for trademark infringements, threats to free speech, and what some feared to be the militarization of the city through high-level security operations. In the survey, this concern was operationalized through "expectations of being inconvenienced" by the Olympics being held in their city. Figure 7.2 shows that initially there was concern over being inconvenienced by the Games but that this concern

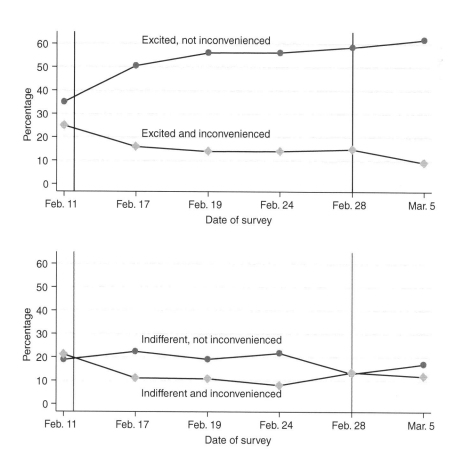

Figure 7.2 Feelings towards the Vancouver Winter Olympics by survey date, Vancouver Metropolitan Area 2010.

dropped off as the Games progressed and people discovered that they were not being inconvenienced.[4] Those who said that they were "excited and not inconvenienced" rose from 35 percent to 62 percent over the course of the Games, and the two categories of not being inconvenienced rose to 80 percent. By the end of the Games, it was clear that, regardless of people's attitude (that is, whether they were "excited" or "indifferent" about the Olympics), the expectations about being inconvenienced had been reduced. About 20 percent of urban residents still did feel inconvenienced (whether "excited and inconvenienced" or "indifferent and inconvenienced") by the Games. These results suggest that while some were inconvenienced, residents anticipated far worse inconvenience than actually occurred, and the fear of being inconvenienced may have played a significant role in producing negative attitudes towards the Games as the actual event approached.

Another question which blended two variables looked at attitudes towards protest and the idea that the Games were a waste of money. Respondents were asked to state their level of agreement or disagreement with the statement "Some people and groups have staged protests against the Vancouver Winter Olympics saying that the event is a waste of money that could be used for more important things" (Figure 7.3). Agreeing or disagreeing with the legitimacy of public protest was clearly a different theme than questioning whether the money spent on the Games could have been better used for other endeavors – even though in the minds of many they were related. In spite of these interpretive difficulties, the data demonstrate that a shift in public opinion did occur. While the percentage of those who "moderately agreed" with the protest/waste of money statement remained more or less constant at around 30 percent, the percentage of those who "strongly agreed" dropped from 29 percent to 19 percent. By the same token, the percentage of those who "strongly disagreed"

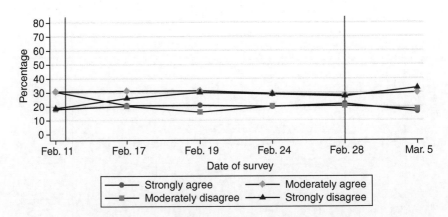

Figure 7.3 Responses to "Some people and groups have staged protests against the Vancouver Winter Olympics, saying that the event is a waste of money that could be used for other more important things" by survey date, Vancouver Metropolitan Area 2010.

with the protest/waste of money idea increased from 16 percent to 32 percent. Whether this shift was a reaction to the violent protest at the Heart Attack March on February 13 or whether it was a shift in attitude due to the euphoria of the event, the opposition to the Olympics as understood connecting protest with the waste of money issue was reduced over the course of the Games, although it still existed. One way to interpret these data is to say that residents were still unsure about the costs of the Games as a priority but that protest lost some of its favor as the Games progressed. The combination of two variables in one question, however, makes any conclusion here somewhat tentative.

One of clearest pieces of evidence of a mood shift during the Olympics is found in Figure 7.4. Respondents were asked to register their feelings on a variety of attitudinal factors that applied to their attitude about the Vancouver Games.[5] The most striking of all was that the Games dramatically increased "national pride" (from 56 percent to 84 percent), which clearly coincided with what was observed in the public realm. "Enthusiasm" about the Games also showed a substantial increase as the Games progressed, from 46 percent to 68 percent. On the other hand, indifference showed a significant drop already in the first week and ultimately from 29 percent to 13 percent, while anger also declined, from 17 percent to 9 percent. These data show that negative emotions about the Games definitely declined as the Games progressed, while positive emotions increased, with patriotic feelings being the strongest.

Respondents were also asked to register their feelings about the Olympics, the athletes, and VANOC. Positive attitudes increased for all three from the first to the last survey wave (data not shown). However, positive feelings towards the Olympics and to the athletes were consistently higher than favorable attitudes towards VANOC. Appreciation of VANOC (enthusiasm) increased as the Games progressed, and anger and disgust moderated, but the

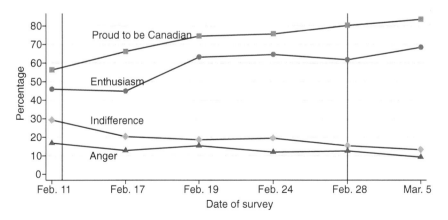

Figure 7.4 Percentages reporting enthusiasm, indifference, anger, and pride about the Vancouver Winter Olympics by survey date, Vancouver Metropolitan Area 2010.

percentages of positive attitudes remained rather low in comparison to residents' perceptions of athletes or the Games in general. After the Games were over, attitudes towards the Olympics, the athletes, and VANOC were compared, and the mean ratings (Figure 7.5) showed that the most positive feelings were held towards the athletes (8.7), followed by the Olympics in general (7.5). VANOC obtained a 5.9 rating. It is clear, then, that the Games had an emotional impact on people and that residents felt increasingly favorable towards the Olympics, and especially towards the athletes. It is not clear why attitudes towards the organizing committee were not as positive, but perhaps it was because of the bureaucratic style required of a goal-directed time-sensitive project that appeared to restructure the city in its own image.

Another clear indicator of an attitude shift assessed residents' view of whether the Olympics had a positive or negative impact on Vancouver (Figure 7.6). A significant shift occurred already from the pre-Olympic period to the eve of the Games, when perceptions of "a positive impact" increased (from 52 percent to 65 percent) and perceptions of "a negative impact" decreased (from 36 percent to 22 percent). It was almost as if there was a sudden recognition that the Games were indeed here and that the positive impact was more easily recognized. In all, the shift in the assessment of "a positive impact" over the course of the Olympics was from 66

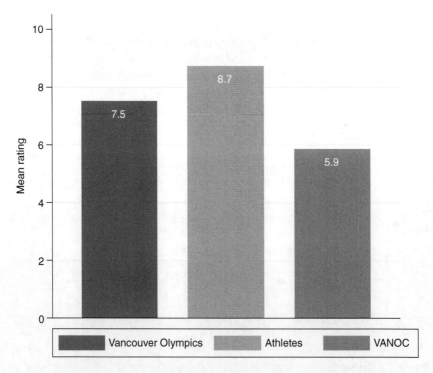

Figure 7.5 Mean ratings of the Vancouver Olympics, the athletes, and VANOC on a scale of 1–10, Vancouver Metropolitan Area, March 5, 2010.

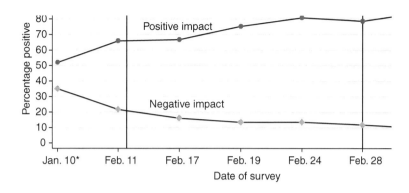

Figure 7.6 Perceived positive and negative impact of the Winter Olympics on Vancouver by survey date, Vancouver Metropolitan Area 2010.

Note
* The January 10 item was asked of a British Columbia sample.

percent to 85 percent. At the same time, perceptions of "a negative impact" kept declining. In the post-Olympic survey, residents were asked to provide their overall assessment of whether the Games had been "a success" or "a failure," and the overwhelming response (82 percent) was that the Games were considered a success (Figure 7.7). More were "not sure" (12.9 percent) than said they were "a failure" (5.5 percent). Clearly, there was a relationship between viewing the Games as a success and perceiving the Games as having a positive impact.

Since one of the major issues from a resident's point of view were the costs involved in hosting the Olympics, it is useful to understand the financial expectations that people had about the Games (Figure 7.8). On the eve of the Games, 63 percent thought that the Games would have a considerable deficit, verifying the fact that a negative financial outcome was prominent in people's minds. That number slowly declined as the Games progressed, but by the conclusion of the Games more people (49 percent) still thought there would be a considerable deficit than any other financial alternative. The next largest category was those who expected there to be a small deficit, which remained rather steady around the mid-teens. The decline in the number of those who expected a considerable deficit is a bit puzzling, although it might be hypothesized that the positive atmosphere of the Games played a role in this attitudinal change. If the Games were considered a success, then people might jump to the conclusion that this success could also be reflected in the financial outcome. However, even though the last survey, which was completed after the Olympics were over, showed the lowest level of an expected considerable deficit, when this category is combined with the rather stable group of those who expected a small deficit, it is clear that about three-quarters of respondents expected some kind of deficit. Only a few expected a considerable surplus. As the Games progressed, the percentage of

UNIVERSITY OF WINCHESTER
LIBRARY

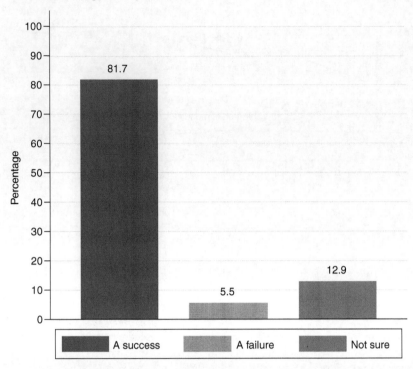

Figure 7.7 Responses to "All things considered, would you describe the Vancouver Winter Olympics as a success or failure?", Vancouver Metropolitan Area, March 5, 2010.

respondents who expected a small surplus increased from 4 percent to 11 percent, but overall an expectation of some kind of deficit was most pronounced. While there was a cluster of people who viewed either a small deficit, a small surplus, or breaking even as a possibility, this cluster accounted for about 38 percent of respondents. The fact that the Games apparently were well run and that residents enjoyed the Games did have some ameliorating effect on expectations of a considerable deficit and a hope for a small surplus, but expectations of a deficit remained the dominant expectation.

There are, then, two counter-trends apparent. One is that most residents thought that the Games were a success while on the other hand there was an acknowledgment that the Games would likely produce a deficit. If the Games were deemed successful and a deficit was the dominant expected fiscal result, did residents think that holding the Games in their city was worth it? That is the question addressed in Figure 7.9. First of all, it is important to note that as the Games progressed, more and more people thought that hosting the Games was indeed "worth it." The percentage that thought the Games were "worth it" began at 49 percent and reached 64 percent by the post-Games survey. While

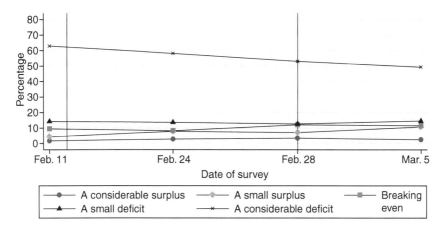

Figure 7.8 Financial expectations for the Winter Olympics by survey date, Vancouver Metropolitan Area 2010.

on the one hand, some might argue that this is not a major shift, it is a shift of note in a matter of seventeen days. Second, while the percentage of those who thought the Games "not worth it" started at 27 percent and held rather steady for the first week, it did decline by the post-Games survey to 20 percent. While some of those initially feeling that the event was "not worth it" became convinced that it was indeed "worth it" by the time the Games concluded, it is also likely that others who considered themselves "unsure" of whether it was worth it or not became convinced that it was worth it. Those "not sure" of whether it was worth it started at 24 percent but finished at 16 percent. This would suggest

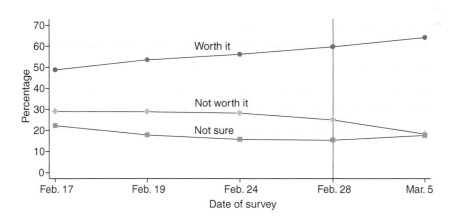

Figure 7.9 Responses to "All things considered, do you think holding the Winter Olympics in Vancouver was worth it or not worth it?" by survey date, Vancouver Metropolitan Area 2010.

that the question of economic value was a puzzling one for a significant minority (about one-third) of residents. One of the reasons could have been that the financial results of the Games were not known and people were apprehensive about the outcome. Nevertheless, it is notable that as a result of experiencing the Games, the percentage of people who did conclude that hosting them was "worth it" did increase.

At the end of the survey, participants were provided an opportunity for further comment. While most chose not to make any further substantive remarks, the respondents who did choose to do so were more likely to focus on finances than any other thing. For these people, the public money spent on the Olympics was unconscionable and the Games were associated with elitism and misplaced priorities. In short, the Olympics benefited only a few, and expenditures on other, more needed public services were neglected. Some did express disappointment that their earlier expectations about how the Olympics would benefit other non-sporting aspects of the city were dashed by ultimate realities. These comments provide further evidence that perceived costs to the host city were the primary basis for opposition and negative attitudes about the Games.

Explaining the results

Using a variety of statistical techniques, it was possible to test for statistical significance and determine the effects of demographic and item measures on the responses (Hiller and Wanner 2011). Demographic variables exhibited some significant effects on attitudes. Gender was only significant on the protest/waste of money variable, with males about 26 percent less likely to agree with this idea – although the effect disappears when party vote is controlled for. Age had a significant effect on all measures except the "worth it" variable. Older persons had more positive feelings about the Olympics and VANOC, felt that the effect on the city was positive, and tended to disagree more with the protesters. But once again, party vote becomes significant, suggesting that Liberal voters tended to be older. Persons who had at least some post-secondary education or who held a degree had less positive feelings towards VANOC and the Olympics than those with a high school diploma or less. The strongest effects among the demographic variables are found for household income. People with higher household income were more than twice as likely to see the impact of the Games as positive, half as likely to agree with the protest/waste of money idea, and 50 percent more likely to view hosting the Games as "worth it." These effects decline in strength with the addition of control for party vote, as Liberal voters were more likely to be in the higher income categories.

As already noted, a linear time trend was evident on many items but was particularly significant on the "positive/negative impact" and "worth it" items. The negative linear trend in attitudes towards protest can be explained by the fact that persons who voted Liberal in the last provincial election were most likely to disagree with the assertion that protest against the Olympics as a waste of money was appropriate, and this relationship was consistent over time. Liberal voters were over three times more likely to say that the Olympics had a "positive impact" on Vancouver, four and a half times more likely to say that hosting the Olympics was "worth it," and only one-fourth as likely to agree with the protest/waste of money theme. Cutler and Matthews's (2005) study of the 2002 Vancouver civic election found a clear link between ideological orientations and provincial partisanship, with local economic evaluations or local issues playing only a small role in electoral choices. City residents' assessments of the Games in the case of Vancouver, then, are closely related to provincial political preferences. Thus, having voted for the Liberal Party (the governing provincial party at the time of the Olympics) was a major explanatory variable in accounting for a positive assessment of the Games. This finding establishes support for the conclusion that the Olympics are viewed by residents as a policy instrument of the governing party and that opposition to that party can be linked to less enthusiasm for the Olympics as a hosted event.

The second explanatory variable with strong effects is related to participation in Olympic events, whether paid or free. Five options were available: attendance at Olympic sporting events, attendance at Cultural Olympiad events, attendance at victory ceremonies, participation at free concerts, and visiting pavilions. The first three were ticketed events that required payment.[6] Events in the last two categories were essentially free. Figure 7.10 shows the percentage of respondents that participated in each category. The fact that roughly one-quarter attended Olympic sporting events or events that were part of the Cultural Olympiad is overall much higher than expected. While there had been some public concern over the fact that tickets to Olympic events were difficult to obtain, a substantial proportion of the population were actually able to attend Olympic events. Attending events that were part of the Cultural Olympiad reached a similar level, although it should be acknowledged that the Cultural Olympiad occurred over a period of three years, which lengthened the time period for participation in these activities. Olympic victory ceremonies were much less patronized and, of course, were limited to the actual period of the Games. What is rather dramatic, however, is the much higher percentage of people who attended the free events (concerts 39 percent) and visited the pavilions (44 percent). The implication here is that non-ticketed events were a major factor in citizen participation in the Olympics. This was confirmed in further analysis which revealed that having attended free events consistently had stronger effects on attitudes towards the Olympics than having attended paid events. Residents having attended free events were nearly three and a half times more likely to perceive the impact of the Olympics on Vancouver as positive, almost four times as likely to believe that hosting the Olympics was "worth it," and only 40 percent as likely to agree with the protest/waste of money scenario. The feelings about the Olympics and VANOC were only slightly higher if residents had attended free events. Overall, however, the evidence is clear that not only is party voting an important factor in explaining people's attitudes towards the Olympics, but so also is whether people actually participated in

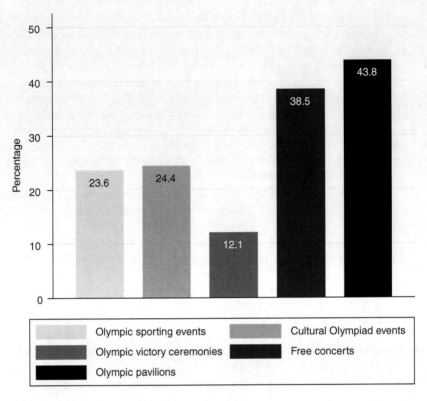

Figure 7.10 Percentages reporting attending Vancouver Olympic events in post-Olympic survey, Vancouver Metropolitan Area, March 5, 2010.

Olympic-related events. In that regard, participation in free events was particularly important in generating positive attitudes about the value of the Olympics for the city.

Conclusion

The most important observation to make about the result of these opinion surveys is that over the course of the Vancouver Games there was indeed a significant shift of public opinion in a relatively short period of time. Shifts in public opinion over short periods of time are relatively rare and are usually associated with things like catastrophes (Skocpol 2002) or assassinations (Esaisson and Granberg 1996), where the element of shock is present. Previous studies in other Olympic host cities cited earlier demonstrated more consistent public support for the Games over time. In the case of the Olympics in Vancouver, the swing in public opinion is much more pronounced and appears to be directly related to "experiencing" the Olympics rather than just debating the value of the Games. In comparison to other sudden shifts in public opinion, it appears that a more positive attitude or mood emerged as the result of some form of citizen participation, which then led to increased support for the Games. One can only assume that the interaction created by participation in Olympic-related events (including the public realm, as noted earlier) played a major role in creating a shift in attitudes about the Olympics. Other factors such as the success of Canadian athletes (and particularly the hockey teams) or the unusual elevated expressions of patriotism cannot be ignored either. The ego enhancement value of associating with a sports team that is winning has been well documented and has a clear effect on mood (Mahoney *et al.* 2000). Local news media may also have played a role in shifting public opinion (McCombs *et al.* 2011) as coverage during the Games shifted away from controversy to positive reports of the Olympics as a human experience, whether among athletes as human actors or in the city as residents interacted with each other in the Olympic atmosphere.[7] All of these points suggest that the dynamics of the event itself had a huge impact on public opinion. And it was primarily through experiencing the Olympics in one way or the other that attitudes began to change – even rather dramatically. While the issue of cost did not disappear as a critical issue, it was considerably attenuated by the event itself. Assessments by residents of the positive impact of the Games on Vancouver and whether hosting them was "worth it" or not reveal the most consistent upward trend over time.

Demographic explanatory variables for these findings were statistically significant only in a few instances. Age, gender, and education had limited utility, although income had some explanatory power, with those of higher incomes being more favorably predisposed to the Games. However, the two most powerful explanatory variables were voting behavior and attendance at Games-related activities. Having voted for the Liberal Party (the party in power at the time of the Olympics) in the last provincial election was a very strong predictor of positive attitudes towards the Games. But of equal importance were the participation variables. Attending non-ticketed events was especially linked to positive attitudes towards the Games. These non-ticketed events included free concerts and pavilion visits, but other activities in the public realm were not mentioned. If they had been, it would likely have increased the extent of participation even more. Being part of any Olympic activity in the downtown core would almost inevitably have contributed to more participation in the public realm. But conversely, many who participated in the public realm would not necessarily have held tickets to paid events. In short, there appears to be a clear link between becoming part of the Olympic experience in a personal way (whether through attending ticketed or non-ticketed events) and having increasingly positive attitudes towards the Games. These forms of participation did not ameliorate other concerns but they did allow a greater number of people to feel a part of the Olympics and to experience them as an event.

These forms of participation indicate how interaction prompted by Olympic-related activity created a sense of civic vibrancy. The fact that such a large proportion of residents participated in the public realm meant that they necessarily made direct contact with many others doing the same thing, which then enhanced positive feelings about the Olympics. Going to free concerts or visiting pavilions, as well as participating in any ticketed event, almost always was an activity shared with others. Perhaps, then, it is not surprising that residents developed positive attitudes towards the Games, which many described as exciting and unusual, and maybe even euphoric. It is possible that a shift in attitudes contributed to more participation in the public realm. However, it is probably more likely that participation in the public realm played a major role in the attitude shift. Again, the reasons for this may be complex but there is some cause to think that the Olympics as an urban event must be also understood as an interactional activity which brings people together and heightens emotions, much as Collins might have predicted. Interaction generating emotional intensity may produce a sense of solidarity, but, more than that, it creates a sense of a collective experience that can suspend typical emotional states. As one woman perhaps uniquely reflected, "Is it really over? For two weeks it felt as if the ugly things in life had faded, and I don't want to go back. I want us all to stay like this always."[8] While the experience and the feelings that it produces are at best fleeting and do not last,[9] they apparently can play a role in creating goodwill towards the Games as well as potentially serving as an important reference in the personal and collective memories of citizens. Whether it was the arrival of the torch relay in the city that was the emotional spark that created new public interest as it weaved its way through local streets, as some have claimed, or whether it was a more complex set of factors that began the transformation of public opinion, the evidence presented here makes it clear that the Olympics did have an almost unexpected impact on city residents. All of this supports the notion that the Olympics must be viewed as an urban event which local residents experience rather than the typical conception of the Games as merely a mediated spectacle.

8   Conclusion

One of the key themes of this book has been that the Olympics must be understood as a unique urban project, one that generates a wide range of responses from within the host city. It is no longer adequate to assume that local residents are all supportive of the Games, or that most are supportive with the exception of a few opponents, or that attitudes towards the Games among residents are constant and consistent over time, or that residents are even sure what to make of hosting the Games. It is also no longer adequate to view host city residents as either irrelevant or merely a supporting cast to the Games themselves. Instead, local residents must be understood as participants in the Olympics and part of the Games, as a drama that requires many different actors. The city is not a container for the Games; the host city is the stage for the Games, ensuring that local residents are actors on that stage at the same time that they are an audience for the action that does occur. This interpretation is possible because the Olympics are understood as a drama beyond the competition venues, a drama that involves many segments of the city, where acts, scenes, and episodes enrich and broaden the dramatic and participative quality of the event. From the host city's perspective, the Olympics is not a seventeen-day event; it is a drama of many years from the consideration of bidding to the decision to bid, to winning the bid, to preparing for the Games, to hosting the Games, to dealing with the consequences of having hosted the Games. It is this lengthy time period of actions and decisions, of debates and dilemmas, that makes the meaning of the Olympics for local residents quite different from the viewpoint of outsiders and non-residents.

The contribution of a micro approach

Hosting the Games is a complex undertaking involving a variety of organizations, structures, and participants in which a myriad of micro encounters or chains of face-to-face interactions occur. The International Olympic Committee and the sport federations involve such interaction chains. By the same token, the host city should be viewed not as a single organization or entity but as a chain of interacting individuals and interlocking groups of persons in which a diversity of interpretations and action preferences about the Olympic project are generated. Hosting the Games may require the retooling of existing organizations or the emergence of new organizations, but these structures are created through the interaction of individuals and issues that give the Games in each city its distinctive character. The focus on interaction chains helps us to understand public attitudes at the grass roots as well as how and why shifts in public opinion can occur. It is not that macrostructures are not important but that what is critical is how people in interaction build macrostructures. These constructions are related to interpretations or frames that residents develop, which are reflected in their meaning-seeking and behavioral choices (Brissett and Edgley 2005). On the one hand, this focus on micro-interactions implies that there is a plurality of interpretive frames which develop. On the other hand, not all interpretive frames have equal power and there is inevitably a dominant frame that is embraced by elites. In a city deciding to bid or having won the bid, the dominant frame is that the Olympics are a project that should be embraced by all. The focus on micro-interactions makes it clearer that while in some ways the dominant frame may appear monolithic and even hegemonic, host cities are sites for a variety of shifting responses to the Games. These dynamics are seldom represented in final reports of the Games in each Olympic city but they are an important undercurrent, one that tells us much about the dynamics of that particular Olympic city and tells us a great deal about how the Games impact a city in which the Olympics are hosted. For these two reasons, analyzing the Olympics as an urban project provides a useful window for understanding the character and issues that undergird a particular city as well as how the Olympics as a powerful event affects normal urban processes.

A neglected aspect in the analysis of the relationship between host cities and the Olympics is how the host city can be energized by the chains of micro-encounters that are rooted in the Olympic project. While Olympic organizers are often given to self-serving platitudes, John Furlong, the CEO of the Vancouver Organizing Committee (VANOC), made an interesting observation that reflects the approach that has been developed here. He said, "People [in Vancouver] didn't watch the Olympics. They lived it" (Lee 2011). While what he meant may be somewhat different from what is proposed here, in many ways his statement accurately portrays what the Games do to a city. "Living it" does not always mean laudatory perceptions or supportive encounters but it does mean multiple years of dealing with the Olympics as a priority project. Host city residents experience the Games because they are at ground zero and virtually cannot escape them. While media outlets keep residents abreast of issues, events, and outcomes, the Olympics as a policy topic and actual experience provokes interaction for discussion and debate supported by small groups and interpersonal communication. As has already been noted, the Olympics raise issues about the goals and priorities of a city for its residents that invariably spark considerable dialogue and the exchange of ideas.

The contribution of dramaturgy

The dramaturgical approach has been shown to be useful because it reveals how the city as a whole becomes a type of giant production studio. The Olympics provide the occasion for the drama, in which there are many roles to play, and the result is wide-ranging forms of participation. There is a master narrative to the script of the drama and yet the script is constantly evolving as the result of planning decisions and conflicting pressures. Participants in the drama are constantly improvising with their roles and adjusting to changing circumstances. Thus, while there are expectations about the outcome of the drama, the actual outcome is unknown in spite of the principles or rules under which the drama is structured. The performance date, time, and place are known but human agency interjects a sense of unfolding unpredictability that heightens the intrigue of the drama. While emotions may be triggered as the drama unfolds, emotions reach a peak in the final act, which is the Games themselves. City residents, who are both actors and audience, are moved by the Olympics as an experience, though it quickly becomes a fleeting memory as normal routines are embraced once again and new issues emerge to shift the focus of attention when the Games are over. The interaction approach developed here demonstrates how *emotion* must be part of our analysis, for host city residents *experience* the Olympics in a different way than visitors and external observers.

The focus in this book has been on how host city residents encounter the Games. The Olympics have been shown to be a performance that involves people playing roles which are interpreted by individuals and small groups that interact with others about what they hear and observe. Some people play roles in the Olympic performance that have official status (e.g., Olympic volunteers), while others play unofficial roles such as sharing opinions about the Olympics with their neighbors over the back fence or discussing in their advocacy groups how they might use the Olympics for their own purposes. Local residents discover that the Olympics provide a platform for a variety of causes, and even local residents seek to use the Olympics for their own group interests. The dramaturgical perspective can also be taken beyond host cities and given a more international focus. The host city can be viewed as putting on a performance for a global audience. Caffrey (2011), for example, has shown how the Beijing Olympics was a production serving as an opening act for a city and nation that desired to communicate new images about itself. Vancouver hoped that the Olympics would provide the stage that would supply dramatic evidence for why it has been considered to be one of "the world's most livable cities." It is not surprising, then, that local residents would ultimately (and maybe only temporarily) put aside their debates and controversies in order to "put on a good show" for the international audience. The need to maintain public order to ensure that the stage, the props and stage set, and the script proceed according to plan to suitably convince the international audience of the civic spirit and pride of the host city is a powerful force in all Olympic cities. Ironically, in Vancouver's case it was another scene one year later (June 2011), the Stanley Cup (the National Hockey League Championship) riots, that provided a counter-drama for a global audience, one that raised new issues for the city.

The dramaturgical and interactionist perspective developed here has also hinted at the fact that it could be applied to other aspects of the Olympic movement beyond host cities. The role of interaction effects in the IOC or among corporate sponsors or affiliated sport federations is also important and is certainly critical among cities experiencing bid failure. The focus on micro-interactions makes it clearer how the structures, organizations, and symbols that emerge are the product of different ways in which people encounter the Olympics beyond sporting events themselves.

The urban perspective

Another important contribution of this book has been to point out the importance of urban spaces beyond competition venues in any analysis of Olympic cities. Particular attention was drawn to what is called the public realm. In many ways, the Games segregate people. Being able to afford tickets is one thing, but so also is the luck of the draw and connections with people or organizations that have tickets, allowing some people to observe official Olympic activities in person while for others the Olympics is a mediated experience. Local residents are divided by this differential access and many have no personal access at all to official Olympic events. Yet, as we have seen, they interact with the Olympics in their own way. Olympic visitors are segregated in that those who are part of the Olympic family have privileges and access to a range of events that others do not have. Athletes have their own self-contained "village." Some event visitors stay in upscale hotels and eat at upscale restaurants while others depend on fast-food franchises or food banks, or bunk in with friends. What changes everything is the public realm. It is here that athletes, visitors, and local residents meet. Whether this means that the Games should be called a festival can be debated, but what is important is that the public realm serves as a critical transitional space to private spaces and to spaces of controlled access. It is a meeting ground in which normal urban routines are confounded and confused with spontaneous mingling. Even though the public realm is short-term and temporary, its egalitarian character plays an enormous role in creating effervescent feelings. It is the public realm that stirs emotions, creates a sense of energy, and plays a major role in shifts in attitude. It is the public realm that transforms the Olympics from an elitist event to an urban experience.

From the perspective of an urbanist focusing on the host city, the Olympics as a project can also be observed as participating in all the post-modern issues raised in the transformation process occurring in contemporary cities. The shift from managerial to entrepreneurial cities, the shift from production to consumption, the emergence of the symbolic economy in which powerful images can be conveyed through mega-events and their iconic structures, the reinvention of urban spaces through regeneration programs, and the increasing prominence of leisure spaces and consumer culture are all part of how the Olympics as a spectacle participate in the processes of urban change (Hiller 2006b). As cities are increasingly defined as places to play and consume, and not just places to live and work (Hetherington and Cronin 2008), the Olympics, as one genre of mega-events, are increasingly contributing to urban transformations. For this reason, the Olympics in a host city can provide a special laboratory for the study of urbanism. These macro observations, however, cannot obscure the micro responses of individuals who live in cities. If cities must be understood from the perspective of the experience of local residents, so also must the Olympics in host cities be understood as something that is experienced by local residents. And if cities have the double character which Lefebvre (1996:170) notes as places of consumption as well as places that consume place, so also must cities be understood as places of experience as well as places where people can experience place in fresh and unique ways.

Economic value versus other outcomes

One of the questions that have plagued the Olympic movement for some time is whether the escalating costs involved in hosting the Games are indeed worth it. The IOC has become aware of the problems created for cities by the increasing scale of the Olympics as a hosted event. While this is a concern for the Summer Games, the Winter Games have also experienced these pressures, because larger host cities are more capable of meeting the requirements of the Games than smaller mountain cities. Nevertheless, when all the costs are added in, is there value in hosting the Games that supports the financial outlay involved? This has been a particularly thorny issue for cities where a sense of having hosted successful Games is offset by other countervailing realities – and particularly economic costs and debt. Successful Games from the point of view of the IOC, then, might not be considered successful by at least some persons in a host city where the consequences of having hosted the Games are encountered for many years (e.g., debt and venue after-use issues in Athens). An interactionist approach provides a useful tool in understanding how different groups of people interpret these consequences.

Because financial issues seem to be at the core of debates about whether hosting the Games has been worth it, it is not surprising that reports of complete costs and all outcomes are difficult to obtain.[1] Separating infrastructural costs from operational costs usually results in conclusions, to be shared with host city residents, that the Games roughly broke even because major infrastructural costs are included in other government budgets. Whether reported Olympic costs are realistic may be debated, but there are similar difficulties in determining the degree of public subsidies for the Olympic project. One justification that is difficult to quantify is the value of place marketing which the Olympics provides to a host city. Is whatever international exposure a host city and host country receive via the Olympics worth the cost? Supporters of this argument answer in the affirmative. But another argument that is also made is difficult to evaluate and quantify: the feelings and emotions felt by host residents. Civic pride, global prestige, warm memories, conviviality, moments of celebration, and the feel-good factor are all soft legacies that are difficult to quantify and evaluate.[2] While some would see this as a fallback position when the economic arguments are less than convincing, others argue that these are positive impacts that also have value.

Spilling (1996:340), for example, concluded that for the 1994 Lillehammer Games, costs were out of proportion to the returns generated – particularly the long-term returns. But he did acknowledge that the Games had significant value in providing the region with an extraordinary experience that stimulated mobilization and celebration, and that this might even be "the main reason" for hosting the Games. Kavetsos and Szymanski (2010) have shown that mega sports events do not generate the long-term economic benefits that are often claimed but that these events do positively impact life satisfaction and heighten the feel-good factor. Repeatedly, analysts have acknowledged the existence of these soft legacies in host cities, and local citizens have often also reported them, but it is difficult to relate these qualitative outcomes to fiscal evaluations of a quantitative nature. This book does not try to answer the question of whether soft legacies justify economic expenditures. However, it does show how the Games serve as a catalyst for interaction within a city in relation to a short-term project of global significance. Whether these conclusions make it "worth it" to have hosted the Games is, of course, a debatable issue.

In contrast to crises such as mass emergencies or disasters, which also mobilize responses and participation, the Olympics are an unusual organizational project that mobilizes people in a variety of ways crossing typical boundaries. The Olympics have the potential to generate considerable debate about what kind of city local residents want or need. They can also raise questions about how public money should be spent. It is not surprising, then, that the notion of "planning legacies" has become an important goal of organizing committees. While this notion of legacy normally refers to the hard legacies of sport venues or infrastructural improvements, the soft legacies are the ones open to considerable disagreement about their value and importance. This book does not answer the ultimate question regarding their value, but it does show that there are soft legacies of various kinds that are the result of hosting the Games, and that they are quite powerful.

It must be reaffirmed, in keeping with the position taken by this book, that people encounter the Olympics within the host city in different ways. For example, if euphoria is a dominant public mood, it clearly does not characterize everyone, whether publicly or privately. But the Olympics do raise interesting questions about its contribution to the social psychology of urban life. Roche (2003) points out that in late modernity, it is important for people to periodically experience non-routine extraordinary special events such as personal or collective rites of passage, or other charismatic and ritual celebrations. Among other things, these events mark the passing of time and give time structure to individuals and to society beyond the routine. The Olympics may provide opportunities for dramatic experiences that reanimate and recover the time structure dimension. Furthermore, Roche argues that the Olympics are not only multinational but also a multigenerational/multi-age activity in comparison to much age-specific and age-exclusionary activity within society. In his words, the

Olympics provide "distinctive occasions for intergenerational and multigenerational co-experience and communication in the lived present of the event. They also provide for the construction and mediatization of collective memories that are accessible intergenerationally" (ibid.:112). These sweeping statements may need further evaluation, but the interactionist approach developed here seems to provide some support for these assertions.

For sports enthusiasts, the Vancouver 2010 Games will be marked by the fact that a country that had hosted two previous Olympics and had never won a gold medal on its own soil had won more gold medals (fourteen) than any other competing country in these Games. However, these Games also provide an excellent illustration of how an interactionist approach can be used to interpret and analyze the significance of the Olympics for a host city. Strategy, ideology, patriotism, merchandising, mobilization, legitimation, power, and resistance were all acted out as performance on the urban stage as celebration, opposition, or advocacy, with a variety of emotions ranging from joy and anger to humor and fear. While some of the role-playing required sometimes followed scripts, at other times it resulted in more spontaneous realities that reflected issues in the city in all its diversity. The Olympics made the host city a stage with the appropriate floodlights to reveal the city as a collectivity in which a full range of tensions and conflicts as well as assets and liabilities exist, and in which city dwellers are all participants.

The symbolic interactionist approach taken in this book is meant to open a new window in the study of the Olympic Games. The goal has not been to substitute this perspective for political economy, cultural studies, or any other interpretive scheme. Rather, in the spirit of Max Weber (1958:183), the objective has been to trace the meaning and role of the Games from one particular direction in order to add to our understanding of a very complex phenomenon or event. Or, to put it in the words of Erving Goffman (1961:xiv), whose work undergirds much of this analysis, "Better, perhaps, different coats to clothe the children well than a single splendid tent in which they all shiver."

UNIVERSITY OF WINCHESTER LIBRARY

Notes

Introduction

1 One of the earliest and most comprehensive attempts by a city to use the Olympics to address urban issues was the bid of a Third World city, namely Cape Town, South Africa, for the 2004 Summer Games (Hiller 2000a).

2 See, for example, the United Nations Population Fund report (Leidl 2007), which contrasted Vancouver's beautiful location and prosperity, making it one of the world's most livable cities, with the Downtown Eastside neighborhood, which housed the very poor and had a HIV prevalence rate that was the same as Botswana's.

1 Building an interpretive model: from macro to micro

1 Todd (2010) referred to the "inspirational image of social acceptance" which this event created as the global public being "awestruck" by the fact that a man in a wheelchair was not stigmatized but moved about the platform twirling the Olympic flag as an elected leader of an Olympic city.

2 Robert Merton (1995) claimed that this was probably "the single most consequential sentence" ever put in print by an American sociologist because it pointed out how behavior is related to how people interpret their circumstances.

3 I borrow selectively from Collins.

4 There is considerable debate among symbolic interactionists about how to interpret Goffman, and Collins is just one among many interpreters. Goffman himself did not prefer the term "symbolic interaction" to describe his own work. There are also many streams of thought within symbolic interaction, and many social theorists interact with Goffman's signal contributions (e.g., Giddens 1984) The analysis developed here is not intended to be part of any debates among symbolic interactionists (Riggins 1990; Lemert 1997); rather, it aims to use symbolic interaction selectively as a tool to bring a fresh perspective to understanding the Olympics.

5 For an alternative view, see Lenskyj (1996), who argues that winning cities are really losers.

6 Fine and Harrington (2004) argue that small groups are a significant repository of civic memory.

2 The Olympics as dramaturgy

1 This matter is often very difficult, as the city of Chicago experienced when bidding for the 2016 Games. The city council was reluctant to provide all the financial guarantees in order to protect its own citizens and the city's financial status because other levels of government did not step to the plate as they did in Canada. Eventually the

city council supported the guarantee but the delay may have hindered Chicago's bid, which was eventually lost.

2 See Cochrane *et al.* (1996), who show how charismatic entrepreneurs can be related to the trend towards urban entrepreneurialism. Surborg *et al.* (2008) argue that it is not cities that compete for the Olympics but leaders made up of locally grounded elites.

3 Burbank *et al.* (2001:169) use regime theory in their interpretation of the relationship between the Olympics and local politics but conclude their analysis by noting that regime theory does not capture all the nuances of the relationship. The discussion here attempts to propose other elements besides economic interests and urban economic growth strategies.

4 Regime theory, from the perspective of this study, involves networks of interpersonal relationships among elites built over time through repeated interaction or as a consequence of their being holders of leadership positions that summon them for community-based projects. Because these relationships and associations are formed outside of normal established structures, they take on a life of their own, especially as a mobilizing strategy for special projects. Presidents or CEOs of companies can call up other executives because they know them from previous interaction. Similarly, they bring more authority in contacting political leaders and government officials to solicit their support. Politicians who endorse the bid idea can thereby lend their cautious support to an idea that does not have legislative approval while at the same time an independent entity pursues the initiative. The point is that it is the personal interaction and networking between elites that make the Olympic project potentially viable.

5 It is important to note that the mandate of the Calgary Booster Club was to support the development of sport, particularly in young athletes. This is somewhat different from the idea of boosterism as city advocacy and urban economic development. On the other hand, the Calgary Booster Club included many key economic leaders in the city.

6 As another example, see McGeoch with Korporaal's (1995) story of the Sydney Olympic bid.

7 The goal here is to show how the model often articulated (e.g., Roche 2003:126) – that elites make decisions about the Games and the public is expected to passively follow – requires modification (at least in western countries).

8 Because of the process required by provincial law, it was impossible to hold a referendum that would have been binding, given the short timeline. It would have also been more costly. While the mayor wanted the voice of the people to be heard, he made it clear that he was in favor of hosting the Games.

9 The bid committee survey indicated 62 percent support in Vancouver (although 80 percent support in Canada), which was fairly close to the 64 percent in the plebiscite. The IOC survey indicated 58 percent support in British Columbia (compared to 65 percent national support), although 25 percent were opposed and 17 percent had no opinion (International Olympic Committee 2003).

10 An interesting comparison can be made with Salt Lake City, where a referendum also produced less than compelling results for the Olympics. A statewide (rather than city) referendum was held in Salt Lake City in 1989 to authorize the spending of money for Olympic construction which passed by 57 percent "Yes" to 43 percent "No." Much of this opposition was directed at responsible public spending and was less vocal after the vote. Perhaps this issue was overwhelmed by the scandals that later tarnished the 2002 Games.

3 Framing: interpreting the Olympic project

1 For a discussion of Olympic resistance movements that have emerged in a variety of international cities, see Lenskyj (2000, 2008).

2 MacRury and Poynter (2008) discuss conceptions of the Olympics as a commodity versus the Olympics as a gift.

3 Berkaak (1999:51) pointed out that hyperbole became a symbolic form in legitimating the Lillehammer Games and that the notion of the Olympics as a global spectacle supported an "ideology of exponentiality."

4 Shaw was a resident of Vancouver. Another expression of this counter-frame by a Toronto resident but with application to Vancouver can be found in Lenskyj (2008).

5 This point was confirmed in the survey reported in Chapter 7, when participants made comments at the end of the survey that the options presented to them did not give enough opportunity to express nuanced or conflicted feelings about the Games. See also Gamson and Modigliani (1989) for a discussion on simple yes–no alternatives with regard to public opinion about nuclear power.

6 See Fowlie (2009) for a review of the discussions about improving this roadway.

7 The reason for this decision is that Canada has another speedskating oval that is the legacy of the 1988 Winter Olympics in Calgary. The ice is much faster in Calgary, owing to its higher elevation and dryer air in comparison to Vancouver with its higher humidity and slower ice.

8 The outcome of this issue was still unknown at the time of writing.

9 For an analysis of protests at the Sydney Olympics, see Neilson (2002) and Lenskyj (2002), and for London 2012, see Fussey *et al.* (2011:211–231).

10 As reported by the Office of the Auditor General of Canada, Petition No. 168.

11 In reality, four aboriginal groups agreed to serve as host nations for the Olympics, but oppositional groups did not accept their authority. In addition, eighty of 203 bands who were members of the Union of BC Indian Chiefs refused to endorse the Games (Pemberton 2010).

12 For a review of the goals and accomplishments of the IOCC, see Edelson (2011).

13 For a discussion of the sanitizing of public space during the Olympics, see Kennelly and Watt (2011). The role of safety and security in relation to urban planning and the Olympic presence is discussed by Fussey *et al.* (2011).

14 For example, "ensure people are not made homeless as a result of the Winter Games," ensure residents are not evicted or displaced as the result of Games-related unreasonable rent increases. Any action undertaken would be done "in the context of existing government activities and take into account fiscal limits." See the 2010 Winter Games Inner-City Inclusive Commitment Statement.

15 The Olympic Stadium in Montreal ("the big O") is often referred to as "the big Owe" because of its structural problems and huge costs that took thirty years to pay off.

16 Shaw (2008:266) refers to continuous opposition as part of a global process of discouraging other cities from hosting the Olympics.

17 Available at: http://vancouver.mediacoop.ca/olympics/native-warriors-take-olympic-flag/6313.

18 See Ha and Caffrey (2011) for a discussion of grassroots reaction to the controls instituted for the Olympics in Beijing.

19 The British Columbia Teachers' Federation said that it had not taken a position either in support of or in opposition to the Games but that of course it did not approve of the diversion of funds to the Olympics if it meant cuts to education. The Vancouver Elementary School Teachers Association did agree to promoting an event called Teaching 2010 Resistance, a curriculum organized by some teachers and the Olympic Resistance Network (ORN), to help teachers raise critical questions about the Olympics (Steffenhagen 2009).

4   The public realm

1 The data discussed here come from Angus Reid Public Opinion, November 20, 2009 and January 21, 2010.

2 The tension between festival, ritual, and spectacle in the Olympics is also discussed by Brown (2005).

3 The Torch Relay was not just an opportunity for people to relate to the Olympics in a supportive way but also a significant opportunity for people to participate in opposition to the Olympics. Protest activities took place at many points on the cross-Canada tour.

4 There were 12,000 torchbearers in the 2010 Olympic Relay. In comparison, there were 5,000 athletes and officials and 10,000 media representatives.

5 Whereas venues serving food were normally inspected once per year, venues related to high Olympic usage were inspected three times during the Olympic month – especially temporary venues. Hospital emergency rooms showed a definite spike in patients in comparison to normal volumes.

6 One furniture store on the pedestrian corridor gave up trying to sell furniture during the Olympics and instead rearranged its furniture to create an Olympic viewing gallery around a large-screen television set.

7 Based on data provided by Vivonet. Restaurants outside the downtown core such as on Broadway or in the suburbs demonstrated little increase in sales. Full-service restaurants with television sets did better in sales than restaurants without television sets. Yaletown restaurants showed the largest increases.

8 The construction of high-rise residential buildings on a mixed-use base creating a high-density residential area while still maintaining view corridors is known in the architectural urban planning community around the world as Vancouverism. The concept of "living first" is analyzed by Kataoka (2009).

9 Most people think of the Cultural Olympiad as involving ticketed events or exhibitions in dedicated spaces normally used for these purposes. However, live sites and some pavilions held free concerts that were part of the Cultural Olympiad. It is unclear, however, whether street entertainers were considered part of the Cultural Olympiad. See Garcia (2008) for the history of cultural events at the Olympics.

10 Rowe (2000) has argued that screen-based live sites in Sydney played a significant role in allowing people to feel that they were actually in attendance at an Olympic event even though they were watching on television, because they were surrounded by others who were watching, creating a crowd effect.

11 For a similar observation from the analyses of other instances of crowd behavior, see McPhail (2006).

12 McPhail (1991:165) refers to the clustering that occurs when people come with companions, stay with them, and leave with them as pedestrian clusters.

13 See Fralic (2010) for a review of some of the street costuming by people from different countries.

14 There were 15,000 Royal Canadian Mounted Police, city police, military, and private security, including 1,700 police from cities across the country, 4,000 Canadian forces, and 4,800 private security personnel in the city during the Olympics. Bajc (2007) examined surveillance at presidential inaugurations in the United States and referred to the need for a higher level of ordering to ensure a public collective activity as a meta-ritual.

15 The approximate size of this protest is open to some debate; 1,500–2,000 is the number frequently mentioned. Ward (2010) suggests that given the length of time organizers had to rally supporters for this action, the number of participants was surprisingly low. As the study of protest was not the primary focus of this research, I am not in a position to evaluate the magnitude of this or any other protest.

16 An anti-anti-Olympic counter-protest of Olympic supporters was proposed for the same time and same place but organizers were discouraged from setting the stage for a street confrontation.

17 There was considerable apprehension in Vancouver about how protest would be dealt with in the light of the experiences of the 1997 Asia-Pacific Economic Cooperation

(APEC) summit. Vancouver lawyer Leo McGrady published a book entitled *Protesters' Guide to the Law of Civil Disobedience in BC: Olympic Edition* in 2009 that
explained how to protest lawfully without getting arrested by engaging in illegal acts.
The Civil Liberties Advisory Committee was also aware of this issue and stated that
it expected the police to deal with illegal activity, but also asked for restraint during
the Olympics. However, two incidents seemed to turn away moderate protesters. The
first was the Resist the Torch action at Victory Square on the margins of the Downtown Eastside, where protesters offended elderly veterans who had been waiting for
the torch to pass. The second incident was the Heart Attack March, which used a
"diversity of tactics" aiming to disturb "business as unusual" and led to violence (Sin
and Colebourn 2010). This is not the place to evaluate Olympic protest but it is clear
that violence splintered and weakened the anti-Olympic movement. "Black-clad
anarchists" wearing black clothing and balaclavas made opposition to the Olympics
into a fringe political subculture that lost the connectivity with the left-liberal middle
class (Ward 2010). Even some of the leaders of the Olympic Resistance Network, as
reported by Ward, could see that their attempt to demonize the Olympics may have
led to their being marginalized during the Games, given the readily observable strong
mass participation in Olympic street life.
18 There were actually many small protests at other places in the city too numerous to
list here, such as at Langara College and even in the downtown area.
19 See Blomley (2004) for an interesting discussion of the relationship between public
and private space in the Downtown Eastside and how localized property can be considered as a community resource.
20 There are many illustrations of the suspension of normal routines such as the closure
of some schools and the changing of work schedules, including being given paid time
off and working from home.
21 Compare MacAloon (1995:183), who came to a similar conclusion about Barcelona.
22 Anderson (2003) discovered a similar outcome among those who attended Expos.
People's recollections centered on their interactional experiences at the Expos more
than the content of the exhibitions.
23 On weekends, there were some problems among young people with drinking alcohol
on the streets, which created some civility issues late at night. These problems were
controlled by closing liquor stores early in the evening in the downtown area.
24 As has already been noted, the police strategy was focused on making connections
with people and meeting and greeting rather than arresting. The police were highly
visible through wearing yellow vests but sought to engage the crowds rather than
confront them.

5 The host city as a symbolic field

1 Dawson (2006:13) has shown how the Commonwealth Games in Vancouver generated a "multiplicity of vernacular understandings" and multiple and conflicting meanings rather than simply unitary or binary meanings.
2 For example, the IOC distributes funds to national Olympic committees and international federations. For a discussion of Olympic financing, see the Olympic Marketing
Fact File, 2011 edition, International Olympic Committee.
3 Cashman (2006:78) notes that in Australia a TV series called *The Games* utilized the
preparation period as light-hearted entertainment by parodying the organizing committee as bumbling and incompetent.
4 Real (2009:168), following Edge, has pointed out that the Vancouver area media
market is the most monopolistic in North America. Both major Vancouver newspapers are owned by one company, CanWest, which also owns other major dailies in
Canada. CanWest also owned the largest television station in Vancouver. CanWest
had a sponsorship agreement with VANOC which declared that CanWest was

obviously supportive of the Olympics. But it did not exercise strong editorial control, and opposing opinions were rife in the media.

5 See Cardinal (2007) for further discussion on how Vancouver businesses could benefit from the Olympics. Cardinal calls for people to be neutral about the Olympics while still benefiting from them.

6 The idea that sporting events can be appropriated for a variety of social and political endeavors has also been suggested by Dawson (2006), who studied the British Empire/Commonwealth Games in Vancouver in 1954. He argues that such spectacles generate multiple, partial, and conflicting meanings that go beyond simple distinctions between being supportive or oppositional.

7 No attempt will be made here to list all groups or organizations that mounted special programs or activities in relation to the Olympics or around the time of the Olympics. Two more examples include the Wal-Mart Green Business Summit or the British Columbia Council for International Education, which held seminars to encourage visitors to study in the province.

8 Most churches in the downtown core opened their doors as places of quietness or as places to watch the Olympics or talk with others over refreshments. A special issue of the *B.C. Catholic* was published, entitled "We Believe: A Catholic Guide to the 2010 Winter Games."

9 The position taken here is that the sale of Olympic-related merchandise was motivated not so much by the need to express a sense of belonging but rather by what could be considered event-appropriate attire and the desire to join in its spirit. For a discussion of such behavior in relation to the literature on fads, see Lilly and Nelson (2003).

10 The Census Metropolitan Area of Vancouver includes the cities of Vancouver, Burnaby, Coquitlam, Port Coquitlam, Richmond, North Vancouver, West Vancouver, Port Moody, New Westminster, Delta, and Surrey.

11 Schrag (2011:89–90) points out that in the context of the Olympics, flying the flag is viewed not as a political statement or an expression of nationalist identity but as an opportunity to identify with the nation as a fan or as a symbol with which supporting fans can identify.

12 It is debatable whether the Olympics in Canada served as the kind of iconic event that Leavy (2007:107) refers to as a major marker in national identity formation whereby the state utilizes the Games to renegotiate or promote national priorities and tighten the link between the nation and the individual. On the other hand, these goals were evident in a variety of ways and undergirded the rationale for federal financial support.

13 Leavy (2007) demonstrates how the media play an important role in interpreting and filtering iconic events to the public, thereby creating a mediated version of what occurred.

14 The captivating nature of this game is demonstrated by the fact that nearly half of all Canadians watched the entire game and 80 percent watched parts of it. The game captured 85 percent of all Canadians watching television at that time (Bell Media, Day 17).

15 Two interesting illustrations prove this point. Spiritual meetings at two mosques that included many new immigrants to Canada (from countries where hockey was not part of their culture) were interrupted to watch the gold medal men's hockey game on a screen brought in for this purpose. A somewhat humorous report from Metro Vancouver Utilities System showed how the gold medal game had captivated the city television audience (Sinoski 2010). Toilet flushes increased so dramatically between periods of the game that special consumption measures had to be taken to ensure adequate operating levels.

16 Roche (2000) argues that mega-events such as the Olympics can serve as life events or rites of passage in individual and community biographies.

6 The social media and urban interaction

1 Maurice Cardinal (2007) also advocated citizen journalism in his book *Leveraging Olympic Momentum*.

2 Goode (2009) acknowledges that there are a variety of forms of citizen journalism, some of which are more serious and deliberate and some of which are more haphazard. He uses the term "metajournalism."

3 For a review of how the Olympic Winter Games have grown in terms of participants, costs, audiences, and revenues, see Chappelet (2002).

4 The data in this paragraph were obtained from "Vancouver 2010 Olympic Winter Games Global Television and Online Media Overview" (IOC 2010), "Factsheet Vancouver Facts and Figures Update February 2011" (IOC, February 24, 2011), and the IOC Marketing Report, Vancouver 2010.

5 Some out-of-country access was blocked, such as Canadian access to NBC streaming. It is not known what other country-specific blocking occurred.

6 *Legacies of North American Olympic Winter Games*, vol. 4: Vancouver 2010 (no publisher but commissioned by VANOC).

7 The size of the Canadian television audience for Vancouver 2010 was almost triple the Canadian audience for the Calgary 1988 Games.

8 Twitter has become of increasing interest to researchers because it is considered a valuable database of sentiments and shifts in public opinion (Pang and Lee 2008).

9 There is no way to determine whether all persons tweeting using a particular hashtag were from Vancouver or not. However, the nature of the tweets suggests that most users were local.

10 The data available do not indicate how many tweets there were in raw numbers but just indicate the proportion and variation of tweets over time. The websites that made these data available are no longer publicly available as of March 21, 2011 as a result of a decision by Twitter.

11 Victory Square celebrates World War II and recognizes those who fought in that war and gave their lives, which is why veterans and a pipe band were present.

7 The consequences of interaction: public opinion and the Olympics

1 Abad (1995) discusses this transformation not only in terms of urban spaces but also in terms of changing mental attitudes.

2 See MacAloon (2008), who refers to the use of the term "legacy" as managerial discourse.

3 The study uses longitudinal data rather than panel data, meaning that each sample was independent of the others. For more details of the study and the statistical measures and modeling employed, see Hiller and Wanner (2011).

4 Unfortunately, the question asked combined two different variables, inconvenienced/not inconvenienced and excitement/indifference, which made it difficult to sort out the independent effects of attitude and being inconvenienced. Therefore, these data need to be interpreted more cautiously.

5 Respondents could choose the emotions or attitudes that applied to them, meaning that percentages do not reflect the responses of all participants in the study.

6 There may be some confusion about what is included in the Cultural Olympiad from the respondent's point of view as the Cultural Olympiad officially included ticketed events as well as activities that did not involve paid admission. However, the assumption here is that people who were more aware of having been part of the Cultural Olympiad were more likely to have paid admission fees to attend this kind of event.

7 Cashman (2006:78) refers to the media criticism before the Games but tremendous approval during the Games and in the immediate aftermath of the Games as a paradox.

8 Letter to the Editor, *Vancouver Sun*, March 4, 2010.
9 Cashman's (2006:27) analysis of the Sydney Games acknowledges the heightened euphoria in the city during the Games and the sense of loss or the "post-Games depression" when the Games were over. He refers to the psychology of the city as a "bittersweet awakening" as the memory of the Games recedes and residents struggle with the difference between a successful Games and actual long-term benefits (ibid.:241).

8 Conclusion

1 The IOC established the Olympic Games Impact (OGI) study requirement to address this issue. The result is a compendium of statistics and facts that still must be interpreted through a set of values and ideals that reflect individual preferences.
2 For a discussion of soft legacies, particularly memories of a mega-event, see Kenneally and Sloan's (2010:18–19) discussion of Expo 67 in Montreal.

References

Abad, Josep Miquel (1995). "A Summary of the Activities of the COOB '92." Pp. 11–17 in Miquel de Moragas and Miquel Botella (eds.), *The Keys to Success: The Social, Sporting, Economic and Communications Impact of Barcelona '92*. Barcelona: Universitat Autònoma de Barcelona.

Abendroth, Lisa J. and Kristin Diehl (2006). "Now or Never: Effects of Limited Purchase Opportunities on Patterns of Regret over Time." *Journal of Consumer Research* 33(3):342–351.

Alexander, David (2005). "Vancouver's Support of the 2010 Winter Olympic Bid: An Analysis of the 2003 Olympic Plebiscite." MA thesis, Royal Roads University, Victoria.

Anderson, David (2003). "Visitors' Long-Term Memories of World Expositions." *Curator: The Museum Journal* 46(4):401–420.

Bajc, Vida (2007). "Surveillance in Public Rituals: Security Meta-ritual and the 2005 U.S. Presidential Inauguration." *American Behavioral Scientist* 50(12):1648–1673.

Barnes, Trevor and Thomas Hutton (2009). "Situating the New Economy: Contingencies of Regeneration and Dislocation in Vancouver's Inner City." *Urban Studies* 46(5–6):1247–1269.

Barney, Robert K., Stephen R. Wenn, and Scott G. Martyn (2004). *Selling the Five Rings: The International Olympic Committee and the Rise of Olympic Commercialism*. Salt Lake City: University of Utah Press.

Bell Media, *Day Recaps*, at www.bellmediapr.ca/ctv/release (accessed March 12, 2011).

Benford, Robert D. and Scott A. Hunt (1992). "Dramaturgy and Social Movements: The Social Construction and Communication of Power." *Sociological Inquiry* 62(1):36–55.

Benford, Robert D. and David A. Snow (2000). "Framing Processes and Social Movements: An Overview and Assessment." *Annual Review of Sociology* 26:611–639.

Berelowitz, Lance (2005). *Dream City: Vancouver and the Global Imagination*. Vancouver: Douglas & McIntyre.

Berger, Jonah and Chip Heath (2007). "Where Consumers Diverge from Others: Identity Signaling and Product Domains." *Journal of Consumer Research* 34(2):121–134.

Berkaak, Odd Are (1999). "'In the Heart of the Volcano': The Olympic Games as Mega Drama." Pp. 49–74 in Arne Martin Klausen (ed.), *Olympic Games as Performance and Public Event: The Case of the XVII Winter Olympic Games in Norway*. New York: Berghahn.

Best, Joel (1987). "Rhetoric in Claims-Making: Constructing the Missing Children Problem." *Social Problems* 34(2):101–121.

Black, David (2007). "The Symbolic Politics of Sport Mega-events: 2010 in Comparative Perspective." *Politikon* 34(3):261–276.

Blomley, Nicholas (2004). *Unsettling the City: Urban Land and the Politics of Property*. New York: Routledge.

Blumer, Herbert (1969). *Symbolic Interactionism: Perspective and Method*. Berkeley: University of California Press.

Boei, William (2003). "Basking in Olympic Glory." *Vancouver Sun*, July 3, 2003.

Boltanski, Luc and Eve Chiapello (2005). *The New Spirit of Capitalism*. London: Verso.

Borch, Christian (2009). "Body to Body: On the Political Anatomy of Crowds." *Sociological Theory* 27(3):271–290.

Boykoff, Jules (2011). "Space Matters: The 2010 Winter Olympics and Its Discontents." *Human Geography* 4(2):48–60.

Brissett, Dennis and Charles Edgley (2005). *Life as Theater: A Dramaturgical Sourcebook*, 2nd ed. New Brunswick, NJ: Transaction.

Brown, Douglas (2005). "The Olympic Games Experience: Origins and Early Challenges." Pp. 19–41 in Kevin Young and Kevin B. Walmsley (eds.), *Global Olympics: Historical and Sociological Studies of the Modern Games*. Amsterdam: Elsevier.

Burbank, Matthew J., Charles H. Heying, and Gregory D. Andranovich (2000). "Anti-growth Politics or Piecemeal Resistance? Citizen Opposition to Olympic-Related Economic Growth." *Urban Affairs Review* 35(3):334–357.

Burbank, Matthew J., Gregory D. Andranovich, and Charles H. Heying (2001). *Olympic Dreams: The Impact of Mega-events on Local Politics*. Boulder, CO: Lynne Rienner.

Caffrey, Kevin (2011). *The Beijing Olympics: Promoting China: Soft and Hard Power in Global Politics*. London: Routledge.

Cardinal, Maurice (2007). *Leverage Olympic Momentum*. Vancouver: Area46 Media.

Cashman, Richard (2006). *The Bitter-Sweet Awakening: The Legacy of the Sydney 2000 Olympic Games*. Sydney: Walla Walla Press.

Cashman, Richard and Anthony Hughes (1999). *Staging the Olympics: The Event and Its Impact*. Sydney: University of New South Wales Press.

Castells, Manuel (1989). *The Informational City: Informational Technology, Economic Restructuring and the Urban-Regional Process*. Oxford: Blackwell.

Centre on Housing Rights and Evictions (COHRE) (2007). *Fair Play for Housing Rights: Mega-events, Olympic Games and Housing Rights*. Geneva: COHRE.

Cernetig, Miro (2010). "Including First Nations in Games Planning Pays Off Both Ways." *Vancouver Sun*, January 19, 2010.

Chappelet, Jean-Loup (2002). "From Lake Placid to Salt Lake City: The Challenging Growth of the Olympic Winter Games since 1980." *European Journal of Sport Science* 2(3):1–21.

Cochrane, Allan, Jamie Peck and Adam Tickell (1996). "Manchester Plays Games: Exploring the Local Politics of Globalisation." *Urban Studies* 33(8):1319–1336.

Collins, Randall (2004). *Interaction Ritual Chains*. Princeton, NJ: Princeton University Press.

Cutler, Fred and J. Scott Matthews (2005). "The Challenge of Municipal Voting: Vancouver 2002." *Canadian Journal of Political Science* 38(2): 359–382.

Dansero, Egidio, Domenico DeLeonardis, and Alfredo Mela (2006). "Torino 2006: Territorial and Environmental Transformations." Pp. 359–376 in Norbert Müller, Manfred Messing, and Holger Preuß (eds.), *From Chamonix to Turin: The Winter Games in the Scope of Olympic Research*. Kassel, Germany: Agon Sportverlag.

Dawson, Michael (2006). "Acting Global, Thinking Local: 'Liquid Imperialism' and the Multiple Meanings of the 1954 British Empire and Commonwealth Games." *International Journal of the History of Sport* 23(1):3–27.

Debord, Guy (1994). *The Society of the Spectacle*. New York: Zone Books.

de Moragas, Miquel, Nancy Rivenburgh, and Núria Garcia (1995). "Television and the Construction of Identity: Barcelona, Olympic Host." Pp. 76–106 in Miquel de Moragas and Miquel Botella (eds.), *The Keys to Success: The Social, Sporting, Economic, and Communication Impact of Barcelona '92*. Barcelona: Universitat Autònoma de Barcelona.

Drury, John and Steve Reicher (2009). "Collective Psychological Empowerment as a Model of Social Change: Researching Crowds and Power." *Journal of Social Issues* 65(4):707–725.

Edelson, Nathan (2011). "Inclusivity as an Olympic Event at the 2010 Vancouver Winter Games." *Urban Geography* 32(6):804–822.

Edgley, Charles (2003). "The Dramaturgical Genre." Pp. 141–172 in Larry Reynolds and Nancy J. Herman (eds.), *Handbook of Symbolic Interactionism*. Walnut Creek, CA: AltaMira Press.

Eisinger, Peter (2000). "The Politics of Bread and Circuses: Building the City for the Visitor Class." *Urban Affairs Review* 35(3):316–333.

Esaisson, Peter and Donald Granberg (1996). "Attitudes towards a Fallen Leader: Evaluations of Olaf Palme before and after the Assassination." *British Journal of Political Science* 26(3):429–439.

Espy, Richard (1979). *The Politics of the Olympic Games*. Berkeley: University of California Press.

Fine, Gary Alan (1991). "On the Macrofoundations of Microsociology: Constraint and the Exterior Reality of Structure." *Sociological Quarterly* 32(2):161–177.

Fine, Gary Alan (2010). "The Sociology of the Local: Action and Its Publics." *Sociological Theory* 28(4):355–376.

Fine, Gary Alan and Brooke Harrington (2004). "Tiny Publics: Small Groups and Civil Society." *Sociological Theory* 22(3):341–356.

Fowlie, Jonathan (2009). "Sea to Sky Highway: A Long Run to Olympics", *Vancouver Sun*, October 28, 2009.

Fox, Susannah, Kathryn Zickuhr, and Aaron Smith (2009). *Twitter and Status Updating, Fall 2009*. Washington, DC: Pew Internet and American Life Project.

Fralic, Shelley (2010). "The Chi of Fandemonium." *Vancouver Sun*, March 2, 2010.

Furlong, John (2011). *Patriot Hearts: Inside the Olympics That Changed a Country*. Toronto: Douglas & McIntyre.

Fussey, Pete, Jon Coaffee, Gary Armstrong, and Dick Hobbs (2011). *Securing and Sustaining the Olympic City: Reconfiguring London for 2012 and Beyond*. Farnham, UK: Ashgate.

Gamson, William A. (1992). "The Social Psychology of Collective Action." Pp. 53–76 in Aldon D. Morris and Carol McClurg Mueller (eds.), *Frontiers in Social Movement Theory*. New Haven, CT: Yale University Press.

Gamson, William A. and Andre Modigliani (1989). "Media Discourse and Public Opinion on Nuclear Power: A Constructionist Approach." *American Journal of Sociology* 95(1):1–37.

Garcia, Beatriz (2008). "One Hundred Years of Cultural Programming within the Olympic Games (1912–2012): Origins, Evolution and Projections." *International Journal of Cultural Policy* 14(4):361–376.

Geertz, Clifford (1983). *Local Knowledge: Further Essays in Interpretive Anthropology*. New York: Basic Books.

Giddens, Anthony (1984). *The Constitution of Society*. Cambridge: Polity Press.

Goffman, Erving (1959). *The Presentation of Self in Everyday Life*. New York: Doubleday.

Goffman, Erving (1961). *Asylums*. Chicago: Aldine.

Goffman, Erving (1974). *Frame Analysis: An Essay on the Organization of Experience*. New York: Harper & Row.

Gold, Margaret M. and George Revill (2011). "The Cultural Olympiads: Reviving the Panegyris." Pp. 80–107 in John R. Gold and Margaret M. Gold (eds.), *Olympic Cities: City Agendas, Planning, and the World's Games, 1896–2016*, 2nd ed. London: Routledge.

Goode, Louis (2009). "Social News, Citizen Journalism, and Democracy." *New Media and Society* 11(8):1287–1305.

Gruzd, A., S. Doiron, and P. Mai (2011). "Is Happiness Contagious Online? A Case of Twitter and the 2010 Winter Olympics." *Proceedings of the 44th Hawaii International Conference on System Sciences (HICSS)*, January 4–7, Kauai, HI. DOI: 10.1109/HICSS.2011.259.

Guala, Chito (2009). "To Bid or Not to Bid: Public Opinion before and after the Games: The Case of Turin." Pp. 21–30 in James Kennell, Charles Bladon, and Elizabeth Booth (eds.), *The Olympic Legacy: People, Place, Enterprise*. London: University of Greenwich.

Ha Guangtian and Kevin Caffrey (2011). "Olympian Ghosts: Apprehensions and Apparitions of the Beijing Spectacle." Pp. 61–79 in Kevin Caffrey (ed.), *The Beijing Olympics: Promoting China*. London: Routledge.

Hall, C. Michael and Julie Hodges (1996). "The Party's Great but What about the Hangover? The Housing and Social Impacts of Mega-events with Special Reference to the 2000 Sydney Olympics." *Festival Management and Event Tourism* 4:13–20.

Handelman, Don (1990). *Models and Mirrors: Towards an Anthropology of Public Events*. Cambridge: Cambridge University Press.

Harcourt, Mike and Ken Cameron with Sean Rossiter (2007). *City Making in Paradise: Nine Decisions That Saved Vancouver*. Vancouver: Douglas & McIntyre.

Hare, A. Paul and Herbert H. Blumberg (1988). *Dramaturgical Analysis of Social Interaction*. New York: Praeger.

Harvey, David (1989). *The Condition of Postmodernity*. London: Blackwell.

Hayes, Graeme and John Horne (2011). "Sustainable Development, Shock and Awe? London 2012 and Civil Society." *Sociology* 45(5):749–764.

Hetherington, Kevin and Anne M. Cronin (2008). *Consuming the Entrepreneurial City*. New York: Routledge.

Hiller, Harry H. (1990). "The Urban Transformation of a Landmark Event: The 1988 Calgary Winter Olympics." *Urban Affairs Quarterly* 26(1):118–137.

Hiller, Harry H. (1998). "Assessing the Impact of Mega-Events: A Linkage Model." *Current Issues in Tourism* 1:47–57.

Hiller, Harry H. (2000a). "Mega-events, Urban Boosterism, and Growth Strategies: An Analysis of the Cape Town 2004 Olympic Bid." *International Journal of Urban and Regional Research* 24:457–476.

Hiller, Harry H. (2000b). "Towards an Urban Sociology of Mega-events." *Research in Urban Sociology* 5:181–205.

Hiller, Harry H. (2006a). *Canadian Society: A Macro Analysis*. Toronto: Pearson/Prentice-Hall.

Hiller, Harry H. (2006b). "Post-event Outcomes and the Post-modern Turn: The Olympics and Urban Transformations." *European Sport Management Quarterly* 6(4):317–332.

Hiller, Harry H. and Richard A. Wanner (2011). "Public Opinion in Host Olympic Cities: The Case of the 2010 Vancouver Winter Games." *Sociology* 45(5):883–899.

Huberman, Bernardo, Daniel M. Romero, and Fang Wu (2009). "Social Networks That Matter: Twitter under the Microscope." *First Monday* 14(1), January 5.

Hutchins, Brett and Janine Mikosza (2010). "The Web 2.0 Olympics: Athlete Blogging, Social Networking and Policy Contradictions at the 2008 Beijing Games." *Convergence: The International Journal of Research into New Media Technologies* 16(3): 279–297.

Hutton, Thomas (2004). "Post-industrialism, Post-modernism and the Reproduction of Vancouver's Central Area: Retheorising the 21st-Century City." *Urban Studies* 41(10):1953–1982.

International Olympic Committee (2003). *Report of the IOC Evaluation Commission for the XXI Olympic Winter Games in 2010*. Lausanne.

Ito, Mizuko (2008). Introduction. Pp. 1–14 in Kazys Varnelis (ed.), *Networked Publics*. Cambridge, MA: MIT Press.

Jansen, Bernard J., Mimi Zhang, Kate Sobel, and Abdur Chowdury (2009). "Twitter Power: Tweets as Electronic Word of Mouth." *Journal of the American Society for Information Science and Technology* 60(11):2169–2188.

Java, Akshay, Xiaodan Song, Tim Finin, and Bella Tseng (2007). "Why We Twitter: Understanding Microblogging Usage and Communities." Pp. 56–65 in *Proceedings of the Joint 9th WEBKDD and 1st SNA-KDD Workshop*. New York: ACM Press.

Judd, Ron C. (2009). *The Winter Olympics: An Insider's Guide to the Legends, the Lore, and the Games*. Seattle: Mountaineers Books.

Kataoka, Serena (2009). "Vancouverism: Actualizing the Livable City Paradox." *Berkeley Planning Journal* 22:42–57.

Kavetsos, Georgios and Stefan Szymanski (2010). "National Well-Being and International Sports Events." *Journal of Economic Psychology* 31(2):158–171.

Kayden, Jerold S. (2000). *Privately Owned Public Space*. New York: John Wiley.

Kenneally, Rhona Richman and Johanne Sloan (2010). *Expo 67: Not Just a Souvenir*. Toronto: University of Toronto Press.

Kennelly, Jacqueline and Paul Watt (2011). "Sanitizing Public Space in Olympic Host Cities: The Spatial Experiences of Marginalized Youth in 2010 Vancouver and 2012 London." *Sociology* 45(5):765–781.

Kidd, Bruce (1992). "The Toronto Olympic Commitment: Towards a Social Contract for the Olympic Games." *Olympika: The International Journal of Olympic Studies* 1:154–167.

Kines, Lindsay (2010). "Rogge Praises Great Atmosphere." *Vancouver Sun*, March 1.

King, Frank (1991). *It's How You Play the Game: The Inside Story of the Calgary Olympics*. Calgary: Script, The Writer's Group.

Knight, Graham, Margaret MacNeill, and Peter Donnelly (2005). "The Disappointment Games: Narratives of Olympic Failure in Canada and New Zealand." *International Review for the Sociology of Sport* 40(1): 25–51.

Kniss, Fred (1997). "Culture Wars(?): Remapping the Battleground." Pp. 259–280 in Rhys H. Williams (ed.), *Cultural Wars in American Politics*. New York: Aldine de Gruyter.

Leavy, Patricia (2007). *Iconic Events: Media, Politics, and Power in Retelling History*. Lanham, MD: Lexington Books.

Lee, Jeff (2010). "Rogge Picks His Top Games Moments." *Vancouver Sun*, March 1.

Lee, Jeff (2011). "John Furlong Q&A: A Much-Needed Rest for Olympics Maestro." *Vancouver Sun/Postmedia News*, February 11.

Lefebvre, Henri (1991). *The Production of Space*. Oxford: Blackwell.

Lefebvre, Henri (1996). "Perspective or Prospective." Pp. 160–174 in Henri Lefebvre, *Writings on Cities*, ed. Eleonore Kofman and Elizabeth Lebas. Oxford: Blackwell.

Leidl, Patricia (2007). "Vancouver: Prosperity and Poverty Make for Uneasy Bedfellows in the World's Most 'Liveable' City." *State of the World Population 2007: Vancouver Feature*. United Nations Population Fund.

Lemert, Charles (1997). "Goffman." Pp. viii–xliii in Erving Goffman, *The Goffman Reader*, ed. Charles Lemert and Ann Branaman. Oxford: Blackwell.

Lenskyj, Helen (1996). "When Winners Are Losers: Toronto and Sydney Bids for the Summer Olympics." *Journal of Sport and Social Issues* 20(4):392–410.

Lenskyj, Helen (2000). *Inside the Olympic Industry: Power, Politics, and Activism*. Albany: State University of New York Press.

Lenskyj, Helen (2002). *The Best Olympics Ever? Social Impacts of Sydney 2000*. Albany: State University of New York Press.

Lenskyj, Helen (2008). *Olympic Industry Resistance: Challenging Olympic Power and Propaganda*. Albany: State University of New York Press.

Ley, David and Judith Tutchener (2001). "Immigration, Globalisation and House Prices in Canada's Gateway Cities." *Housing Studies* 16(2):199–223.

Liggett, Helen (2003). *Urban Encounters*. Minneapolis: University of Minnesota Press.

Liggett, Helen (2007). "Urban Aesthetics and the Excess of Fact." Pp. 9–23 in Lars Frers and Lars Meier (eds.), *Encountering Urban Places: Visual and Material Performances in the City*. Aldershot, UK: Ashgate.

Lilly, Bryan and Tammy R. Nelson (2003). "Fads: Segmenting the Fad-Buyer Market." *Journal of Consumer Marketing* 20(3):252–265.

Ling, Richard Seyler (2008). *New Tech, New Ties: How Mobile Communication Is Reshaping Social Cohesion*. Cambridge, MA: MIT Press.

Lofland, Lyn H. (1973). *A World of Strangers: Order and Action in Urban Public Space*. New York: Basic Books.

Lofland, Lyn H. (1998). *The Public Realm: Exploring the City's Quintessential Social Territory*. New York: Aldine de Gruyter.

Low, Setha M. (2000). *On the Plaza: The Politics of Public Space and Culture*. Austin: University of Texas Press.

MacAloon, John (1981). *This Great Symbol: Pierre de Coubertin and the Origins of the Modern Olympic Games*. Chicago: University of Chicago Press.

MacAloon, John (1984). *Rite, Drama, Festival, Spectacle: Rehearsals toward a Theory of Cultural Performance*. Philadelphia: Institute for the Study of Human Issues.

MacAloon, John (1989). "Festival, Ritual and Television." Pp. 6-21–6-40 in Roger Jackson and Tom McPhail (eds.), *The Olympic Movement and the Mass Media*. Calgary: Hurford.

MacAloon, John (1995). "Barcelona '92: The Perspective of Cultural Anthropology." Pp. 181–167 in Miquel de Moragas and Miquel Botella (eds.), *The Keys to Success: The Social, Sporting, Economic, and Communication Impact of Barcelona '92*. Barcelona: Universitat Autònoma de Barcelona.

MacAloon, John (2006). "The Theory of Spectacle: Reviewing Olympic Ethnography." Pp. 15–39 in Alan Tomlinson and Christopher Young (eds.), *National Identity and Global Sports Events*. Albany: State University of New York Press.

MacAloon, John (2008). "'Legacy' as Managerial/Magical Discourse in Contemporary Olympic Affairs." *International Journal of the History of Sport* 25(14):2060–2071.

MacRury, Iain (2009). "Branding the Games: Commercialism and the Olympic City." Pp. 43–71 in Gavin Poynter and Iain MacRury (eds.), *Olympic Cities: 2012 and the Remaking of London*. Farnham, UK: Ashgate.

MacRury, Iain and Gavin Poynter (2008). "The Regeneration Games: Commodities, Gifts and the Economics of London 2012." *International Journal of the History of Sport* 25(14):2072–2090.

Madanipour, Ali (2003). *Public and Private Spaces of the City*. New York: Routledge.

Mahoney, Daniel F., Dennis R. Howard, and Robert Madrigal (2000). "BIRGing and CORFing Behaviors by Sport Spectators: High Self-Monitors versus Low Self-Monitors." *International Sports Journal* 1(1):87–106.

Mangan, J.A. (2008). "Prologue: Guarantees of Global Goodwill: Post-Olympic Legacies – Too Many Limping White Elephants?" *International Journal of the History of Sport* 25(14):1869–1883.

Marshall, P. David, Becky Walker, and Nicholas Russo (2010). "Mediating the Olympics." *Convergence: The International Journal of Research into New Media Technologies* 16(3):263–278.

Mason, Gary (2003). "It was a Great Day to be a Canadian." *Vancouver Sun*, July 3.

McCarthy, John D. and Mayer N. Zald (1977). "Resource Mobilization and Social Movements: A Partial Theory." *American Journal of Sociology* 82(6): 1212–1241.

McCombs, Max, Lance Holbert, Spiro Kiousis, and Wayne Wanta (2011). *The News and Public Opinion: Media Effects on Civic Life*. Cambridge: Polity Press.

McGeoch, Rod with Glenda Korporaal (1995). *The Bid: Australia's Greatest Marketing Coup*. Melbourne: Heinemann.

McPhail, Clark (1991). *The Myth of the Madding Crowd*. New Brunswick, NJ: Aldine Transaction.

McPhail, Clark (2006). "The Crowd and Collective Behavior: Bringing Symbolic Interaction Back In." *Symbolic Interaction* 29(4):433–463.

Merton, Robert (1995). "The Thomas Theorem and the Matthew Effect." *Social Forces* 74(2):380.

Miah, Andy (2010). "New Media Activism at the Vancouver 2010 Olympic Winter Games." *Culture @ the Olympics* 12(3):14–18.

Mihalik, B. (2001). "Host Population Perceptions of the 1996 Atlanta Olympics: Attendance, Support, Benefits and Liabilities." *Tourism Analysis* 5(1):49–53.

Millard, Gregory, Sarah Riegel, and John Wright (2002). "Here's Where We Get Canadian: English-Canadian Nationalism and Popular Culture." *American Review of Canadian Studies* 32(1):11–34.

Moos, Markus and Andrejs Skaburskis (2010). "The Globalization of Urban Housing Markets: Immigration and Changing Housing Demand in Vancouver." *Urban Geography* 31(6):724–749.

Moss, Laura (2009). "Strategic Cultural Nationalism." *Canadian Literature* 200:6–14.

Neilson, Brett (2002). "Bodies of Protest: Performing Citizenship at the 2000 Olympic Games." *Continuum: Journal of Media and Cultural Studies* 16(1):13–25.

O'Bonsawin, Christine M. (2010). "'No Olympics on Stolen Native Land': Contesting Olympic Narratives and Asserting Indigenous Rights within the Discourse of the 2010 Vancouver Games." *Sport in Society* 13(1):143–156.

O'Brien, Dan (2006). "Strategic Business Leveraging and the Sydney 2000 Olympic Games." *Annals of Tourism Research* 33(1):240–261.

Oliver, Pamela and Daniel J. Myers (1999). "How Events Enter the Public Sphere: Conflict, Location and Sponsorship in Local Newspaper Coverage of Public Events." *American Journal of Sociology* 105(1):38–87.

Pang, Bo and Lillian Lee (2008). "Opinion Mining and Sentiment Analysis." *Foundations and Trends in Information Retrieval* 2(1–2): 1–135.

Panteli, Niki (ed.) (2009). *Virtual Social Networks: Mediated, Massive and Multiplayer Sites*. New York: Palgrave Macmillan.

Pemberton, Kim (2010). "Aboriginal Groups Divided on Whether to Support the Olympics." *Vancouver Sun*, February 6.

Pitt, Leyland, Michael Parent, Pierre Berthon, and Peter G. Steyn (2010). "Event Sponsorship and Ambush Marketing: Lessons from the Beijing Olympics." *Business Horizons* 53:281–290.

Pound, Richard (2004). *Inside the Olympics: A Behind-the-Scenes Look at the Politics, the Scandals, and the Glory of the Games*. Toronto: John Wiley.

Real, Michael (1996). "The Postmodern Olympics: Technology and the Commodification of the Olympic Movement." *Quest* 48(1):9–24.

Real, Michael (2009). "Gold for Whom? Canadian Sports, Mega-events and the 2010 Olympics." Pp. 165–178 in Leslie Regan Shade, *Mediascapes: New Patterns in Canadian Communication*, 3rd ed. Toronto: Thomson Nelson.

Reese, Stephen D., Oscar H. Gandy, Jr., and August E. Grant (2001). *Framing Public Life: Perspectives on Media and Our Understanding of the Social World*. Mahwah, NJ: Lawrence Erlbaum.

Rheingold, Howard (2002). *Smart Mobs: The Next Social Revolution*. New York: Basic Books.

Richins, Marsha L. (1994). "Valuing Things: The Public and Private Meanings of Possessions." *Journal of Consumer Research* 21(3):504–521.

Riggins, Stephen H. (1990). *Beyond Goffman: Studies on Communication, Institution, and Social Interaction*. Berlin: Mouton de Gruyter.

Ritchie, J., R. Brent, and Marcia Lyons (1990). "Olympulse VI: A Post-event Assessment of Resident Reaction to the XV Olympic Winter Games." *Journal of Travel Research* 28(3):14–23.

Roche, Maurice (1994). "Mega-events and Urban Policy." *Annals of Tourism Research* 21(1):1–19.

Roche, Maurice (2000). *Mega-events and Modernity: Olympics and Expos in the Growth of Global Culture*. London: Routledge.

Roche, Maurice (2003). "Mega-events, Time and Modernity: On Time Structures in Global Society." *Time and Society* 12(1):99–126.

Rossel, Jorg and Randall Collins (2006). "Conflict Theory and Interaction Rituals: The Microfoundations of Conflict Theory." Pp. 509–531 in Jonathan A. Turner (ed.), *Handbook of Sociological Theory*. New York: Springer.

Rothenbuhler, Eric W. (1988). "The Living Room Celebration of the Olympic Games." *Journal of Communication* 38(4):61–81.

Rothenbuhler, Eric W. (1989a). "The Olympics in the American Living Room: Celebration of a Media Event." Pp. 6-41–6-50 in Roger Jackson and Tom McPhail (eds.), *The Olympic Movement and the Mass Media*. Calgary: Hurford.

Rothenbuhler, Eric W. (1989b). "Values and Symbols in Orientations to the Olympics." *Critical Studies in Mass Communication* 6(2):138–157.

Rowe, David (2000). "Global Media Events and the Positioning of Presence." *Media International Australia, incorporating Culture and Policy* No. 97:11–21.

Rustin, Michael (2009). "Sport, Spectacle and Society: Understanding the Olympics." Pp. 3–21 in Gavin Poynter and Iain MacRury (eds.), *Olympic Cities: 2012 and the Remaking of London*. Farnham, UK: Ashgate.

Ryan, Denise (2009). "Poverty Olympics Ridicule Games." *Vancouver Sun*, February 9.

Sandstrom, Kent, Daniel D. Martin, and Gary Alan Fine (2001). "Symbolic Interactionism at the End of the Century." Pp. 217–231 in George Ritzer and Barry Smart (eds.), *Handbook of Social Theory*. Thousand Oaks, CA: Sage.

Scamuzzi, S. (2006). "Winter Olympic Games 2006 in Turin: The Rising Weight of Public Opinion." Pp. 343–357 in Norbert Müller, Manfred Messing, and Holger Preuß (eds.), *From Chamonix to Turin: The Winter Games in the Scope of Olympic Research*. Kassel, Germany: Agon Sportverlag.

Scherer, Jay (2011). "Olympic Villages and Large-Scale Urban Development: Crises of Capitalism, Deficits of Democracy?" *Sociology* 45(5):782–797.

Schmitz, Jason K. (2005). "Ambush Marketing: The Off-Field Competition at the Olympic Games." *Northwestern Journal of Technology and Intellectual Property* 3(2):203–208.

Schrag, David (2011). "'Flagging the Nation' in International Sport: A Chinese Olympics and a German World Cup." Pp. 80–100 in Kevin Caffrey (ed.), *The Beijing Olympics: Promoting China*. London: Routledge.

Senn, Alfred E. (1999). *Power, Politics and the Olympic Games*. Champaign, IL: Human Kinetics.

Sennett, Richard (1976). *The Fall of Public Man*. Cambridge: Cambridge University Press.

Shaw, Chris (2008). *Five Ring Circus: Myths and Realities of the Olympic Games*. Gabriola Island, British Columbia: New Society Publishers.

Shirky, Clay (2008). *Here Comes Everybody: The Power of Organizing without Organizations*. New York: Penguin.

Short, John (2008). "Globalization, Cities and the Summer Olympics." *City* 12(3):321–340.

Sin, Lena and John Colebourn (2010). "Peaceful Protest Sours as Criminal Element Takes Over Streets." *Vancouver Province*, February 14.

Simson, Vyv and Andrew Jennings (1992). *The Lords of the Rings: Power, Money, and Drugs in the Modern Olympics*. New York: Simon & Schuster.

Sinoski, Kelly (2010). "Gold Medal Game Kept Fans in Seats." *Vancouver Sun*, March 11.

Skocpol, Theda (2002). "Will 9/11 and the War on Terror Revitalize American Democracy?" *Political Science and Politics* 35(3):537–540.

Snow, David A., and Robert Benford (1992). "Master Frames and Cycles of Protest." Pp. 133–155 in Aldon D. Morris and Carol McClurg Mueller (eds.), *Frontiers in Social Movement Theory*. New Haven, CT: Yale University Press.

Snow, David A., E. Burke Rochford, Jr., Steven K. Worden, and Robert D. Benford (1986). "Frame Alignment Processes, Micromobilization, and Movement Participation." *American Sociological Review* 51(4):464–481.

Song, Felicia Wu (2009). *Virtual Communities: Bowling Alone, Online Together*. New York: Peter Lang.

Spilling, Olav R. (1996). "Mega-event as Strategy for Regional Development: The Case of the 1994 Lillehammer Winter Olympics." *Entrepreneurship and Regional Development* 8(4):321–343.

Srinivasan, Nirmala (1990). "The Cross-cultural Relevance of Goffman's Concept of Individual Agency." Pp. 141–161 in Stephen Harold Riggins (ed.), *Beyond Goffman: Studies on Communication, Institution and Social Interaction*. New York: Mouton de Gruyter.

Statistics Canada (2006). *Immigration in Canada: A Portrait of the Foreign-Born Population, 2006 Census: Portraits of Major Metropolitan Centres*. Ottawa: Government of Canada.

Steffenhagen, Janet (2009). "Teachers Urged to Critique Games." *Vancouver Sun*, October 15.

Summers-Effler, Erika (2006). "Ritual Theory." Pp. 135–154 in Jan E. Stets and Jonathan Turner (eds.), *Handbook of the Sociology of Emotions*. New York: Springer.

Surborg, Björn, Rob VanWynsberghe, and Elvin Wyly (2008). "Mapping the Olympic Growth Machine: Transnational Urbanism and the Growth Machine Diaspora." *City* 12(3):341–355.

Swart, Kamilla and Urmilla Bob (2004). "The Seductive Discourse of Development: The Cape Town 2004 Olympic Bid." *Third World Quarterly* 25(7):1311–1324.

Tang, Tang and Roger Cooper (2011). "The First Online Olympics: The Interactions between Internet Use and Sports Viewing." *Journal of Sports Media* 6(1):1–22.

Todd, Douglas (2010). "The Changing Face of Vancouver's Games." *Vancouver Sun*, February 9.

Tomlinson, Alan and Garry Whannel (1984). *Five-Ring Circus: Money, Power and Politics at the Olympic Games*. London: Pluto Press.

Tomlinson, Alan and Christopher Young (2005). *National Identity and Global Sports Events: Culture, Politics, and Spectacle in the Olympics and Football World Cup*. Albany, NY: State University of New York Press.

Toohey, Kristine and Tracy Taylor (2008). "Mega-events, Fear and Risk: Terrorism at the Olympic Games." *Journal of Sport Management* 22(4):451–469.

Toohey, Kristine and A.J. Veal (2007). *The Olympic Games: A Social Science Perspective*. Wallingford, UK: CABI.

Tromp, Stanley (2003). "Let the Voting Begin." *Vancouver Courier*, February 20.

Turner, Victor (1969). *The Ritual Process: Structure and Anti-structure*. Ithaca, NY: Cornell University Press.

Turner, Victor (1982). *From Ritual to Theatre: The Human Seriousness of Play*. New York: Performing Arts Journal Publications.

Ueberroth, Peter (1985). *Made in America: His Own Story*. New York: William Morrow.

van Hilvoorde, Ivo, Agnes Elling, and Ruud Stokvis (2010). "How to Influence National Pride? The Olympic Medal Index as a Unifying Narrative." *International Review for the Sociology of Sport* 45(1):87–102.

Varnelis, Kazys and Anne Friedberg (2008). "Place: The Networking of Public Space." Pp. 15–42 in Kazys Varnelis (ed.), *Networked Publics*. Cambridge, MA: MIT Press.

Ward, Doug (2010). "Black Bloc Taints Anti-Olympic Movement." *Vancouver Sun*, February 27.

Weber, Max (1958). *The Protestant Ethic and the Spirit of Capitalism*. New York: Charles Scribner's.

Whannel, Garry (1984). "The Television Spectacular." Pp. 30–43 in Alan Tomlinson and Garry Whannel (eds.), *Five-Ring Circus: Money, Power and Politics at the Olympic Games*. London: Pluto Press.

Whannel, Garry (2009). "Television and the Transformation of Sport." *Annals of the American Academy of Political Science* 625(1):205–218.

Whitson, David (2004). "Bringing the World to Canada: 'The Periphery of the Centre.'" *Third World Quarterly* 25(7):1215–1232.

Whitson, David and Donald Macintosh (1996). "The Global Circus: International Sport, Tourism, and the Marketing of Cities." *Journal of Sport and Social Issues* 20(3):278–295.

Whyte, William H. (1980). *The Social Life of Small Urban Spaces*. Washington, DC: Conservation Foundation.

Whyte, William H. (2009). *City: Rediscovering the Center*. Philadelphia: University of Pennsylvania Press.

Zhao, Dejin and Mary Beth Rosson (2009). "How and Why People Twitter: The Role That Micro-blogging Plays in Informal Communication at Work." Pp. 243–252 in *Proceedings of the ACM 2009 International Conference on Supporting Group Work (GROUP '09)*. New York: ACM.

Index

UNIVERSITY OF WINCHESTER
LIBRARY

Taylor & Francis

eBooks

ORDER YOUR
FREE 30 DAY
INSTITUTIONAL
TRIAL TODAY!

FOR LIBRARIES

Over 23,000 eBook titles in the Humanities,
Social Sciences, STM and Law from some of the
world's leading imprints.

Choose from a range of subject packages or create your own!

Benefits for **you**

▶ Free MARC records
▶ COUNTER-compliant usage statistics
▶ Flexible purchase and pricing options

Benefits for your **user**

▶ Off-site, anytime access via Athens or referring URL
▶ Print or copy pages or chapters
▶ Full content search
▶ Bookmark, highlight and annotate text
▶ Access to thousands of pages of quality research
  at the click of a button

For more information, pricing enquiries or to order
a free trial, contact your local online sales team.

UK and Rest of World: **online.sales@tandf.co.uk**

US, Canada and Latin America:
e-reference@taylorandfrancis.com

www.ebooksubscriptions.com

ALPSP Award for
BEST eBOOK
PUBLISHER
2009 Finalist

Taylor & Francis eBooks
Taylor & Francis Group

A flexible and dynamic resource for teaching, learning and research.